Little Birch on Aconbury Hill

Little Birch on Aconbury Hill
A History of the Parish and its people

compiled by
**The Little Birch
& King's Thorn
History Group**

The Little Birch & King's Thorn History Group
in association with
Logaston Press

LOGASTON PRESS
Little Logaston Woonton Almeley
Herefordshire HR3 6QH
logastonpress.co.uk

First published by The Little Birch and King's Thorn History Group
and Logaston Press 2006

ISBN 1 904396 64 x
(978 1 904396 65 9)

Set in Times New Roman by Logaston Press
and printed in Great Britain by
Biddles Ltd., King's Lynn

Cover illustrations:
Front: Looking over Little Birch towards Aconbury Hill
Rear (clockwise from top left): Area of the Woodfield, former open-field system,
with Athelstan's Wood beyond; Looking north-east over King's Thorn and
Barrack Hill with Little Birch to the right; Little Birch Methodist Chapel,
Barrack Hill; Church Farm and Little Birch church; Back of the former
Rowlston's Barn (collapsed late 1980s)

Contents

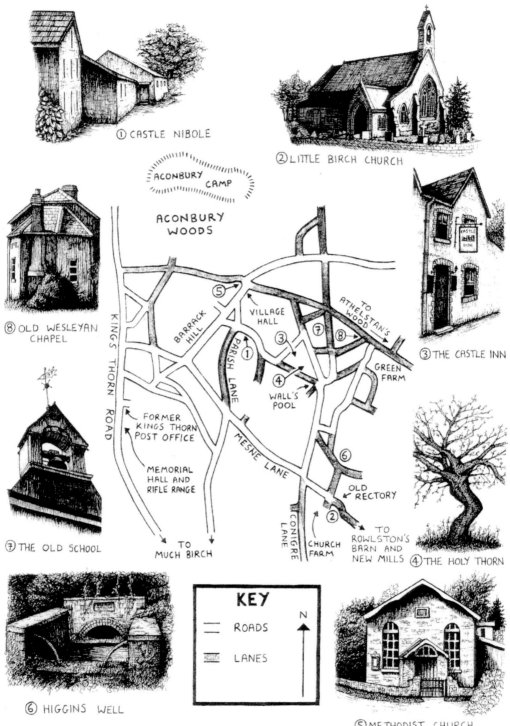

① CASTLE NIBOLE

② LITTLE BIRCH CHURCH

ACONBURY CAMP

ACONBURY WOODS

⑧ OLD WESLEYAN CHAPEL

③ THE CASTLE INN

⑦ THE OLD SCHOOL

④ THE HOLY THORN

⑥ HIGGINS WELL

⑤ METHODIST CHURCH

KING'S THORN ROAD

BARRACK HILL

PARISH LANE

VILLAGE HALL

⑤

①

⑧

⑦

③

④

WALL'S POOL

TO ATHELSTAN'S WOOD

GREEN FARM

⑥

OLD RECTORY

②

MESNE LANE

CONIGRE LANE

CHURCH FARM

FORMER KINGS THORN POST OFFICE

MEMORIAL HALL AND RIFLE RANGE

TO MUCH BIRCH

TO ROWLSTON'S BARN AND NEW MILLS

KEY

N

ROADS

LANES

JOHN SADLER 2005

Acknowledgments

The Little Birch History Group wishes to acknowledge the wide range of advice, assistance and support it has received in the course of preparing this book.

It is grateful to the following specialists: John Freeman, currently preparing the Herefordshire volumes of the English Place-Names survey, for information on local place names; Peter Reavill, local Finds Liaison Officer of Portable Antiquities Scheme, for information and advice on Bronze Age artefacts and boundaries; Rosamund Skelton for advice on deserted mediaeval sites; Jim and Muriel Tonkin for advice and opinion on local buildings.

The group has received consistent and valuable help from the custodians of a variety of local collections and archives. It would particularly like to thank:

Kate Andrew and the staff at Hereford Museum; Robin Hill and the staff at Hereford City Library; Sue Hubbard, Elizabeth Semper O'Keefe and the staff of the Herefordshire Record Office; Jackie Jonson and Gwilym Rees – honorary librarians of the Woolhope Naturalists' Field Club; Rebecca Roseff and the other staff working on the Herefordshire Sites and Monuments Record; Geraint James, Carolyn Jacob and other staff at Merthyr Tydfil Library and Record Office; Staff at Gloucestershire Record Office.

The group would also like to thank the following for their assistance, advice and support: Christine Harvey, Heather Hurley (particularly for material on Aconbury Gate Accounts and Holme Lacy estate sale), Virginia Morgan, Dr Tony Murgatroyd, Dr David Potter, Ruth Richardson, Mark and Janet Robinson (particularly for information on Stephen Thackwell's friendship with Thomas Walsh), Geraint Rogers at the Duchy of Cornwall, Guy Rogers and David Whitehead.

Without the knowledge and assistance of many local people, the writing of sections of this book would not have been possible. We are very grateful to them all, they include: Hilda Andrews, Percy Bristow, Alwyn and John Bulbeck (for information from their deeds), Frank Cooke, Sylvia Cooke, Ivor Crum, John and Kate Dillon, John Evans, Dennis Hands, Geoff Jones, Susan Jones, Peter Lee, Iris Lloyd, the late Dulcie Morgan, Margaret Mullins, Thelma Murphy, Bill Powell (for information and access to his deeds), Mark Roberts, Anne Rooke, Muriel Saunders, Gerald Skyrme, Diane Smith, Victor Townsend, Marion Turner, Percy Verry and John Walker.

We also thank the following for their contributions to the illustrations in this book: Frontispiece, 2.1, 13.15(b) – By kind permission of John Sadler who drew these sketches for us; 1.1, 1.4, 3.1, 8.1, 9.1, 9.9 – By kind permission of

Jonathan Porter who prepared these maps for us; 1.2 – By kind permission of Alan McDougall; 1.3(a), 13.3 – from a range of postcards of the area taken in early 1930s and sold at Kings Thorn shop at that time; 2.2, 2.4 – with kind permission of Hereford Museum; 2.3 – with kind permission of Ivor Crum; 4.2 – with permission of The Master and Fellows of Balliol College, Oxford; 5.1, 10.6 – from a survey carried out by Mr Dennis Hands, with his kind permission; 6.1, 11.1, 11.2 – with permission of the Priest-in-Charge, Rev Preb Kay Garlick; 6.2 – by kind permission of the Bishop of Hereford/ Diocesan Office; 9.2 – with kind permission of Gerald Skyrme; 9.3 – from the late Mr Derek Hackett; 9.6, 9.8, 10.2, 10.4, 10.8, 10.9, 13.9. 13.10, 14.3, 14.4, 15.7 were all taken from the Millennium Photographic Record of Little Birch and Kings Thorn; 10.1 – with kind permission of Mr Fred Druce; 10.3, 12.4, 14.2 – by kind permission of Mrs Sylvia Cooke; 12.5 – from the late Mrs Gwen Andrews; 13.1, 13.2 – from the collection of the late Cmdr H Bromby by kind permission of his executors; 13.4, 13.5 – with permission of the preist in charge and Parochial Church Council; 13.16 – given by the late Miss Elizabeth Jones; 13.15(b) – taken with kind permission of Mr J Langford; 13.6, 13.17, 13.18 – by kind permission of Mr Geoff Jones; 14.1 – by kind permission of Mr Michael Symonds; 14.5 – in the possession of the Village Hall Committee, with their permission; 15.1, 15.2, 15.3, 15.4, 15.5, 15.6 – by kind permission of Peter Lee. Thanks are due to John Elphick who scanned some of these photographs. The remaining illustrations were photographed, scanned or prepared by members of the group.

We owe a debt of gratitude to the partners of the authors for their extraordinary patience and tolerance during the preparation of this book.

Finally, and most importantly, as a working group of amateur historians, we would like to express our thanks to our publisher, Andy Johnson of Logaston Press, for the generous exercise of his professional expertise on our behalf.

Foreword

I am sure there has always been an interest in the past in this area, particularly as the Iron Age fort on Aconbury Hill is such an impressive monument to it. However, nothing has ever been put together in the form of a book and most knowledge has been, in the age-old tradition, passed on from generation to generation, with a little embellishment on the way. In the 1970s, a desire to discover and record more about the past resulted in the formation of a local history group. One of the founder members of this was Adrian Harvey, who then lived in the village. He was warned at the time by other historians in the area that they wished him the best of luck since there was so little documented about Little Birch. Undaunted, he pressed on and some of what he found then is included in this book. Other events took over in people's lives and the group was disbanded after a few years. Nothing was ever published apart from in a local Handbook.

To celebrate the Millennium, it was decided to take up the offer of a grant for the purpose and compile a photographic record of all the buildings in the west end of Little Birch and Kings Thorn. This, together with information which each householder provided about their property's history, stimulated interest in studying local history once again and the Little Birch and Kings Thorn History Group was born.

Progress was slow initially although one of the earliest projects was to interview as many of the older people, who had lived in parish all or most of their lives, as soon as possible. Sadly, one died before we interviewed her and another passed away soon after. Realising how much valuable information has been lost in this way makes us all frustrated that we had not questioned and listened more carefully to people in the past. However, bit by bit, tasks were allotted and research began. The membership has fluctuated over the years. One of the early members was Joan Ingram, who was a very keen local and family historian as well as running the village shop. She was already suffering from the illness from which she, sadly, died in 2002. We hope she would have approved of this final result.

We decided that we should concentrate on the parish of Little Birch but would, inevitably, encompass much of the postal district of King's Thorn which overlaps adjacent parishes. In fact, this old Aconbury Common area nowadays forms a fairly well-defined community.

After a while we realised that, with the information we had gathered, we should embark on writing. Further research, which would become needed as we wrote, could then be carried out. Inevitably, teasing out documentary fact from anecdotal evidence proved a challenge. By now the membership of the group had, more or less, settled down to the present members. We allocated the writing of chapters and decided to set ourselves a target for finishing the text and publishing by the end of 2006. The difficulty sometimes comes in knowing when to stop and we have already realised that there are many tantalising possible new discoveries which have not made it into the book. This will, however, provide focus for the group in the future and we hope that the discovery of the history of Little Birch on Aconbury Hill will go on and maybe encompass more of the surrounding area. We discovered that, if you do not have a cut-off point, nothing will ever go into print. In fact, the whole exercise of researching, writing, illustrating and compiling this book has been a steep learning curve for all of us.

Members of the Little Birch and Kings Thorn History Group who all contributed to this book are:

John Bryant
Alison Clarke
Adrian Harvey
Jennifer Jones
Barbara Kilby
Michael Morley
Graham Philpott
Gillian Porter
Ian Porter

Alison Clarke
Little Birch, 2006

1 The Parish, its Physical Environment and Natural History

Little Birch parish lies about 6 miles due south of Hereford city on the south-facing slopes of Aconbury Hill which reaches a height of 276m (910ft). Much of the most inhabited part of the parish is above 190m (630ft), a fact reinforced by the temperature often being 2°C lower than that on the surrounding Herefordshire plains, and by the growing season being up to two weeks behind.

The parish is elongated in a north-west/south-east direction and falls into three main areas. Firstly, the most inhabited area on Aconbury Hill; secondly, that which encompasses most of Athelstan's Wood and thirdly, that which is beyond this and to the south which is mainly farmland belonging to Rowlston, New Mills, Bromley and Church Farms. The southern boundary borders Church Farm and follows the Wrigglebrook. The extreme south-east end of the parish actually lies on the other side of the Much Birch to Hoarwithy road.

The most inhabited part shares the southern slopes of Aconbury Hill with the neighbouring parishes of Much Birch and Aconbury and with a small part of Much Dewchurch. This whole area originally formed Aconbury Common — an area of generally poor land above the surrounding plains, which was largely uncultivated until the time of the Enclosures in the early 1800s. The steep slopes of parts of the area make it less than ideal for cultivation.

The deep valleys in the parish have been cut by three streams. The main one, the Wrigglebrook, rises near Warren Farm, though between here and the Wrigglebrook area it only flows in wet weather. It then proceeds in a south-easterly direction along Wrigglebrook valley, skirting the southern boundary of the parish, towards New Mills. A second stream rises somewhere below Uplands and, again, runs only in wet weather, along to Newtown Well and along the valley to Higgins Well where it is joined by water from the well which always runs. It skirts the southern edge of Athelstan's Wood and joins the Wrigglebrook just south of the wood. The third rises below Merrivale Farm and flows through Athelstan's Wood

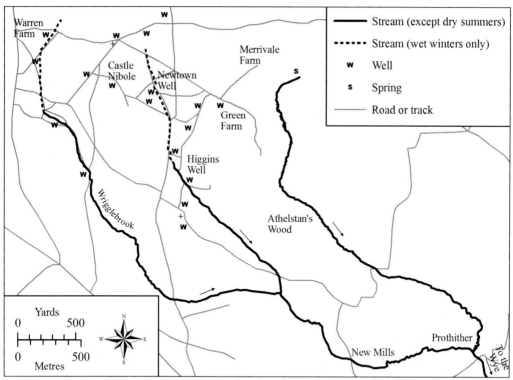

Fig. 1.1 Map of wells and streams rising
on Aconbury Hill in Little Birch parish

Fig 1.2 Sketch of a blossom on the
Holy Thorn by Alan McDougall from
the front cover of the King's Thorn
Community handbook, the first edition
of which received a Village Ventures
Award in 1984 sponsored by Shell

and then on to Prothither where it meets
the Wrigglebrook. This finally flows into
the Wye at Hoarwithy. New Mills was
the first of four mills along the length
of Wrigglebrook. There were others at
Prothither, Tresseck and Hoarwithy.

These streams generally run very low
in summer when most of the numerous
springs and wells in the area run dry. The
existence of so many springs and wells is
due to layers of less permeable sandstone
interspersed between more porous layers.
The position of the springs and wells has
obviously had an impact on the siting of the
centres of habitation. Little Birch church,
the Rectory, Church Farm and a few
cottages to the north of this represent what

Fig. 1.3 Photos taken from behind the Memorial Hall on the Kings Thorn road looking north, with Barrack Hill on the left, the Wrigglebrook area middle right and Little Birch in the distance to the right. The upper photograph was taken in the 1930s and the lower in 2006. Notice the difference in the number of buildings

was once the centre of Little Birch, close to Higgins Well which continues to flow through the driest of summers. Another centre including the Castle Inn developed near Newtown Well. There were other centres at Upper and Lower Wrigglebrook.

As alternative water sources have been made available housing increased, particularly in the area of Wrigglebrook Lane, Little Birch Road and Barrack Hill. This area became known as King's Thorn, a name created as a postal district in the 1840s and taken from the holy thorn, reputedly a cutting from the original Glastonbury thorn, which is located in Little Birch near the Castle Inn. This variety (*Crataegus monogyna praecox*) flowers in January. A local legend claims that it was planted to commemorate a visit by Charles I to the area one Christmas. A cutting of this thorn is to be planted alongside its parent tree which is soon likely to expire. Another thorn tree of this type is now growing well at the bottom of the hill known as The Thorn thereby giving its name some credence!

There is much confusion in relation to the parishes of Little Birch, Much Birch and Aconbury and the district of King's Thorn. So much so that some people are uncertain as to exactly where they live (see Fig. 1.4).

Geologically, this area of Aconbury Hill is formed of cornstone, a type of red marl which is rich in calcium carbonate creating a kind of rubbly limestone. This was rather more resistant to the effects of the Wye glacier. This flowed during the glacial periods of the last 200,000 years from the ice-covered areas west of Hereford in the direction followed by the present Wye, scouring out the softer sandstones but having less effect on areas of harder cornstone. This resulted in hills such as Aconbury and Dinedor remaining in the somewhat flatter Hereford plain. Some of the area has red fertile soils indicative of old red sandstone but the presence of lime near the surface may possibly be indicated by the several small pits scattered through Aconbury wood where lime would have been dug for agricultural purposes. Indeed, there are remains of two limekilns in adjacent Wallbrook Wood. There are also areas in fields well known to have rubbly stone near the surface making cultivation difficult. One particular site is on Green Farm, near to Athelstan's Wood. Despite this limestone, there seems to be a layer of neutral to slightly acidic soil over much of the area.

Much of the area is farmed but, as a result of the topography and as a legacy of the enclosure of the common, there still exist a large number of small fields. Where the slopes are less steep, larger fields are cultivated and a variety of crops (potatoes, beet, barley and maize) are grown but the steeper slopes mostly provide grazing for cattle, sheep and horses.

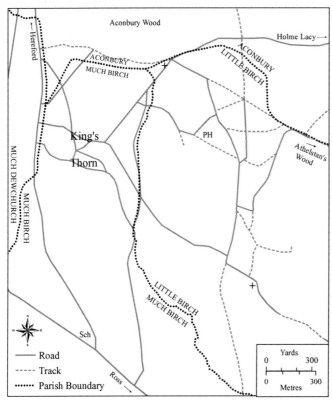

Fig. 1.4 Map showing the parish boundaries on Aconbury Common area superimposed on the road network

In some areas the underlying rock is close to the surface, and so easy to quarry for building stone, which has been used for all the surviving older cottages. These cottages tend to be scattered over the area (often on the fringes of the old common) and each would have originally had one or more small fields. In some cases these fields have been sold for building, a process which occurred throughout the second half of the 20th century, and has resulted in a fairly concentrated area of housing along Wrigglebrook Lane and Little Birch road, also extending up Parish Lane and Barrack Hill. There is a smaller concentration of housing around the Castle Inn in Little Birch. In other cases, the land was amalgamated into farms such as Castle Nibole. A small number of properties retain a few acres for their own use.

As a result of the small fields and the multitude of lanes (a legacy of the Enclosures; see Fig. 12.3) there is a great extent of hedgerows and ditches providing habitats for a wide diversity of wildlife. The hedgerows contain the usual variety of woody species but do not generally contain calcareous indicator species. Wild hops are to be found in several places trailing through the hedges. Round some fields damson trees are still to be found in the hedges, a reminder of when every square foot was made to grow something useful. The bases of the hedgerows and edges of the green lanes are adorned in spring with bluebells — a strong indicator that this area was formerly woodland, and foxgloves growing in profusion also demonstrate this. Wild daffodils still grow in a few hedgerows and in two fields — a relic of the huge numbers allegedly carpeting the orchards which themselves once covered much of the area (and of which hardly any remain). Gorse and bracken are in evidence as a legacy of the uncultivated common grassland, the bracken also indicates a soil verging on the acidic. Uncultivated areas which remain, including the roadside verges, support the usual variety of grassland species. Of these cow parsley — Queen Anne's lace — is a feature of the early summer lanes. Shady damp areas, particularly around Higgins Well, support many ferns, including the harts tongue, and many mosses and liverworts.

In the mixed woodland areas of Athelstan's and neighbouring Aconbury, wood anemone and wild garlic are to be found carpeting some areas and, of course, bluebells which thrive particularly well where there is a hazel understorey. Blackberry/ bramble covers the ground in some parts of the woodland and grows through many hedgerows providing delicious pickings in the autumn. Stinging nettles, which indicate high phosphate levels in the soil, show where there have been humans and farm animals over a long period of time, (urine contains phosphate!). Their presence, in places distant from other habitations, is an indicator of the possible site of former dwellings and can be seen on several such locations in Little Birch.

Brambles and stinging nettles both provide food plants for the caterpillars of a range of butterflies so many of these are present in summer, including the tortoiseshell and peacock butterflies. A wide variety of moths are also to be seen — when lights are on and windows open at night! — thanks to the uncultivated areas which support their food plants.

The usual farmland and garden invertebrates, together with rich pickings of fruits and seeds from the gardens and hedgerows, provide food for a wide diversity of birds. The area also benefits from some birds associated more with woodland. Apart from common ones such as robins, blackbirds, various tits, finches and sparrows (making a comeback), less common ones such as the goldcrest nest in the village. Woodpeckers are quite frequently seen and heard and buzzards are often spotted wheeling overhead, as are some ravens. Sparrowhawks swoop along the lanes leaving telltale piles of feathers and peregrines have occasionally been seen. Tawny owls are to be heard on occasions at night. Summer visitors, particularly martins, swallows and swifts, breed well in the many suitable nest sites, the swifts, particularly, delighting us with their swooping and shrieking as they feed on the multitude of flying insects. Large flocks of fieldfares and redwings descend on the area in some winters, stripping the remaining berries in the hedgerows. Wood pigeons and collared doves are present in some numbers, the latter having been known to nest in January. The heron is not viewed with pleasure when it makes all too frequent visits to garden ponds. The first cuckoo arrives with remarkable consistency from 19 to 23 April.

Mammals abound, although less frequently seen, and can be recognised by the various types of evidence which they leave. Deer, roe and muntjac, from Aconbury wood spill out into the neighbouring fields. Badgers and foxes burrow their way into many banks as does the large population of rabbits. The numerous foxes ensure that poultry-keeping is a hazardous exercise. The grey squirrel is another only too successful species, damaging trees and raiding bird tables. Hedgehogs are common, as are moles, which leave their rows of tumps across fields and gardens. Rats, mice and voles are commonly in evidence, often as prey of the numerous domestic cats. Hares have been spotted occasionally and polecats have been seen in the area. Bats are present and take advantage of the many flying insects at night.

We are fortunate in the wide diversity of wildlife in this area, due in large measure to the fact that little of the area is intensively farmed and many of the hedgerows are in a relatively unkempt state. Not to be forgotten are the many gardens, which offer much for birds in particular and in which the proliferation of garden ponds ensures the continued presence of frogs, toads and newts.

Though by no means unique, Little Birch area has many features, both natural and historical, which make it a place worthy of investigation as well as being a most congenial place to live.

2   The Pre-history of Aconbury Hill

The name 'Birch' — or as it first appears, 'Birches' — is not recorded until the middle of the twelfth century. Clearly, however, the area which includes Little Birch was inhabited for many thousands of years before this. The most obvious physical indication of early human occupation is the large Iron Age hill fort which girdles the summit of Aconbury Hill and whose southern rampart lies 400 metres or so north of the northernmost stretch of the parish boundary.

When the hill fort was constructed its site was almost certainly already clear of trees and it seems to have remained unwooded throughout most of the succeeding centuries, long after it had ceased to be inhabited. There are early references to Wallbrook Wood, Holloway Bank Wood and Held Wood but all these woods lie on the slopes of the hill and not around its summit; indeed their actual names derive from their geographical situation. ('Helde' is the Old English word denoting a slope or declivity.) In 1625 Richard Kidley of Bromley was responsible to Sir James Scudamore for the maintenance of a beacon on Aconbury Hill, and 20 years later when Parliament's Scottish allies besieged Hereford they apparently posted detachments of troops on both Aconbury and Dinedor Hills, presumably to keep watch for any attempt to harass the besiegers by the Royalist garrisons at Monmouth and Raglan. Neither of these facts would make sense if the top of the hill had then been densely wooded as it was during the twentieth century. The drawings made by the surveyor in 1815 in preparation for the production of the first Ordnance Survey map of the county (published in 1831) still show the camp as clear, as indeed was the entire area extending southwards from the camp to the lane which marks the southern boundary of the present-day woodland.[1]

In June, 1885, however, when members of the Woolhope Club visited the site, it was noted that it had been planted with trees about 50 years earlier. Before that time they understood it had been used as a rabbit warren enclosed by a stone wall. This is confirmed by the account given in a report prepared for the Court of Committee of Guy's Hospital in 1754, which describes 'the Warren at Aconbury with a farm adjoining let at will to Edward Bevan for a rent of £15 p.a.' The account continues that the rent had been abated to £5 because the warren was out of stock (presumably of rabbits). The authors of the report clearly believed this abatement was unnecessary and that the absence of rabbits would be an advantage to the farm rather than otherwise. The 'farm adjoining' was evidently not the present Warren Farm but the property called Warren House on the 1815 surveyor's drawing and lying to the south of the hill fort about half-way between the southern rampart and the lane running along the edge of the present woodland; the remains of this can still be seen in the wood. A detailed map of the Aconbury estate was prepared for Guy's Hospital in 1757, but unfortunately the western sheet, showing the hill fort, is lost.[2]

The decision to plant up the top of the hill with trees was presumably taken by Whaley Armitage, who was the agent for the Hospital's Herefordshire estates between 1809 and 1849. Armitage was anxious to improve the income yielded by the estate after decades of indifferent management and was impressed by the suitability of the soil of Aconbury for forestry. In the notebook which records the timber valuations for the estate between 1810 and 1890 there is no mention of the new plantation until 1868 and 1869 when it is described as the Warren or Warren Plantation and as yielding 341 larch poles and 62 acres of coppice wood. The estate map of 1852 shows the whole area as wooded and called the Warren.[3]

It is particularly unfortunate that after so long as open ground the area that contains the hill fort should have been afforested in the early nineteenth century. Scientific archaeology in Britain really dates back to the 1880s — about the time the Woolhope Club visited Aconbury — when a retired general, Sir Augustus Pitt-Rivers, carried out his pioneering excavations on Cranborne Chase in Wiltshire. By this time the top of Aconbury Hill was irrevocably compromised as a site for detailed excavation and no full archaeological study of it has been possible. To obtain an idea of what it would have been like at the time of its occupation we have to depend on what has been learnt from modern excavations at other Herefordshire hill forts, most importantly those by Dr Kathleen Kenyon at Sutton Walls and by Dr S.C. Stanford at Croft Ambrey, in north Herefordshire and at Credenhill. When Dr Kenyon was carrying out her work at Sutton Walls between 1948 and 1951, she arranged for supplementary small-scale excavations at a number of other hill forts in the county, including Aconbury, to provide comparative information about the types of occupation. Given the nature of the site the excavations at Aconbury were particularly perfunctory — 'little more than surface scratching' as Dr Kenyon put it — but they provided some important clues about continuity of occupation.[4]

The summit of Aconbury Hill is 276 metres above sea-level and dominates the central Herefordshire basin. The eastern rampart of the hill fort lies just to the

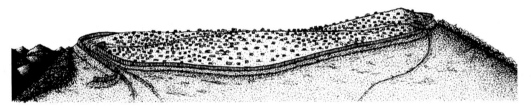

Fig. 2.1 Sketch of a reconstruction of how Aconbury hill fort might have looked in the Iron Age

east of the trig point marking the summit and the maximum length of the defended area is somewhat under 600 metres east to west; the width from north to south varies but nowhere exceeds 200 metres; the total area enclosed is about 7 hectares, making the fort one of the largest in the county (though nowhere near as large as Credenhill at 20 hectares). The northern and western approaches are very steep. Unlike Maiden Castle in Dorset — or locally Risbury — the fort is univallate, its defences consisting of a single rampart, sections of which still stand as high as 5 metres. Much of the original outer ditch has disappeared though it partially remains on the southern and eastern sides. The excavation team in 1951 thought it likely that the rampart had originally been constructed with some sort of revetment of timber or stone. At the south-eastern and south-western corners are original in-turned entrances; the first is a comparatively simple straight passage-way, but the one at the south-western corner is more elaborate — a winding entrance created by the southern rampart being built in a wide inward curve around a tighter curve in the northern rampart; there is also a steep ramp outside leading to this entrance. These entrances are clearly designed for effective defence; the other simple entrances cut through the rampart are pretty certainly relatively modern.[5]

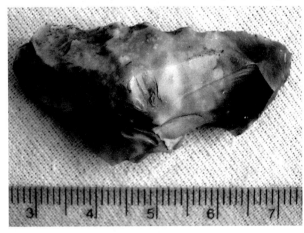

Fig. 2.2. Flint scraper found at Rock Cottage, Aconbury, from earlier than 2000BC. The top surface was sharpened to scrape flesh off hides. The notch on the lower surface was possibly for stripping bark of willow to prepare it for basket weaving (scale in cm)

The size and nature of Aconbury Camp led Dr Stanford to conclude that it was probably constructed in the fifth century BC. Whether earlier occupation on the site preceded this is

9

uncertain. At Sutton Walls there is clear evidence of occupation before the earthen ramparts were raised, but the kind of detailed excavation needed to establish such a fact was impossible at Aconbury. Two casual finds in the vicinity, however, indicate earlier human activity. A Neolithic flint scraper found near Rock Cottage probably dates from before 2000 BC. Then there is the discovery by Mr Ivor Crum of part of a bronze spear-head, probably of late Bronze Age date (900–700BC) near Warren Farm.[6]

Fig. 2.3 Bronze spear-head found at Warren Farm from 900–700BC

One of the most important aspects of Dr Stanford's work at Croft Ambrey and Credenhill, as well as at Midsummer Hill in the Malverns, was the investigation of the structures contained within the Herefordshire group of hill forts. These turned out to be not the large round houses associated with Iron Age settlements in much of southern Britain but smaller, rectangular four-post buildings, some square, others slightly larger and oblong. They were fairly densely distributed and, making due allowance for some being dwellings and others storage facilities of various kinds, Dr Stanford arrived at some tentative guidelines for estimating the population of individual hill forts. His suggestion of between 180 and 240 people per hectare would give Aconbury a population of somewhere between 1,260 and 1,680. Of course, no structures within Aconbury have ever

Fig. 2.4 Spindle-whorl found on Bromley Farm from the Iron Age/Roman period (scale in cm)

been excavated but the quantity of Iron Age pottery sherds found during the very limited digging in 1951 impressed the archaeologists and does not suggest that Aconbury was comparatively sparsely inhabited.[7]

It is true to say that some archaeologists have proposed considerably lower population densities for Iron Age hill forts in Britain as a whole. On the other hand it should be remembered that for the last 80 years historians have steadily been revising upwards their estimates of the total population of Britain in the late Iron Age and the Roman period. Figures as high as 5 million or more have been suggested. This would mean that the population of Britain at the beginning of the Christian era was far higher than at the time the Domesday Book was compiled or indeed than during the reign of Henry VIII. Even if the population of Aconbury was only a half or two thirds of Dr Stanford's lower estimate, it would still be substantial when set against the numbers that can be inferred from parish records for the area in the seventeenth century (see section 7 below).[8]

Of course a population reckoned in four figures would imply the control of a sizable hinterland around Aconbury devoted to the agricultural activity necessary to support such a large number of people. This hinterland would presumably have extended towards the boundaries of similar hinterlands controlled by neighbouring hill forts — most notably Dinedor, 4 kilometres to the north-east, and Gaer Cop, near St Owen's Cross, 8 kilometres to the south-east. The upper part of an Iron Age stone quern, used for grinding grain, has been found at Minster Farm in Much Birch. At Bromley, at the south-eastern edge of Little Birch, an Iron Age spindle-whorl has been discovered; this is the bottom part of a simple drop-spindle, commonly used for spinning wool before the development of more advanced tools such as the spinning wheel. These finds tend to confirm both the extent of settlement and the existence of a mixed farming economy. They may also imply that the people of Aconbury practised some sort of transhumance, i.e. living for part of the year in the hill fort and for part in outlying settlements. The work being undertaken by the Landscape Origins of the Wye Valley project during 2005 and 2006 on the 12 riverside parishes between Fownhope and Bridstow will, when complete and written up, almost certainly confirm the view of an extensively inhabited and exploited landscape.[9]

Who were the people of the Aconbury hill fort? As the inhabitants of Iron Age Britain had not learned to read or write, we depend for our information — apart from what can be gleaned from the archaeological record — upon the accounts of their Roman conquerors. The great majority — if not all — of the population of late Iron Age Britain seems to have belonged to the Britonnic group of Celtic peoples, i.e. those speaking a language which subsequently developed into modern Welsh, Cornish and Breton. To the Romans they were of course barbarians, but some of them were recognized as being more advanced and sophisticated than the remoter peoples of central and north-eastern Europe. They often congregated in large settlements — almost embryonic towns; they engaged in trade, and their social structures were complex, with a warrior aristocracy and a priestly caste. One interesting feature of many Roman accounts concerns their physical appearance: that by Roman standards they were tall. In this context it is interesting to note that when the excavations at Sutton Walls were carried out the remains of about two dozen skeletons, probably all male, were found near the western entrance. The manner in which these men met their deaths will be considered below, but for the moment the main point of interest is the estimates that experts have been able to make from examining their bones of their height. The shortest was apparently 5ft 4½ins and the tallest 6ft 0¾ in. The average height was 5ft 8¼ins, which compares with the average for British males in 1950 of 5ft 7½ins.[10]

Roman sources make it clear that the people of Britain were divided into tribal groupings. The names of the tribes are recorded by several authorities, together with some idea of which part of the island each inhabited. These authorities, however, are sometimes contradictory, and the precise boundaries of each tribe's territory are usually unclear. This means that there are some areas where tribal links cannot be firmly established and, unfortunately, one such area is what is now Herefordshire. To the south-east and east lay the territory of the Dobunni. They were one of the more advanced tribes of Iron Age Britain; they had been producing their own primitive coinage since around 35 BC and the tribal capital that was established under Roman rule, *Corinium* (Cirencester), was to become Roman Britain's second city after London. To the south-west and west were the Silures, distinguished by the Roman historian Tacitus for their obdurate resistance to the Roman conquest. And to the north, in modern Shropshire, were the Cornovii.

It has been most usual to identify Herefordshire — or at least its central plain — with the Dobunni. The most significant piece of evidence for this identification is the Roman milestone found at Kenchester in 1796 and dating from the reign of the emperor Numerian (283–284). At the end of the inscription on the stone are the letters RPCD, usually interpreted as standing for 'Res Publica Civitatis Dobunnorum' — 'the government of the state of the Dobunni'. Some historians, taking into account the importance of the Wye as a boundary in later periods, have suggested that the territory south and west of the river might have belonged to the Silures. Neither solution is wholly satisfactory. Though Dobunnic coins have been found at *Ariconium* (Weston-under-Penyard), these have been interpreted as showing that *Ariconium* was a trading outpost for the Dobunni rather than a part of their tribal area; Dobunnic coins have not frequently been found in other parts of Herefordshire.[11]

The most experienced excavator of Herefordshire hill forts, Dr S.C. Stanford, noting the cultural similarity of the Iron Age sites across the county, has proposed a third theory. This involves interpreting the 'D' on the Kenchester milestone as standing not for 'Dobunnorum' — 'of the Dobunni' — but for 'Decangorum' — 'of the Decangi'. It is a complex argument. There seems to have been a tribe called the Deceangli in north-east Wales, and it has generally been assumed that the reference to the Decangi in the *Annals* of Tacitus represents a corrupted spelling of the same name. Stanford, however, argues that there were actually two distinct tribes — the Deceangli in Flintshire and the Decangi in Herefordshire. It is fair to say that there is still controversy about this theory and that therefore the tribal identity of the inhabitants of Aconbury hill fort is still an open question. As a footnote to this debate about tribal identity, a find of considerable local archaeological importance made in a nearby parish in 2005 is worth attention. This included a hoard of Bronze Age axes of several distinct types. There are many theories about why such hoards were deposited but one at least is related to the marking of boundaries. This part of Herefordshire may well have been a boundary area in the Bronze Age, as well as in the Iron Age and — as we shall see later — for long after that.[12]

It remains to say something of how these people made the transition from pre-history to being a part of the Roman Empire and thus the subject for the first time of written records. This happened about half-way through the first century AD. In fact, Julius Caesar had led two expeditions to Britain in 55 and 54 BC. These had been little more than exploratory raids and not serious attempts to colonise the island — a task which had to await the emperor Claudius in 43 AD. However, Caesar's expeditions established treaties of alliance with some tribes. Consequently, the Romans were able in 43 to follow their preferred practice of wooing some tribes away from opposition and thus dividing their potential enemies. Tacitus comments that a major cause of the Romans' success was the inability of the Britons to combine effectively against them. The subjugation of Britain proceeded deliberately and purposefully; the annexation of the Welsh Marches seems to have been accomplished during the periods of rule of the second and third provincial governors, Ostorius Scapula (47–52 AD) and Didius Gallus (52–57 AD).

The historical record suggests that, more probably than not, the advance of the Romans in Herefordshire met resistance. At least the southern portion of the Dobunni appear to have opposed the Romans into the time of Scapula. He also had to campaign vigorously against the tribe called by Tacitus the Decangi. The Silures, immune alike to severity or clemency, obstructed the Roman advance for longer than any other tribe.

The excavations at Sutton Walls have supplied supporting archaeological evidence. Mention has already been made of the remains of a number of male skeletons found near the western entrance. They had apparently been thrown haphazardly into the ditch and barely covered with earth. The ditch itself had recently been re-cut. From the reconstruction that was possible most seemed to have been in the prime of life when they died. Most showed signs of serious wounds, some obviously fatal; six of the bodies had been decapitated. This looks suspiciously like a punitive Roman massacre following the storming of the fort, which had recently had its defences repaired. Strictly speaking such harsh treatment was reserved for rebels, so it may be that an act of resistance had followed an earlier acceptance of Roman rule; or it may be that even initial resistance by a tribal group was interpreted as rebellion once the subjugation of the island was well underway. Interestingly there is a tradition in Kings Caple that, when the drive to the rebuilt Poulstone Court was being relaid in 1877, workmen found a number of skeletons buried; all were very tall and all had been decapitated.[13]

3 The Roman Period

Most of lowland Britain was a part of the Roman Empire for 350 years — a period equal in length to that between the English Civil War and the present day — which had an impact on our landscape and settlement patterns that can be clearly seen today. The basis of our road system, with major routes radiating out from the Roman provincial capital, London, and the development of London itself and other urban centres are legacies of Roman occupation. Herefordshire shows many obvious signs of its Roman past, though it was on the edge of the lowland zone and nothing has yet been found to match the proliferation of great villas in the Gloucestershire Cotswolds or the opulent town houses whose mosaics are preserved in Cirencester's Corinium Museum.

The area controlled by the Iron Age hill fort of Aconbury lay almost exactly half-way between two significant Roman settlements. About 12km north-west, in the present-day parish of Kenchester, lay the town of *Magnis*. There had apparently been occupation on the site in the Iron Age before the arrival of the Romans. Though classed as one of the smaller towns of Roman Britain, *Magnis* was clearly a place of some importance. It covered about 9 hectares and was enclosed by defences which, by the fourth century at least, consisted of substantial stone walls. The town had a planned street pattern and some buildings which, judging by their excavated remains, were very imposing. Of course, if Dr Stanford is correct in his theory about the Decangi, *Magnis* must have been a *civitas* capital, i.e. the administrative centre of a government unit based on the territory of one of Britain's tribes. Even if he is not correct, some experts believe Magnis could have become the capital of a *pagus*, a sub-tribal Roman administrative unit.[1]

No such claim can be made for the other Roman settlement, 14km south-east of Little Birch. This is *Ariconium* in the parish of Weston-under-Penyard. It was not walled nor apparently had a planned layout in the manner of *Magnis*. The widespread remains of iron slag and furnaces discovered in excavations reveal that it must have been an important industrial centre exploiting the mineral wealth

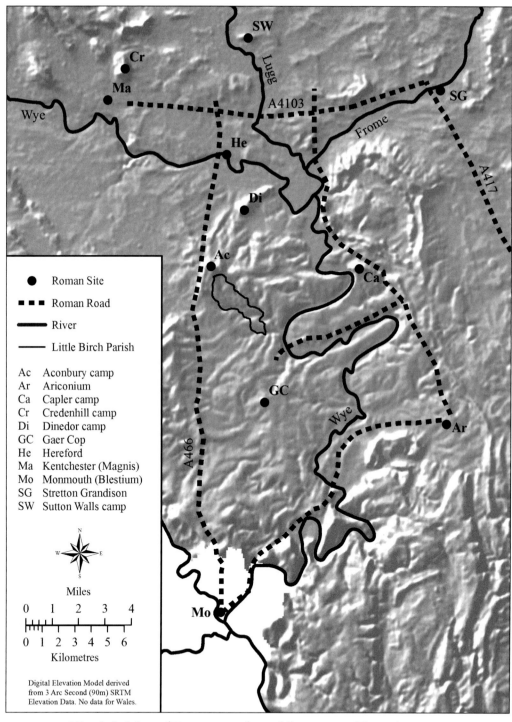

Fig. 3.1 Map of Roman roads and Roman and Iron Age sites in south Herefordshire

of the Forest of Dean. Its name, as we shall see, was to survive through ensuing centuries.[2]

Roman Herefordshire was certainly integrated into the road system which the Romans bequeathed Britain. Unfortunately, as noted by I.D. Margary in the standard modern study, *Roman Roads in Britain*, it is not always easy to trace the course of such roads in the hillier areas of Wales and the Marches. It is necessary in many instances to piece together the complete course of a particular road, or as much of it as possible, from isolated stretches still visible, from sources such as the *Antonine Itinerary*, a third century list of routes with place-names and distances, and finally from informed guesswork. Given the difficulties, a full picture of the network of Roman roads in the county is only likely to become clear when (and if) a detailed local survey is carried out on the lines of that undertaken in the south-east Midlands in the 1950s and 1960s by the group calling itself the Viatores.

Margary's account suggests that Little Birch lies within an approximate quadrilateral of Roman roads, To the north is a road that passes from east to west through the middle of *Magnis*; it seems to have extended to the east at least as far as Stretton Grandison and to the west to Clifford, Clyro and beyond. This probably represented the line of the Romans' original advance into central Wales. Today we are familiar with part of it as the Roman Road, which runs along the northern edge of Hereford. It was crossed near the Starting Gate Inn by another road leading from *Bravonium* (Leintwardine), and running for much of its course along the present A4110. This second road traversed Widemarsh Common and crossed the Wye probably near the Old Bridge. Margary believes its destination must have been *Blestium* (Monmouth) and that its only feasible course would have been the modern one, i.e. the A49/A466. (It would presumably have followed the old route through Callow village not the new more contoured route cut in 1835.) Such a road would have passed only a few hundred metres from the western rampart of Aconbury Camp.

The only one of the four roads of the quadrilateral to appear in the *Antonine Itinerary* is that which links *Blestium* and *Ariconium*, a section of the long Iter XIII, which ran from *Isca* (Caerleon) to *Calleva* (Silchester). The precise course of this road is not clear. Even more problematic is the road which Margary believes must have run north from *Ariconium*. This apparently crossed the road from Stretton Grandison to *Magnis* at Bartestree; north of this point there are a number of clear alignments as far as Ashton, near Leominster, but southwards from Mordiford its route is entirely conjectural.[3]

This quadrilateral of roads is fully discussed in Margary's definitive modern study, but there is, in addition, a locally attested road that bisects the area bounded by the quadrilateral and passes just over a kilometre south of the Little Birch parish boundary. Today the most easily identifiable section of this road runs from the cross-roads by the old school at Kings Caple, past Kings Caple church and Pennoxstone Court to the Wye; across the river at Red Rail (an anglicised form of the Welsh 'rhydd yr heol' — 'ford of the street') the alignment continues until it joins a track leading from Llanfrother to Kynaston, which gives it a slightly different alignment to Hentland church. In 1969 an excavation was carried out across a section of the road about 80 metres from the east bank of the river. This revealed at a depth of just over a metre (from the natural ground level to the crown of the road) a metalled surface; two layers of river cobbles sandwiched a layer of finer gravel, and the overall width of the road appeared to be about 7.3 metres. The excavators were confident they had found the original Roman road. In 2005, under the auspices of the Landscape Origins of the Wye Valley project, an excavation at Red Rail across a section of the road between the west bank of the river and the Hoarwithy — Sellack road also revealed a metalled surface, this time of cobbles at a depth of about 0.7 metres; however the fragments of eighteenth-century pottery discovered both immediately above and below this metalling showed that it could not be Roman but was more likely to give access to a riverside wharf marked on nineteenth-century maps.[4]

Despite the results of the 2005 excavation, this road is almost certainly Roman, even if in many parts its original surface has been overlaid by later ones. A telling argument is the fact that the name 'Capul streete' is recorded as early as 1453. East of Kings Caple old school its course, apart from one or two kinks, is reasonably straight to How Caple, somewhere near which it presumably joined the road north from *Ariconium*. Beyond Kynaston its course is more confusing; the path that leads from Hentland church to the A49 by Pengethley Manor, though reputed to be Roman, scarcely looks such. All this may prompt thoughts about what we mean by the term 'Roman road'. Do we mean a major strategically aligned road surveyed and engineered by Roman or Roman-trained professionals or do we also include earlier trackways still used in the Roman period, perhaps with some sections re-laid to Roman specifications? This latter definition might certainly explain the central section of the Red Rail road — a piece perhaps of professional Roman upgrading to carry the road across the damp Wye flood-plain. It may also be useful to bear in mind when examining the evidence for a Roman road actually traversing the parish of Little Birch (see section 12 below).[5]

There is no evidence that in Roman Britain as a whole there was any marked decline in population from the comparatively high levels of the late Iron Age — at least until the fifth century. The Sites and Monuments Record pages of the Historic Herefordshire On-line website indicate 494 entries for the Roman period (as opposed to 122 for the Iron Age). A reasonable proportion of these relates to sites outside the concentrations in major settlements such as *Magnis*, *Bravonium* and *Ariconium*. There are, however, no entries for Little Birch. This should not be taken as evidence that there was no activity or habitation there in the Roman period. One of the most significant developments in this period was the availability for the first time of mass-produced pottery, and many of the scattered Roman finds are of potsherds. These are most easily turned up by field walking in recently ploughed arable land; in parishes with a substantial proportion of pasture, such as Little Birch, there is less scope for this activity. Some parishes have also benefited from the attentions of a well-informed local enthusiast such as the late Elizabeth Taylor in Kings Caple.[6]

These factors may help to explain the apparent imbalance in the distribution of Roman finds and to put into perspective what has been found. Pottery finds have been recorded in Brockhampton, Kings Caple, Hentland, Sellack and Peterstow. In Little Dewchurch some potsherds were unearthed when the natural gas pipeline was being laid in 1970. Aerial photography has revealed the site of a possible Roman building near Penallt in Kings Caple. One of the interesting aspects of the discoveries in Sellack (near Upper Pengethley Farm) and Peterstow is that they seem to be associated with traces of iron-working, which suggests that the industrial activity of *Ariconium* may have been diffused westwards and across the Wye.[7]

In the end, however, perhaps the most significant fact may be the evidence for occupation during the Roman period in the Iron Age hill forts. The 1950 excavations at Aconbury and Dinedor revealed sherds of Roman as well as of Iron Age pottery, though the excavations were not sufficiently exhaustive to generate a detailed chronology for occupation after the Roman conquest. In central Herefordshire only the digs at Sutton Walls and Credenhill have been large enough to provide such information and their findings are intriguingly different. At Credenhill there seems to have been little activity after about 90 AD, whereas at Sutton Walls, despite the likely military onslaught at the time of the first Roman occupation, a part of the hill fort remained inhabited until about 300. The explanation usually proposed for this difference is that Credenhill lay only two kilometres from *Magnis*, and there would have been a progressive transfer of population as the Roman town developed; Sutton Walls, on the other hand, was not adjacent to a major Roman centre and so remained a substantial settlement in its own right. If this hypothesis is correct, it seems likely that Aconbury and Dinedor would have resembled Sutton Walls in their settlement history.[8]

In all probability then the Little Birch area in Roman times would have been similar to, or would have seen a very gradual development from, what it had been in the Iron Age. It is significant that the Bromley spindle-whorl mentioned above, though of Iron Age type, could well date from the Roman period. People would have lived in many of the same places in the same sort of houses. Roman administration brought better communications, some sort of money economy, more trade, more access to goods such as pottery and, almost certainly, greater political stability. The price was Roman taxation.

4   Archenfield

During the years around 400 AD all the regular units of the Roman army were progressively withdrawn from Britain. They went either to combat the barbarian incursions into the Empire in mainland Europe or to support the imperial aspirations of various ambitious generals. Such withdrawals had happened before, but this time the soldiers did not return. In 410 the Emperor Honorius apparently wrote to the cities of Britain advising them to make arrangements for their own defence.

At this time Roman Britain was confronted by three principal enemies. In the far north of the island were the unconquered northern Caledonian tribes known in later Roman Britain as the *Picti* or Picts; from across the Irish Sea there were raids and invasions by Goidelic Celts; and from across the North Sea there were increasingly heavy raids by Germanic tribes — most notably Angles and Saxons. The history of the two centuries from 400 to 600 is extremely obscure but one fact that seems fairly clear is that, of all the areas of Roman Britain, the area that became south-east Wales and the southern Marches was one of the last to be affected by the invasions and folk movements that convulsed the rest of the island. It was too far south to be threatened by the Picts and too far east to face serious incursions by the Irish, whose influence does not seem to have extended beyond Brycheiniog (Breconshire). The most dangerous adversaries of the Britons in the long term, the Angles and Saxons, took a long time to reach so far westward from their original settlements along the east coast. Not until 577 did a victory by the West Saxons at Dyrham in south Gloucestershire destroy the British kingdoms of the lower Severn valley. There is some evidence that a few years later a Saxon advance to the Wye was repulsed at Tintern.[1]

For 200 years, therefore, after the departure of Roman troops the territory bounded by the quadrilateral of Roman roads described by Margary, with *Magnis* at its north-west corner and *Ariconium* at its south-east, survived comparatively unscathed by invasion. This does not mean that the pattern of Romano-British life remained unchanged. Throughout Britain at this time there are signs of epidemic disease and population decline not directly related to warfare. The money economy disappeared, mass produced pottery was no longer available, and building techniques reverted to the use of timber and other non-durable materials. All this means that the archaeological record of the period in south Herefordshire is scanty — much more so even than that for the pre-Roman Iron Age.[2]

The most important survival in this area from the Roman period was Christianity. Christianity had been the religion of the Empire from the time of the Emperor Constantine (306–337), but the earliest Anglo-Saxon kingdoms preserved the paganism of their European origins. In the west of Britain, however, contacts were maintained across the sea to the western seaboard of Europe and the post-Roman church there.

Perhaps the earliest figure of the so-called Age of the Saints in south-west Britain was Dubricius or Dyfrig. He appears to have lived in the late fifth and early sixth centuries. An account of his life was not written down until the early twelfth century and, at such a distance in time, this was really rather a 'collection of traditions and local legends' than a true biography. On the other hand, he features prominently in a Life of the Breton saint Samson (who had been born in Wales), a work which is believed to date from the early seventh century. Dubricius is here referred to as *episcopus* — 'bishop' — and *papa* — 'father' — both of which terms suggest continuity with the institutions of a late Romano-British diocese. The centre of his cult was clearly in south Herefordshire; the seven churches dedicated to him include those of Ballingham, Hentland, St Devereux and Whitchurch. But his influence extended beyond this base. There are two church dedications to him in Wales — Gwenddwr, near Builth Wells and Llanfaches, between Newport and Chepstow — as well as one across the Bristol Channel at Porlock in Somerset.[3]

The twelfth-century Life (*Vita Dubrici*) recounts how he established and maintained for seven years a large centre for religious study at *hennlann super ripam Gui* — 'Hentland on the bank of the Wye'. The most likely — though not the only — identification for this place is Llanfrother, which lies south-west of the centre of Hoarwithy. The earlier forms of the name were *Hendresroudre* and *Henfrowther* — probably 'the old place of the brethren'. The farm at Llanfrother, where the seventeenth-century antiquarian, Silas Taylor, reported that the foundations of Dubricius' monastery were still visible, is on a ridge above the west bank of the Wye, but the site also slopes down to stream valleys to the west and the north. It is only just within Hentland parish, the boundary with Harewood lying a few metres away. Significantly, the long south-easterly extension of Little Birch protrudes to the stream running to the north of Llanfrother, the Red Brook, only about 700 metres distant. And Little Dewchurch parish extends south to near Prothither, just over a kilometre away. It seems as if Llanfrother may have been sited at the boundary between two large estates existing in the centuries before the Norman Conquest (see below).[4]

Discussion of Dubricius leads us to the most difficult problem in understanding our area in the so-called Dark Ages, the way in which it was ruled and administered. Roman political and administrative institutions did not survive for many decades after the departure of the army. Britain became an island of small kingdoms; in the east were the various kingdoms of the English invaders; in the west were those of the British, the peoples whom the English began to call Welsh (*walh* — 'foreigner', 'serf') and who began to call themselves Cymry (*combroges* — 'fellow-countrymen'). These kingdoms were unstable, and the smaller ones tended to be absorbed and become parts of larger ones. In southern Herefordshire was located the kingdom of Erging. This does not seem to have had any independent existence after the early seventh century but survived as some sort of semi-autonomous district dependent on a neighbouring authority until the Norman Conquest and as a division of civil or ecclesiastical administration even after that. The earliest form of the name was *Ercic* and the English anglicized it as *Arcenefelde*, which gives us the modern Archenfield.[5]

Before embarking on an account of Archenfield, it is necessary to say something of our sources of information about it. Although its existence is mentioned in various works such as the Anglo-Saxon Chronicle, most of the relevant material is found in the *Liber Landavensis*, or Book of Llandaff. However, the Book of Llandaff is a very problematic source. It was compiled in the twelfth century, much of it between 1120 and 1130 at the instigation of Urban, Bishop of Llandaff from 1107 to 1134. As well as saints' lives (including that of St Dubricius already referred to) it contains a series of charters recording grants of land to religious foundations during preceding centuries; many of these charters are prefaced by passages of historical narrative. The problem with the material arises from the motivation for its original compilation. Urban was engaged in a lengthy, and ultimately unsuccessful, attempt to persuade the Pope that considerable parts of the dioceses of Hereford and St Davids properly belonged to the diocese of Llandaff. It is rather like reading a scientific treatise on lung disease produced by the tobacco industry to prove that its products are harmless. But despite the clear special pleading in the Book of Llandaff, modern scholars have proved that the charters, though corrupt in places, also incorporate much probably genuine early material and so, used carefully, provide valuable information for the historian.[6]

Erging was later described as the land lying between the Wye, the Monnow and Worm Brook. But there is plenty of evidence to suggest that in its earliest existence it must have extended well beyond these limits. For a start there is its name, which, it is generally agreed, is a Welsh derivation from the British name

Ariconium, a place lying nearly five kilometres east of the Wye. In the fourteenth century there was apparently a longstanding ecclesiastical link between the church of Lugwardine and five churches in Archenfield, and in the sixteenth century a chapel dedicated to St Dubricius was recorded at Woolhope. As well as evidence for Archenfield once having controlled territory east of the Wye, there are hints of its extension north and west of Worm Brook as far as the Wye west of Hereford. The Life of St Dubricius tells us that he was born at Madley and was the grandson of Peibiau, king of Archenfield, whose seat was described as being at Moccas.[7]

When and how this earlier 'greater' Archenfield was reduced in size is not clear. It may have been during the reign of the expansionist king Aethelbald or his even more formidable successor, Offa, who between them ruled Mercia for 80 years. Both the Anglo-Saxon Chronicle and the Welsh Annals speak of war between the English and Welsh in the early and middle parts of the eighth century; the Annals record a battle at a place called *Pencoet* — very probably Pencoyd, four kilometres south of Little Birch — in 721, and another battle at Hereford in 760.[8]

The later north-eastern boundary of Archenfield was described in the *Liber Landavensis* as following 'the Guormuy up to its source, from the source of the Guormuy to Caer Rein, from Caer Rein to the source of the Taratyr, along the Taratyr till it falls into the Wye, along the Wye ...'. The Guormuy here is Worm Brook, which derives its name not from the English *wurm*, meaning a snake or dragon, but from the Welsh *gwrm*, meaning dark or dusky. Caer Rein is Aconbury Camp. The origin of the name *Rein* is obscure; it probably derives from an early Welsh personal name, and the most likely candidate is Rhain Dremrudd, a king of Brycheiniog (Brecon), perhaps in the late sixth century. Erging probably ceased to be an independent kingdom about this time, but it is not clear whether there is any connexion between these two rather shadowy scraps of information. Finally we have the stream or river called the Taratyr. There have been various speculations about this. What is clear is that as late as 1639 there was a mill on the Wye known as Abbot Tarretts Mill; it was situated on the west bank just within the parish of Bolstone, where the river bends sharply eastward to run below Ballingham Hill; its name was a corruption of the earlier form *Abertarader* — 'the mouth of the Tarader'. The problem is that two streams enter the Wye near this point and a third about 700 metres to the north. It has been suggested that this third stream — the longest of the three — has at some time in the past been diverted, that it originally joined the course of the middle stream to enter the Wye, and that it was the Taratyr.[9]

This account of the boundary of Archenfield is obviously expressed briefly and approximately. It seems that the eastern boundary probably did not exactly follow the Wye, where the river's meanders are especially pronounced between Bolstone and Ross. According to the Domesday Book, Kings Caple, on the eastern bank, lay in Archenfield, while Foy and much of Sellack, on the western bank, apparently constituted a small English hundred. There are in addition two descriptions of the boundary of the manor of Wormelow, dating from 1639 and 1816. The northern boundary of this manor is likely to follow the much earlier northern boundary of

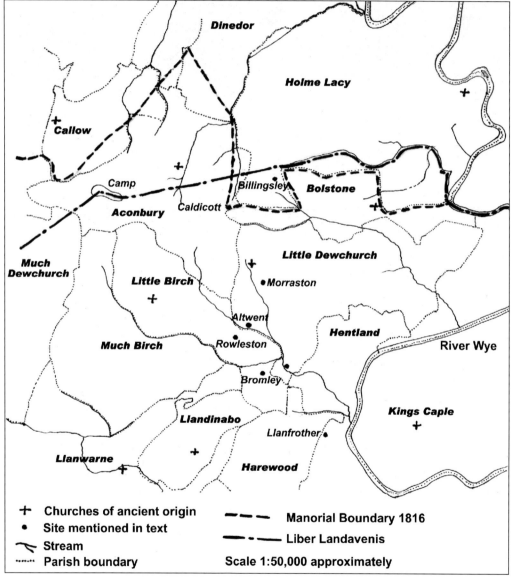

Fig. 4.1 Map of Archenfield showing its northern boundary as indicated in the Liber Landavensis *and by the description of the bounds of the Manor of Wormelow in 1816*

Archenfield. Unfortunately part of the 1639 document is missing and the description extends only as far east as 'Aconburies Mill' — probably Tar's Mill. In the 1816 description, which is complete and, for most of the boundary, extremely detailed, there are only two named points between Pullaston and Caldicot, namely Dinedor Cross and 'Torr's Mills'. Almost certainly the boundary line between Pullaston and Caldicot would in detail have followed streams and parish boundaries rather than run in straight lines. Even so, it is clear from these manorial documents that the boundary of Archenfield is likely to have been drawn not along the top of Aconbury Hill but rather to include most of the land to the north sloping up to the hill — that is the whole of what became the parish of Aconbury, much of which lies to the north of the hill, as well perhaps as part of the future parish of Dinedor. The only part of the boundary which approaches a ridge affording a prospect south into Archenfield is between Cold Nose, near Callow, and Pullaston. Finally, like Domesday, the 1816 boundary includes land east of the Wye in Kings Caple and Fawley.[10]

Whatever the precise dividing line between English territory and the Welsh area of Archenfield at the end of the eighth century, the district around Aconbury Hill was now obviously situated on a political and racial frontier, though one where the strategic allocation of territory seems to have favoured the Welsh. The charters granting land contained in the *Liber Landavensis*, apart from some very early (seventh-century) grants around Madley and in the Golden Valley, do not include any which relate to land north of the boundary established by 800. The nearest grant to Little Birch was made about 850 for a place called *Ecclesia Cum Mouric* — which has tentatively been identified with Moraston in Little Dewchurch, about 700 metres from the Little Birch/Little Dewchurch parish boundary. There is a fairly detailed description of the boundaries of the land granted in this charter mentioning a stream called the Iguern, which it has been suggested may be the stream that flows through Athelstan's Wood; there is also mention of an additional grant of land *trans viam* — 'across the road' — which may give an early indication of the existence of the road linking Aconbury, Caldicot, Little Dewchurch and Hoarwithy. Other nearby grants of land in the Llandaff Charters relate to Llandinabo and Ballingham.[11]

By the early tenth century, though the boundaries of Archenfield had probably not changed, there had evidently been an evolution of the political arrangements which applied to it. These may have come about in the wake of the events of the year 914. Herefordshire was so situated as to escape the most serious Viking attacks, but in that year a raid launched from Brittany came up the Severn estuary and evidently penetrated to Archenfield since the bishop of Archenfield, who bore the irreproachably Welsh name of Cyfeiliog, was captured. He had to be ransomed by the English king and subsequently, as the Anglo-Saxon Chronicle tells us, the men of Gloucester, Hereford and other neighbouring boroughs combined together to attack the raiders, killing many of them including Hroald, one of the two leaders of the expedition; eventually, after further fighting, the depleted remnants of the Viking force were compelled to retreat to Ireland.[12]

It was about a dozen years after this, in the reign of the English king Athelstan, that the curious document known as *The Ordinance concerning the Dunsaete* was written. The Dunsaete evidently constituted a group of people containing both English and Welsh communities who lived on either side of a substantial river. Most scholars are agreed that all the evidence points to the territory of the Dunsaete equating to, or at least including, Archenfield. As we have seen, there was little left of Archenfield on the eastern bank of the Wye by this time and it is not clear how much English settlement had occurred on the west bank, south of the Taratyr. There is a good deal of reference in the *Ordinance* to the river bank and crossing the river, with the implication that to a large degree the river was a racial boundary, so the Dunsaete may have included English settlements outside Archenfield. The dykes which still survive in the parishes of Foy and Kings Caple may well indicate early boundaries between English and Welsh settlements. The *Ordinance* itself is a set of procedures designed to moderate, where the two races lived close together, between the different laws of the English and Welsh, particularly in relation to crimes such as murder and cattle raiding. The picture presented is a bit like that seen later in the provinces of the Ottoman Empire where different racial and religious communities were allowed to retain their own laws and customs under a single political authority within the same district.[13]

This apparently harmonious arrangement was to be abruptly terminated 150 years later in the middle of the eleventh century. The agency for this upheaval was not, however, the Norman Conquest but what occurred ten years earlier. To understand what probably happened we need to look more closely at the events of the early tenth century. It had been an English king who ransomed the Welsh bishop Cyfeiliog and English volunteers who had expelled the Viking aggressors. The final paragraphs of the *Ordinance* suggest strongly that the Dunsaete — Welsh as well as English — owed their political allegiance to the English authorities. This is confirmed and amplified by an interesting paragraph near the beginning of the Domesday Book for Herefordshire, which reveals the price that had to be paid for English protection. The paragraph occurs in an account of the customs of the Welshmen of Archenfield before 1066. Most of the account deals with the same legal issues addressed in the *Ordinance*, but at the end comes a clear statement of military obligation: 'When the army advances on the enemy, these men by custom form the vanguard and on their return the rearguard.'[14]

It may be imagined that these arrangements did not always make the men of Archenfield popular with the independent Welsh communities living to the west of them. The history of Wales from the period of the first arrival of the English in Britain to the end of the Middle Ages is generally one of disunity and fragmentation, but every so often a leader arose with the drive and charisma to unify the country and challenge English dominance. One such man in the eleventh century was Gruffydd ap Llywelyn. He became king of Gwynedd in 1039 and gradually succeeded in gaining control of the whole of Wales. This left him free to turn his attention to England, and the border county of Herefordshire bore the brunt of his onslaughts. It should be said that Gruffydd was quite prepared to attack Welshmen in any part of Wales who contested his supremacy and to ally himself with Englishmen, like the rebel Earl Aelfgar, who found themselves in opposition to the government of the English king, Edward the Confessor.[15]

The most devastating of Gruffydd's attacks came in 1055 when he, with Aelfgar, advanced on Hereford. The local forces raised to defend it were defeated and the Welsh army captured and sacked the town, burning down the cathedral and killing seven of its priests. The English were forced to call up their most formidable commander, Earl Harold Godwinsson, the future King Harold. He compelled Gruffydd to withdraw up the Golden Valley but was unable to defeat him. Negotiations followed, which led to some sort of peace agreement. The peace talks were conducted at a place the Anglo-Saxon Chronicle calls *Bylgeslege*, which can only have been the settlement we now know as Billingsley, the farm lying to the east of the road leading from Caldicot to Holme Lacy and just over two kilometres from the Little Birch parish boundary. Billingsley, of course, was sited on the political and racial boundary between Archenfield and English Herefordshire (see above and map).[16]

The facts that Harold and Gruffydd met here, that Harold had advanced against Gruffydd from Gloucester and that the campaign had penetrated as far as the Golden Valley, suggest that it was this campaign that wreaked the worst of the terrible destruction in Archenfield described 30 years later in the Domesday Book. The compilers of Domesday were required to report, amongst other things, on the conditions applying in each place 'in the time of King Edward' — i.e. before the Norman Conquest. Explaining the scanty information they provided for Archenfield, they said: 'King Grifin and Blein [Gruffydd's half-brother, Bleddyn] laid this land waste in the time of King Edward; therefore what it was like at that time is not known.' There were probably other reasons apart from this devastation that caused the information on Archenfield in Domesday to be somewhat limited, but there are some revealing comments on other areas in western Herefordshire which were better documented in Domesday and had also suffered from Gruffydd's activities. In Clifford and around Kington it seems that there were considerable areas that had been depopulated and, by 1086, were reverting to woodland; it is quite likely that parts of Archenfield were similarly affected.[17]

It may be asked whether and how the history of Archenfield, now 1,000 years and more in the past, is relevant to the Little Birch of modern times. The answer is that the so-called 'Dark Ages' decisively shaped the pattern of settlement in the area as they did in almost every place in rural Britain. In Archenfield it is the half submerged but still visible Celtic foundations that are most significant. Three examples will serve to demonstrate this.

First there is the distribution of settlement. In Welsh communities the unit of settlement was the *tref* (plural *trefi*). Where the inhabitants were free men (the more usual situation) a *tref* was an estate of somewhere around 125 acres with a settlement consisting of a homestead or a small number of homesteads (*tyddynod*); initially these *trefi* were probably inhabited by members of one kin or extended family. Though in the *trefi* of bondmen the homesteads were grouped together, the number of homesteads in each was likely to be small. Given such settlements, individual churches would probably not serve individual *trefi*. This essentially produced a different type of settlement pattern from the large but more compact nucleated villages common to some parts of England. Individual homesteads and small hamlets were dispersed across the landscape and churches were sometimes isolated.[18]

In Archenfield as a whole many examples of these features survive. In Little Birch it is difficult to determine what the settlement pattern in the north-west part of the parish might have been like. The parish as a unit almost certainly did not exist until the late eleventh or early twelfth century and there is no evidence for a church before this time. More recently, there has obviously been at some stages a rather larger settlement around the church than now exists but it is by no means certain what sort of settlement was there before the Norman Conquest. What is clear is that at the other end of the parish are two estates that look very like the successors of *trefi*. Bromley and Rowlston (or as we should now describe the latter, New Mills Farm) are almost entirely separated from the other farms in the parish by Athelstan's Wood. The history of their ownership is also separate and distinct as are their field systems (see section 8). The existence of both is evidenced in the Middle Ages (Bromley from 1334 and Rowlston from 1254). Both are also of roughly the same size that scholars have considered normal for *trefi*; when the tithe map for Little Birch was drawn up in 1841, New Mills Farm comprised 147 acres and Bromley 144 acres. Apart from such settlements in Little Birch, there are other very similar ones in neighbouring parishes; two which apparently existed before the Norman Conquest and have already been mentioned are Billingsley on the boundary between Holme Lacy and Bolstone parishes and Moraston in Little Dewchurch.[19]

In view of the Welsh pattern of settlement we would not be surprised to find a high proportion of place names of Welsh origin. This is generally true of Archenfield as a whole. Many parish names are of Welsh origin (for example Hentland, Sellack, Garway, Llanwarne, Llandinabo), and so are a large number of surviving settlement names. Many of the latter are listed in the most recent study of the Celtic impact on place names in England, *Celtic voices, English places*, but the authors of this work note that far more will be added to the list when a full study of Herefordshire place names is eventually completed. There are also several church dedications to Welsh saints in the area. Apart from the dedications to Dubricius, already mentioned, there are three to St David (Much and Little Dewchurch and Kilpeck), and one each to St Dinabo (Llandinabo), St Tysilio (Sellack), St Deinst (Llangarren), and St Weonard (St Weonards). Little Birch, however, though indisputably part of Archenfield, has no surviving settlement names of Welsh origin that can clearly be traced back to the Middle Ages. There are a handful of Welsh field names; in the early seventeenth century one of the village's surviving open fields was called the Myndfield. There is the stream name 'Wenleys' recorded in the thirteenth century, probably derived from the Welsh *gwyn + glais* — 'white stream' — which may be an early name for Wriggle Brook. From the same period there is one settlement name — Hendre Thomas — but it is not certain that this referred to a place in rather than adjoining Little Birch, and in any case the name did not survive. Castle Nibole, though an interesting and suggestive name, is not found in documents earlier than 1670. The possible reasons for this absence of Welsh names will be further discussed below.[20]

One final and very curious survival from Archenfield's Welsh past is worth particular comment. This concerns the laws and customs relating to the inheritance of land. It seems likely, though it is not certain, that in Anglo-Saxon communities prior to the Norman Conquest some sort of division of land among the sons of a deceased land-holder was usual. Whatever the reality, such a practice gave place after the Conquest to the system of primogeniture, where the landed estate went solely to the eldest son. In mediaeval Welsh law the land of a land-owner in a free *tref* was shared equally among his sons after his death — a custom that came to be known as gavelkind; involved rules existed which attempted to control and rationalise the complications which such arrangements could lead to as generation succeeded generation. In Archenfield gavelkind seems to have been retained even when the area was more fully integrated into Herefordshire after 1066. Indeed, it survived in Wales after the Edwardian conquest at the end of the thirteenth century. The laws of independent Wales were finally abolished by the Act of Union in 1536 during the reign of Henry VIII. But Archenfield was not in Wales or even in the Welsh March and here at least gavelkind continued after 1536. Two documents dated 1596 and 1600 give an account of arrangements to apportion rights between co-heirs to gavelkind lands in Orcop and St Weonards. It certainly seems to have survived in Little Birch even to the end of the eighteenth century. Details of this survival and its significance in shaping the local landscape will be considered in section 8.[21]

In 1063 Gruffydd ap Llywelyn was killed by his own countrymen. After several more years' fighting, some of it in Herefordshire, he had eventually been driven into Snowdonia by Harold, and deserted by his followers. Three years later, after a brief reign as King of England, Harold was himself killed at Hastings. England, including Archenfield, was purposefully re-organized on feudal principles by the comparatively small group of French-speaking Norman knights and barons who had supported William the Conqueror in his English adventure. A fairly early feature of this process was the compilation of the Domesday Book, commissioned by William in 1085 and compiled during the ensuing year.[22]

For many English villages the Domesday Book provides the first specific reference. The Birches — Much and Little — are no exception, but this did not always seem to be the case. The single volume so far to appear of the *Victoria County History* of Herefordshire, published in 1908, printed the text of the original manuscript, now held in the National Archives with a translation and list of places. There was no mention of Birch. Indeed few places in Archenfield were described and some of these were impossible to identify. Much of the area was disposed of in a summary beginning: 'In Archenfield the King has 100 men, less 4, who have 73 ploughs with their men.' The fact is that recording Archenfield would have presented particular and serious problems. For a start, the area had never been integrated into English administration, and much of the evidence would have concerned customs and obligations not found in most other parts of the country. The devastation of 1055 had, as Domesday itself stated (see above), made it impossible to say what the area was like before that time. Finally, evidence would have had to be taken verbally from people many of whom presumably spoke no English, French or Latin, but rather Welsh.[23]

However, by great good fortune it was found that another manuscript of the Herefordshire section of the Domesday Book had survived. It is in the library of Balliol College, Oxford, apparently part of a bequest to the college by the eighteenth century Herefordshire antiquary, George Coningsby. This manuscript probably dates from between 1160 and 1170. It is in the main a faithful copy of the original, but it contains a number of marginal entries, made apparently to assist officials using the document 80 years or so after the material had first been compiled. The marginalia include place names and one of these links the entry for a hitherto unidentified place — one of the comparatively few individual entries for Archenfield — with the Birches. In translation the main entry is as follows:

> Roger de Laci holds Mainaure. Costelin held it in the time of King Edward. Now his son holds from Roger. 4 ploughs there. He pays 6 sesters of honey and 10 shillings. Roger has 1 Welshman there and he pays 5 shillings and 1 sester of honey.

In the left-hand margin, in red, is the shoulder heading 'Mainaure' and immediately above this has been written 'Birches'. Such is the first mention of Birch by name; it may be brief, yet read carefully, it is extremely informative.[24]

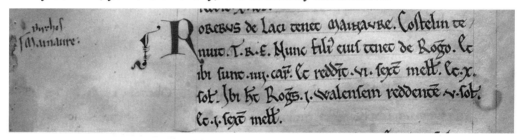

Fig. 4.2 Extract from the twelfth-century transcript of the Domesday Book for Herefordshire held at Balliol College, Oxford

The first point of interest is the name. *Mainaure* is not so much a Welsh place name as a Welsh word. In the early Welsh law-books a *maenor* or *mainaur* was an administrative unit comprising a number of *trefi*. Despite its similarity in appearance to the word *manerium* — 'manor' — it has a quite different derivation, from the Welsh *maen*, meaning 'stone'. It has been suggested that this was because the *llys* or court inhabited by the magnate who controlled the *mainaur* would have been the only stone-built structure that it contained. To make the word *mainaur* into a place name it would normally have been expected for it to be qualified by a further word, usually an adjective. It appears that sometimes a *mainaur* in an upland area was paired with an adjacent lowland *mainaur*. In the Balliol manuscript of the Herefordshire Domesday, a marginal note by another entry refers to a *Meiner Reau*, possibly a mis-hearing of *mainaur fro*, or lowland *mainaur*. The entry to which this marginal note apparently refers is for Harewood. A glance at a map highlighting the local parish boundaries reminds us how a group of parishes sloping down southwards from Aconbury Hill — Much Birch, Little Birch and Little Dewchurch — converge towards a group of parishes on lower ground — Hentland, Harewood and Llandinabo — at or near Llanfrother. It has been suggested that Birch was once part of an upland *mainaur*, linked to a corresponding lowland *mainaur*, which together constituted the territory originally controlled by the Iron Age hill fort of Aconbury.[25]

As far as the status of the land-holders in *Mainaure* is concerned, matters would have been a little different if Domesday had been compiled earlier in William's reign. In 1086 *Mainaure* is listed with other estates directly owned by the king. However, immediately after the Conquest the king had appointed three tough and trusted Norman noblemen to deal with the turbulent Welsh border. The man created Earl of Hereford was William Fitzosbern. Like the newly created Earls of Chester and Shrewsbury he was a palatine earl, that is one directly exerting royal authority and granting land to his own followers. Fitzosbern was killed in 1071; his son was subsequently involved in a plot against the king and dispossessed. Thus the de Lacys, probably originally holding the land from Fitzosbern, held it from the king in 1086.[26]

Costelin is a much greater puzzle. Domesday names very few pre-Conquest land-holders in Archenfield, but of those it does name most, as we might expect, have Welsh names — apart from Earl Harold and King Edward. The exception is Costelin; his name according to the expert on the subject is not Welsh, English or Norman but of continental Germanic origin. What a man with a name like this was doing in Archenfield before 1066 is a matter of conjecture. One explanation is that he might have been one of the foreign soldiers granted land by Edward the Confessor; there would presumably have been plenty of vacant land in Archenfield after the devastation of 1055. Another possibility, not so far researched by any authority, is that the name may after all be Welsh, perhaps a mis-hearing of *Gwasteilo*, a name that appears in the parish in the thirteenth century.[27]

Of the five men with plough-teams mentioned in the entry — presumably the heads of families occupying farms — four are apparently English, one certainly Welsh. In most entries for Archenfield no distinction was made between Welsh and English; such a distinction was probably only made when both Welsh and English lived in the same estate, the Welshmen being the ones specified; in other entries which refer only to 'men' it is usually assumed they are Welsh. Whatever the race of the farmers, the remainder of the material looks Welsh. The money rents and particularly the rents paid in honey (a sester was a measure of volume) were features of Welsh land-holding. The amount of land is described in terms of the number of ploughs — *carucae* — needed to cultivate it, rather than using the Anglo-Saxon unit of land measurement, the hide. However a carucate is generally considered to have been roughly equivalent in size to a hide — about 120 acres. This implies that the land under arable cultivation in *Mainaure* was about 600 acres; the combined size of the present-day parishes of Much and Little Birch is just over 2,300 acres.[28]

So much for the facts. Are there any further inferences to be drawn from them? Here is an estate in the Welsh district of Archenfield, which obviously has Welsh customs; on the other hand, only one of its five farmers is Welsh and its feudal sub-tenant seems to belong to a family of continental Germanic origin. The clue to solving these discrepancies may be the significance of the settlement names. The fact that no Welsh settlement name recorded before 1500 survives in Little Birch today has already been mentioned. Although Little Birch was in Archenfield, it lay very near the latter's northern boundary. It is perhaps significant that the one Archenfield parish north of Little Birch — Aconbury — is also lacking in Welsh settlement names. It is not mentioned by name in Domesday, but Caer Rein appears only in the *Liber Landavensis*. In 1213 it is recorded as Akornebir, from the old English *acweorne* — a squirrel — so 'an old fort inhabited by squirrels'.[29]

In fact, the racial boundary appears at some stage to have moved to the southern boundary of Little Birch parish. Once one goes a few hundred metres into Little Dewchurch, Welsh settlement names or names with Welsh elements abound (for example Altwent, Moraston, Prothither). We cannot be sure when this happened but it could well have been the result of resettlement after the disastrous upheavals of 1055. Though the name *Mainaure* survived in 1086, it seems to have done so only in a truncated form as if the second element the name probably once possessed had been forgotten or not properly understood. By the 1160s it had given way to the English 'Birches', presumably in the plural because two parishes, each with its own church, had been created. As for the settlements taking their name from the birch tree, it is worth noting that birches are among the first trees to colonize waste ground.

5   Aconbury Priory

The Norman Conquest gradually imposed new systems of administration on Archenfield. The feudal organisation of manors in the area, however, seems to have been rather different from that found in other parts of England. Evidently certain of the customs of pre-Conquest Archenfield persisted in some form, particularly in relation to military obligatons.[1]

Judging by the annotations to the twelfth-century transcript of the Herefordshire Domesday (see above) the settlements known collectively as 'The Birches' must have been established by this time. The implication of the annotation is that there were at least two and these were probably Much Birch and Little Birch; this period is the likeliest date for the creation of the present pattern of parishes. The common name 'Birch' and the common dedication of their churches — to St. Mary — suggest that their origins must have been linked, though Much Birch was one of the parishes to change its dedication to St Thomas à Becket in the thirteenth century, that dedication being reversed in the sixteenth century when Henry VIII decreed that Becket should be regarded only as 'Bishop Becket'. It is a curious fact that, despite this apparent early connexion, the ecclesiastical links of the two parishes have, for most of their history been quite different. Much Birch was for centuries a perpetual curacy and chapelry of Much Dewchurch, while the livings of Little Birch was joined with that of Aconbury.[2]

Little Birch's links with Aconbury almost certainly derive from the establishment at Aconbury in the early thirteenth century of a priory. The earliest charters in the cartulary of Aconbury Priory, preserved in the National Archives, are retrospective; they date from the reign of Henry III, citing the original grant of the land for the priory from Henry's father, King John. The only contemporaneous record of the grant for the foundation of the priory is found in the Patent Rolls. It is dated 10 October 1216 from 'Lenne' (King's Lynn) and granted to Margaret, wife of Walter de Lacy, three carucates of land to be assarted from the forest of Aconbury for the foundation of a house for religious women for the souls of

William de Braose (Margaret's father), Matilda (her mother) and William (her brother).[3]

The date and the stated purpose of this foundation, taken together are most significant. In the earlier part of King John's reign, William de Braose had been one of the king's favourites, but there had been a breach in 1207 and William had been declared a traitor. He took refuge in Ireland but was pursued there by John in 1210. Though William managed to escape to France, his wife and son were captured and conveyed to Windsor Castle where they were apparently starved to death — as one historian has put it, 'one of the grimmer examples of the king's merciless love of cruelty'. In 1216 the king arrived in King's Lynn on 9 October, threatened by civil war and an invasion from France. He was immediately struck down with an attack of dysentery which was to kill him nine days later. The implication that the grant to Margaret de Lacy was an act of contrition in the face of approaching death is convincing.[4]

It is worth trying to tease out what King John's grant actually consisted of. Three carucates constituted a not inconsiderable area — about 360 acres. The grant specifically mentions the right to assart, a term which strictly means grubbing up trees and shrubs to create arable land. As far as the term 'forest' is concerned, it can carry the meanings both of woodland and land preserved for hunting and it raises the question of just how much of the area was wooded in 1216. The inhabitants of Archenfield successfully appealed in 1252 for Archenfield to be disafforested, but this clearly implies the removal of laws protecting royal hunting forest rather than wholesale clearance of trees. It has been argued that Athelstan's Wood, which according to documents dating from the reign of Henry III had originally been excluded from John's grant to Margaret de Lacy, was so named because it had originally belonged to Bishop Athelstan of Hereford, who died in 1056. If so, this argues for the existence of substantial woodland in the area at that date. The devastation of Gryffydd ap Llewellyn, as has been pointed out above, very probably led to an extension of woodland growth over depopulated land between 1055 and 1086. The very name Aconbury — 'old fort inhabited by squirrels' — recorded in 1213, suggests the existence of trees at or near the summit. At the other end of the parish the name 'Bromley' recorded in 1334 implies a woodland clearing. Finally it seems that all grants to the priory observed the right of the crown to the 'great timber' of the forest, a situation which persisted at the end of the sixteenth century after the dissolution of the monasteries.[5]

It is tempting to identify part of the area assarted by the priory with the two large areas of cultivated ground south of the priory and which climb the lower northern slopes of Aconbury Hill between Holloway Bank Wood, Wallbrook Wood and Condies Wood. Clearing evidently did not proceed rapidly. Only two of the three caracates had been cleared by 1242. This may have been due to the scarcity of labour in what must have been a remote district. It may, however, have reflected other difficulties. The early years of the priory were beset with problems.[6]

From the rather confused documents it seems that the autonomy of the priory's title to the lands King John had granted was challenged during the early part of the reign of his successor, Henry III, first by unlawful acts committed by William de Cantilupe and Hugh de Kilpec and then, in 1227, by the grant of the king himself of Archenfield to Hugo de Burgh with specific rights to the wood of Aconbury Forest and the advowson of the priory of Aconbury. By 1265 these rights had reverted to the crown. De Burgh's grant had included Athelstan's Wood and when Henry III confirmed the priory's grant, Athelstan's Wood, initially excepted from the grant of King John, was added. This gave the priory its first land in Little Birch. Of the 200 or so acres of Athelstan's Wood about four-fifths lies in Little Birch parish and one-fifth in Aconbury.[7]

More serious, at least from the religious point of view, was the dispute that raged for the first 20 years of the priory's existence about which religious order it should be attached to. When Margaret de Lacy obtained her grant from King John she had intended that it should be attached to the Order of St John of Jerusalem — the Hospitallers — attached to the Order's preceptory at Dinmore. It seems it was her intention that there should be a hospital at Aconbury. Subsequently, however, she realised that even women attached to the Order would be liable for service overseas and attempted to have the nuns transferred to the Augustinian Order. The Order of St John resisted these moves vigorously. The dispute involved two petitions by Margaret to the pope and inquiries by the Bishop of Coventry, the Prior of St Albans, the Bishop of Hereford and the Abbot of Dore. It seems that the arguments even divided the sisters within the priory itself. Margaret's husband, the influential Walter de Lacy, great-grandson of the Roger de Lacy who had held *Mainaure* in 1086, became involved, and the dispute was referred to a papal legate; as a result, in 1237, the priory was finally freed from the rule of the Order of St John and remained a house for Augustinian canonnesses until its dissolution.[8]

Before the end of the thirteenth century, the priory was to gain more land in Little Birch. In 1275 John de Lacy, son of Hugh de Lacy and nephew of Walter and Margaret, released to the prioress and nuns of Aconbury the lands and tenements in 'Rolvestone' which he had by gift from Roger Codach, son of Wasteyl Codach. He accompanied this grant with the original deed of gift from Roger Codach to himself, dating from some time between 1216 and 1272. This grant had to be confirmed in 1278 by the king as it was land held in chief — i.e. directly from the king himself. This was why in 1400 the priory's accounts show a rent of four shillings paid to the king. It appears that Roger's father, Wasteyl, had conveyed the same property, but for a fixed term only, to Sir John de Turbervile in 1254. The land identified in the grant is Rowlston in Little Birch — or perhaps what we should now describe as New Mills Farm.[9]

The names in this document are fascinating. The settlement name has as its second element the English '-*tun*' — 'farmstead', 'estate'; but the earliest forms 'Raueston' or 'Ralfueston' in 1254 indicating the Norman name Ralph — suggests at one stage a Norman occupier. A similar derivation applies to the village of Rowlestone near Ewyas Harold. Who this Ralph might have been is not at all clear. Several Ralphs are named in the Domesday Book entries for Herefordshire and it must be remembered that even before the Conquest, King Edward the Confessor had installed a number of Normans and Anglo-Normans in Herefordshire. One of these was Earl Ralph of Mantes, known as Ralph the Timid for his disastrously ineffective leadership in resisting the first onslaughts of Gruffydd ap Llewelyn. The Anglo-Norman place name of 'Rolvestone' and the completely English name of Bromley suggest that, if, as has been argued, these were originally '*trefi*', there must have been changes of ownership and name resulting from the turmoil of the mid-11th century. However, the man who gave the land to John de Lacy is even more puzzling. He has the solidly Norman forename Roger; his surname clearly gave contemporary scribes trouble, for it appears in different documents as 'Codach', 'Codauh', 'Cadach', etc. It looks Welsh, and his father's name 'Wasteyl' or 'Wastelyn' is certainly Welsh — an Anglo Norman form of 'Gwasteilo', literally 'the servant of (Saint) Teilo'. Nothing could be more indicative of the fact that the racial background to this part of twelfth- and thirteenth-century Archenfield was still very complex even if, as has been argued (in section 4 above), there had been a southward movement of English settlement names in the previous 200 years.[10]

Not quite all of 'Rolvestone' appears to have been included in John de Lacy's release of 1275 to the priory. Although Roger Codach's grant to John de Lacy talked of 'all his lands and tenements in Rolvestone', he had apparently already disposed of some land there to Griffin Cut, described as 'of Llanwarne'. This land, comprising 12 acres, was sold on to Lawrence, variously described as Lawrence de Wyke, Lawrence de Clehongre and Lawrence of Cornbury, from whom it was acquired by Aconbury Priory, Lawrence having obtained from Griffin's widow, Margery, the release of all her interest in it. The original document recording the transfer to Griffin Cut, unfortunately, like the other documents relating to that piece of land, undated, describes it as adjoining Hendre Thomas and extending along the brook called 'Wenleys'.[11]

This series of documents raises some interesting questions about where the various places mentioned were actually located since neither of the names Wenleys or Hendre Thomas survives today. New Mills Farm, which, as has already been noted, seems to represent a land unit of some antiquity, occupies an approximately triangular piece of land bounded on the west by the eastern end of Athelstan's Wood, on the south by Wriggle Brook and on the north by the stream which rises to the south-east of Merrivale Farm, flows through Athelstan's Wood and past Altwent Farm in Little Dewchurch to join Wriggle Brook a little to the north-west of Prothither. The brook called Wenleys must be one of these streams and the balance of probability favours Wriggle Brook. Griffin Cut obviously had property in Llanwarne and there is a short stretch of Wriggle Brook which forms the boundary between the parishes of Llanwarne and Little Birch. New Mills Farm lies on the Little Birch side of this boundary and Blewhenstone on the Llanwarne side; according to the tithe map of 1841 one small field on the Little Birch side of Wriggle Brook is named Blewhenstone Meadow. The brook to the north, flowing through Athelstan's Wood, runs in a deep valley between Little Dewchurch and Little Birch; the fields on the Little Birch side, part of the New Mills Farm property, are very steep and there are no traces of habitation, though on the Little Dewchurch side lie the Crickets and Altwent Farm. This brook has no modern name, but Bruce Coplestone-Crow, in his study of Herefordshire place names, has suggested it may be the stream called 'Iguern', mentioned in a boundary clause of 'Cum Mouric' — often identified with Moraston in Little Dewchurch — in the *Liber Landavensis*. It is not possible to identify whether Hendre Thomas lay within 'Rolvestone' and therefore in Little Birch or outside it, perhaps in Llanwarne. A document in the National Archives dated 1289 speaks of the Prioress of Aconbury having a right to certain land in Hendre Thomas; this may imply it lay within Little Birch.[12]

Another important but uncertain issue is the location of the principal settlement within 'Rolvestone'. The farmhouse of the modern farm is New Mills, situated beside Wriggle Brook and the site of the highest upstream of five water mills that once lay along the brook's course, (the others being Hoarwithy Mill, Tresseck Mill, Middle Mill and Prothither Mill.) The mill leat is clearly marked on the tithe map of 1841 and was apparently only filled in between the two World Wars. There is mention of a mill at Rolvestone in one of the earliest surviving court rolls of the priory in 1304. In 1340 it is referred to as the new mill; it seems probable that a mill existed there before the priory acquired the manor because mills are mentioned in the conveyance to Sir John de Turbervile in 1254. In any case these entries do not tell us conclusively whether the mill was on the site of the principal settlement or not.[13]

The other candidate as a location is the site on the hill above New Mills Farm currently occupied by the collection of agricultural buildings named on modern maps as Rowlston's Barn. The oldest building of this complex is probably the threshing barn on the northern side, of which only the eastern portion remains standing. This seems to date from the earlier half of the seventeenth century as do the earlier parts of New Mills Farm. Both were recorded in considerable detail by Mr Dennis Hands in 1986, fortunately just over a year before the whole of the western section of the barn collapsed. The seventeenth-century building on both sites probably reflects invest-ment by new owners after the Scudamores of Holme Lacy acquired the property

Fig. 5.1 The northern and western sides of Rowlston's barn in c.1982 before it collapsed

from the Parrys in 1592; it may even be contemporaneous with the acquisition of a life interest in the property by Barnabas Scudamore (see section 6). It is not easy to determine what might have preceded the agricultural buildings on the site since there are a number of somewhat later buildings and a yard covering the site to the south of the threshing barn. Some 150 metres west of the barn stood a small holding called Crab's Castle, still standing until after the Second World War. There were, until recently ploughed out, some traces of earlier buildings in the same field as Crab's Castle, but only aerial photography under optimum conditions could reveal more substantial evidence for a deserted mediaeval settlement. It is worth noting, however, that the position of Rowlston's Barn, on an elevated three sided site, bounded on two sides by steep valleys, strongly resembles both Llanfrother and Moraston, settlements with possible pre-Conquest credentials.[14]

By 1300, the religious foundation of Aconbury had survived its early years of difficulty and uncertainty and had acquired all its possessions in its immediate vicinity. Detailed records of the manorial courts held over the years by the Prioresses of Aconbury and of the priory's accounts survive in the National Archives. These demonstrate the agricultural and commercial activities of a typical mediaeval monastic community. There are records of the sale of grain produced on the estate and of the import of fish such as fresh and pickled herrings and conger eels from Lydney. There was probably a freshwater fish pond at the priory; one of the entries for 1317 shows a payment of 12 pence to the fishermen of Wilton for fish in the fishpool — presumably for catching them. There was evidently considerable traffic

Fig. 5.2 New Mills farmhouse in 2006

of goods across the Wye in both directions via ferries at Hoarwithy and Wilton.

The accounts and court rolls of the priory refer frequently not only to Rolvestone, but also to Caldicot — usually described as a manor — and Muryvalefeld or Merrivale. Fines for trespassing refer no doubt to the woodland; one of these in 1304 relates to the chaplain of the Birches and his two brothers; the latter both have Welsh names as do many of the persons who appear before the manorial court. Whatever the depopulation of 1055 and whatever the causes of the almost complete absence of Welsh place names in Little Birch, Welshmen with characteristic Welsh patronyms clearly formed a very large proportion of the population in the later Middle Ages. An interesting feature of the Michaelmas accounts for 1340 is an item for the agistment (a term for the hiring out of pasture for grazing usually in woodland or woodland clearings) for 21 beasts from 'Muchelbirches' in the 'Meenede' for 21 pence. The same accounts also have an item for rusks — tree bark — sold in the 'Meenede' for 32 pence. 'Meenede' is clearly a form of the Welsh 'mynydd' — a mountain or, as has been suggested, in the Forest of Dean sometimes a woodland clearing. In either case the entry must refer to woodland or woodland clearings on Aconbury Hill. These entries suggest both that the priory, perhaps unsurprisingly, had an economic relationship with the communities immediately surrounding it, even if they did not form part of its possessions, and also that the priory managed its resources very flexibly to maximize the return on them.[15]

The place of a small remote parish like Little Birch in the larger pattern of late mediaeval history is necessarily obscure. It may be assumed that it probably suffered in the successive waves of bubonic plague that swept the country after 1348. This will be further explored in section 7. Though it lay a little to the east of the Welsh March, an area notoriously associated with lawless baronial politics, it was certainly not immune to the effects of these politics and the proximity of the Welsh border. Though Wales had been conquered by Edward I, its administration and legal system had not been assimilated into the English system. The rebellion of Owain Glyndwr in the first decade of the fifteenth century was the last of a long series of attempts to establish Welsh independence of the English. Despite the fact that Glyndwr had connexions with the area — his daughter had married Sir John Scudamore of Kentchurch — his warbands pillaged Archenfield in 1404. Some years ago field walking on a recently deeply ploughed field just to the east of Much Dewchurch revealed dark stains on the soil together with scraps of fused daub. These clearly suggested a settlement destroyed by fire and never rebuilt. The pottery finds were of late fourteenth-/early fifteenth-century type. There can be little doubt that this was the lost settlement of Wormeton destroyed by the Welsh. The site is only a little over two kilometres from Little Birch and can be easily viewed from Aconbury Hill and the top of King's Thorn Pitch. The documentation of Aconbury Priory suggests that its property suffered damage at the hands of Glyndwr's men, but this may relate to the priory's possessions in other parts of the county.[16]

It is often seen as convenient to date the end of the Middle Ages to 1485, the year that saw the Battle of Bosworth, the end of the Wars of the Roses and the arrival of the formidable Tudor dynasty. For the inhabitants of Little Birch, however, and villages like it, the really noticeable transition from the mediaeval to the modern world came in the 1530s. This was the decade of the break with Rome and the beginning of the Protestant reformation in England; it was also the decade dominated by Thomas Cromwell as Henry VIII's chief minister.

Three of the changes of this decade may be singled out as particularly significant for Little Birch; all had their origins in legislation of 1536. One was the Act of Union which finally brought Welsh law and administrative practice into line with that of England. Even before the Act of Union, Cromwell had, in 1534, secured the appointment of his friend, Rowland Lee, Bishop of Coventry and Lichfield as President of the Council in the Marches and Lee had vigorously begun the task of bringing the Marches and Wales firmly under central control. These developments meant that border villages like Little Birch would never face the dangers of 1055 and 1404 again.[17]

1536 also saw an Act designed to deal with the problems of poverty, poor-relief and vagrancy. The Act was not as radical as originally intended and was a precursor of the much more important Acts passed in the reign of Queen Elizabeth. One principle, however, that was established was the central role of the parish in poor relief. In 1538 Cromwell issued a mandate requiring every parson, priest or curate to enter all weddings, christenings and burials with the names of the parties in a book. In practice many entries were made on loose sheets until 1598. Little Birch is fortunate in preserving a register that dates back as far as 1557. The importance of the parish as a unit of civil administration has much of its origins in the 1530s and survived for 300 years. Not until the Poor Law Act of 1834 and the Registration of Births Marriages and Deaths Act of 1836 did the first-line responsibility for registration and poor relief move decisively to a supra-parochial level.[18]

But the event which must have had most immediate impact on Little Birch during the 1530s was the dissolution of the monasteries. The neighbouring parish of Aconbury was the location of a small but generously endowed priory which also owned approximately 300 acres (just under one-third) of the land in Little Birch itself. The Act for suppressing minor houses was approved by Parliament in April 1536. In December of that year Rowland Lee wrote to his friend Cromwell, passing on to him the views of 'dyverse of my loving ffrends in thies parties'. It seems the priory performed a valuable function in educating the daughters of the gentry of Herefordshire and the southern Marches 'in virtue and lernyng'. He felt that its good reputation should justify its survival. Lee, as we have seen, was no reactionary cleric but a committed supporter of Cromwell's reforms. This fact, and the fact that as President of the Council in the Marches he could be expected to have his finger on the pulse of local opinion, might have suggested his letter would carry some weight. There were, however, to be no exceptions in the dissolution process.[19]

Though the suppression of the monasteries caused political unrest in some places — Norfolk and Yorkshire for example — and the suppression of a few larger abbeys was achieved through forfeiture and involved execution of the abbot, the dissolution of most minor houses proceeded in an orderly and peaceful manner. Aconbury appears to have been no exception to this pattern. The last prioress, Johanna Scudamore, was awarded a pension of £9 per year. In 1554 she was recorded as living at Holme Lacy — presumably among her kinsmen — still in receipt of the pension. She was described as aged 60 and of virtuous life; she had not married.[20]

The dissolution of a religious house was preceded by a most thorough audit of its buildings, lands and possessions. The dissolution of the monasteries looks at first sight like an act resembling nationalization since all the property of the religious order passed to the crown. In fact, however, privatization is a nearer analogy since it was the government's intention, at least after Cromwell's disgrace and execution in 1540, to sell on all the assets. The acquisition of Aconbury's assets shows that — as in modern privatizations — a certain amount of confusion and speculative investment probably occurred. A document held in the Augmentation

Fig. 5.3 This drawing of 'SW View of Aconbury Chapel' by James Wathen in 1787 also shows Aconbury Court before remodelling. Netherwood rises on the (exaggerated) hill behind. Note the confusion of the east end of the church with the west end: no porch is shown

Office suggests that the manor of Aconbury and that of Rowlston in the parish of Little Birch were to be granted to Sir William Sydney. However in 1542 they were acquired by the mayor and burgesses of Gloucester. This was part of a speculative investment of £493 that the city made in former monastic lands, most of which they sold on within a few years. The Aconbury Priory lands came into the possession of Hugh Parry (or ap Harry) of Poston in Vowchurch. He is shown as a taxpayer at Aconbury in 1545.[21]

The subsequent ownership of the lands which formerly belonged to Aconbury Priory will be discussed in section 8. But in the meantime it is worth saying something about the people involved in the priory's dissolution and their significance for the future history of the area. One of the most important roles in the whole dissolution process was that of receiver. Receivers were appointed for individual counties or groups of counties and the receiver for Herefordshire, Staffordshire, Shropshire and Worcestershire was John Scudamore of Holme Lacy. This was an important step in the rise of the Holme Lacy branch of the family. Although, the Scudamores did not directly acquire lands of Aconbury Priory at this stage, they were to purchase the Parrys' lands in Little Birch before the end of the sixteenth century.[22]

One of the most interesting facts revealed in this episode of Herefordshire's history is the prominence of the Welsh families from the districts of Archenfield,

Ewyas and the Golden Valley. It must be rememberedthattheTudors were by origin Welsh and that Welshmen often prospered in their service. The leading example of this was the man who became Queen Elizabeth's chief minister, William Cecil, later Lord Burghley, whose grandfather was a younger son of the family whose ancestral home was Allt-yr-Ynys in the parish of Walterstone. Another important royal servant was Blanche Parry, the maid of honour to Queen Elizabeth, whose remarkable tomb is the chief object of interest in Bacton Church. Hugh Parry, the eventual purchaser of Aconbury, was a collateral relation of Blanche Parry through a common great-great-great-grandfather. Finally, another Welsh family prominent in southern Herefordshire an the late Middle Ages were the Gwillyms. The last bailiff of Aconbury Priory was John Gwillym of Fawley near Kings Caple. His detailed survey of its lands after its dissolution is

Fig. 5.4 The south side of Aconbury church in 2006 showing a blocked-up door which would have provided entrance to the church from the cloisters of the priory. Note also the 'peephole' which looked into the church from a small room

Fig. 5.5 The porch which dates from the fifteenth century or slightly earlier

45

contained in the augmentation records. He must have been a regular visitor to the parish and his son, Thomas, married Elizabeth, the daughter and heir of George Baylye, one of the principal landowners in Little Birch, establishing a family that was to hold land in the parish for 300 years.[23]

6 Peace and War

The brief reign of Mary Tudor was too short to reverse the religious and administrative changes of the previous 20 years. Queen Elizabeth came to the throne in 1558, the year after the first entry had been made in Little Birch's first parish register. At this time the parish was, as it had been during most of the Middle Ages, poor and comparatively sparsely inhabited; there were almost certainly not above 60 residents (see section 7). But though the sixteenth century was a time of rapid, sometimes painful, economic change, and also, intermittently, of the threat of foreign invasion, it was also a time of virtually unbroken domestic peace. Perhaps not since the days when it had been part of the Roman Empire had the area been so safe from the danger of armed conflict. From 1540 it is almost possible to tell the story of Little Birch in terms of who owned the land, how it was farmed, how and where people lived, where they worshipped and where they were educated. The remaining sections of the book will deal with these topics.[1]

There was, however, one more occasion when Little Birch was, like every community in the land, forced to confront and experience at first hand a great historical crisis. In 1642, after two years of escalating political tension between King Charles I and most of the members of his Parliament, the two sides resorted to war.

We think of Herefordshire as a Royalist county in the Civil War. This does not mean, of course, that some kind of democratic decision was made to support the King. Quite simply a majority of the rich influential men who decided to take any active part at all supported the Royalist cause. These included John, Viscount Scudamore, from the Holme Lacy branch of that family, and Sir Walter Pye of the Mynde in Much Dewchurch. Almost certainly some of the gentry who favoured Parliament kept their heads down at least until 1645 when it became clear that the King was going to lose the war.[2]

Equally likely is the fact that in Little Birch most of the landowners, like most other men with small landed stakes in the community, tried to keep out of trouble. There was one exception. In 1592 the lands once held by Aconbury Priory in Little Birch — Athelstan's Wood and the manor of Rowlston — were acquired by the Holme Lacy Scudamores. The viscount, who had at one time been Charles I's ambassador in Paris, though an unswerving Royalist, was also a cautious one; in April 1643 when Hereford was for a couple of weeks in Parliamentary hands, he took the opportunity to surrender and was conveyed to London where he spent the rest of the war under virtual house arrest, safely away from the danger of taking local actions that might put him at too much risk in the event of a Parliamentary victory.[3]

The viscount, however, had a younger brother. Barnabas Scudamore, born in 1609, was left virtually nothing in the wills of his father and grandfather and adopted the career of a professional soldier. He was active for the King from the beginning of the Civil War, nearly losing an arm in the siege of Coventry in August 1642 and fighting at Edge Hill two months later. By May 1644 he was serving under Colonel Nicholas Mynne, then military governor of Hereford, and, when Mynne was killed in a small but savage battle at Redmarley in August 1644, Barnabas was chosen to succeed him, also becoming sheriff of the county in December. According to John Webb in his *Memorials of the Civil War in Herefordshire* Barnabas had been given possession for life of Rowlston in Little Birch to bolster his meagre income. Quite what the legal arrangement was is not clear; according to a lost Scudamore document (see section 8.1 below) Edward Kidley of Bromley was given power of attorney over the manor of Rowlston by Viscount Scudamore in 1633 and he probably managed the land; it is unlikely Barnabas had much direct contact with it. Technically, however, it is possible that the county's leading Royalist soldier was Little Birch's largest land-owner.[4]

In one respect the parishioners of Little Birch, like those of many villages in Herefordshire, were fortunate during the first three years of the war. The county lay too far to the west to suffer the depredations of the main Parliamentary field armies. The principal ongoing threat was from the Parliamentary stronghold of Gloucester under the leadership of the formidable Colonel Edward Massey (who was responsible for Mynne's defeat and death at Redmarley). Massey certainly raided Herefordshire, but his path normally took him via Ledbury or through Ross towards Monmouth.[5]

Twice during the first year of the war the city of Hereford fell into the hands of small Parliamentary armies; between September and December 1642 it was occupied by the Earl of Stamford and in April and May 1643 by Sir William Waller. Neither of them was able to hold the city for long. On the first of these occasions, Royalist soldiers from the army of Lord Herbert of Raglan (and probably like him, Roman Catholics) deployed on Aconbury Hill as they looked for a means of recapturing Hereford. In November a group of gentry from the area petitioned the Earl of Stamford for relief from the raids of 'the barbarous Cavaliers of the Welsh Parts, who are under the Command of a dangerous Papist.' Among the signatories of this petition, identified by John Webb as probable adherents of the Parliamentarian cause, was John Tyrer, described as Minister of Cornbury. There is no other record of this man. William Higgs was then rector of Aconbury and Little Birch. (A Thomas Tyrer was instituted to the living of Sellack and Kings Caple in 1660.)[6]

The strategic position of Herefordshire was totally altered by the battle of Naseby on 14 June 1645. The almost complete destruction of the King's field army opened the south-west Midlands and southern Welsh border to attack by major Parliamentary forces. In the event it was not the New Model Army but the army of Parliament's Scottish allies — the so-called 'Army of the Solemn League and Covenant' — that came to Herefordshire. This force, which entered the county on 21 July, numbered 15,000 men, by far the largest force seen in the county since the war had begun. Why the Scots chose to besiege Hereford and the reasons for their rather tortuous manoeuvres beforehand is too complex an issue to discuss here. It seems that they approached the city from the south on 30 and 31 July, some probably coming on the western side of the Wye. It also seems they quickly established some sort of command or outlook posts on Dinedor and Aconbury Hills. As noted in section 2, Aconbury Hill was then unwooded; a late eighteenth-century painting by the Hereford watercolourist James Wathen shows that at that time Dinedor had only one solitary tree on its summit. These lookout posts were an obvious precaution since initially any relief of the city seemed most likely to come from the south-west — from Raglan, via Monmouth.[7]

It was not the specifically military activities of the Scottish Army that had the greatest impact on the villages of Herefordshire but rather the systematic plundering practised by its soldiers. By the standards of the time the Army of the Solemn League and Covenant was godly and well disciplined, and its commander, the Earl of Leven, issued the strictest orders forbidding plundering at the beginning of the siege. The problem was that the English Parliament was bound by treaty to pay the Scots for their services, but most of the money promised failed to materialize. In these circumstances the Scots were obliged to live off the land — at 'free quarter' as the contemporary term put it.

Tales of Scottish plundering became deeply embedded in the folk memory of the country people of Herefordshire. John Webb, collecting these around 1825, noted that they should really have been recorded 50 years earlier when it would have been possible to speak to people who had heard them at first hand from contemporary witnesses. Even so some of the stories Webb recounts have a realistic resonance. These include the account of the Scots assembling cattle they had driven off to be slaughtered at Wormelow Tump, and also that of the inhabitants there burying their pewter and flitches of bacon to prevent them falling into Scottish hands. Interestingly the stories do not suggest brutality on the part of the Scots towards the native population — indeed rather the opposite. The farmer of Ash Farm in Much Birch falling in with a Scottish soldier walking between Turkey Tump and Wormelow Tump and noting that he carried a sword, allowed him to cross a stile first and killed him with his bill-hook.[8]

More precise evidence of the effect of Scottish depredations is contained in a pamphlet published in 1650 by a Herefordshire lawyer named Miles Hill. In 1645 Hill had been engaged by the Parliamentary commissioners accompanying the Scottish army to bring in provisions from the county for their use; he had kept a record during and immediately after the siege of the extent of damage and loss reported to him. Much of his pamphlet is taken up with a parish-by-parish list of losses. The entry for Little Birch is fairly typical: 'Taken and plundered from the inhabitants of Little Birch to the value of 0071. 03. 08.'[9]

Hill's figures need interpretation. There are no returns for some villages and in others he thought losses noted might be underestimates. He believed the real losses for the whole county might be double the total of £31,743 5s 2d given in his pamphlet. In any case, parishes varied so greatly in size and wealth that the raw data can give little impression of the impact such losses might have had on the community. One way of obtaining a picture of the loss each parish sustained relative to its wealth is to compare the figures that Hill gives with the estimates of annual values listed in the Herefordshire Militia Assessments of 1663.

Making due allowance for the fact that Hill's figures are, on his own admission, not complete, and that the valuations in the Militia Assessments, which depended on local raters in each parish, may not be wholly accurate and consistent, we can perhaps gain a better sense of what happened to Little Birch and its neighbouring parishes. The annual tax value of its holdings was rated in 1663 at £68. This represents one of the lowest values per acre recorded in Herefordshire — about 1s 4d against the county average of 3s 4d, though there is some reason for thinking that the assessment on the whole of Athelstan's Wood may have been included in the Aconbury assessment. The losses that Hill ascribed to Little Birch actually exceeded its estimated annual assessment value by just over £3. In Aconbury matters were not quite as bad — a loss of £105 10s against an annual tax value of £130. But in Much Birch, the losses Hill recorded — £181 7s — were nearly twice its annual tax value of £98.[10]

The perspective this kind of analysis gives us shows that the apparent concentration of folk memories quoted by Webb in this area may not simply be due to the fact that he was rector of the nearby parish of Tretire. It is clear that some parishes probably escaped such severe plundering because of particular circumstances. Kings Caple for instance, where the losses of £63 11s were only about one-seventh of the annual militia assessment, was protected by the great loop of the River Wye, at that period unbridged between Hereford and Ross. Goodrich, with losses of £38 3s 6d against an annual tax value of £384 16s 2d, was presumably protected by the presence of its castle and Royalist garrison. More surprising are the comparisons with parishes nearer to Hereford. There the losses are usually well below the annual tax values of the parishes in 1663 even though these areas were very close to the Scottish leaguer or camp on Bartonsham meadows.[11]

Why did the Birches suffer so badly? The explanation may be a combination of two separate circumstances. It is clear from the Parliamentary news-sheets published during August 1645 that, before the Scots arrived, the Royalist garrison in Hereford had not only dismantled the suburbs outside the city walls but also had conducted a 'scorched earth' exercise in the surrounding villages, destroying horse quarters, ovens and mills and burning corn. This fact has been hitherto little noted perhaps because the main contemporary continuous narrative of the siege is that written by Barnabas Scudamore, and he for obvious reasons did not want to publicise such activity. In addition, the Earl of Leven had been obliged to send away most of his cavalry sometime around 10 August, to pursue the small Royalist army led by the King, which had slipped away from South Wales and was making for the north Midlands. Cavalry are not much use for military tasks in a siege but they are useful for foraging at a distance. It is probable that the Birches were far enough to have escaped Barnabas Scudamore's destruction but just near enough for the Scots to use as bases for plunder.[12]

The main shortcoming of Hill's pamphlet is not that it is inaccurate but that it is incomplete. Though the data for it must have been collected in 1645 and 1646, Hill did not publish it until 1650. By this time much had changed. King Charles I had been executed and his son had accepted the Presbyterian covenant in return for Scottish support. The leaders of the new English republic were arguing among themselves whether to launch a pre-emptive invasion against their former Scottish allies. Hill was a hard-liner and his pamphlet was overtly intended as a piece of anti-Scottish propaganda. What he therefore did not include was the extent of Royalist plundering and forced contributions in Herefordshire.[13]

The problem for the Royalists was that when the counties of England took sides in 1642, it was the wealthier counties of the south and east that opted for Parliament and the poorer counties of the north and west that supported the King. In 1644 the Scots had entered the war as allies of Parliament, and by the beginning of 1645, the Royalist war effort had to be supported from the shrinking area which Royalist forces controlled — Wales, the West Country and the south-west Midlands. Outbreaks of civil disobedience broke out in many Royalist areas. These risings of 'clubmen' — so called because of the weapons they carried — varied in militancy. The one in Herefordshire in March 1645 was among the most militant, probably because of the ruthlessness with which Scudamore exacted contributions. After a series of escalating acts of provocation and retaliation, there was a skirmish at the Lugg Bridge on 18 March during which a number of villagers were killed by Royalist troopers from Hereford. The next day the city was surrounded by an army of 'clubmen' — estimates of its size varied from 4,000 to 16,000 — and at least a third of them carried not clubs but firearms. Even at the lower estimates, this force must have contained men from all over the county. Scudamore had to call in Prince Rupert for assistance.[14]

After the war there were a number of reckonings of damage. At Goodrich — where the losses attributable to the Scots had been only £38 3s 6d — those perpetrated over two years by the Royalist garrison in Goodrich Castle under Sir Henry Lingen totalled £295 10s. At Clehonger, Herbert Aubrey, a Royalist supporter, lost £300 in plunder and free quarter to the Scots, but £570 to the Royalists, and, what is more, the latter also pulled down his great mansion worth £2,000 (presumably to prevent its falling in to the hands of the Scots). The combined consequences of Royalist and Scottish military activity on the people of Herefordshire in 1645 must have been appalling. No wonder that on 3 September, as the Scottish army withdrew via Fownhope, one of the English Parliamentary commissioners attached to it, Colonel William Purefoy, wrote to the Speaker of the House of Commons of 'the sad and miserable condition of these parts'.[15]

But there was one more circumstance to compound the miseries of 1645. The seventeenth century was in what we now call the 'Little Ice Age'. On 8 December most of the country was plunged into a spell of intensely cold weather which lasted until 28 January. Several men in the Parliamentary force coming from Ledbury on 18 December to attack Hereford died of exposure; the Wye was frozen so hard that 50 Royalists were able to escape from the city by walking across it. These conditions have been paralleled in recent times

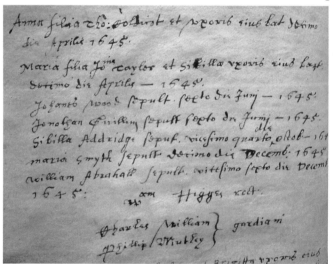

Fig. 6.1 Little Birch Parish Register 1645, showing the abnormally large number of deaths and the characteristic way in which the rector, William Higgs, signed off each year's entries

only in 1946–7 and 1962–3. The effect of such weather, coming on top of all the other privations of 1645, may be imagined. There is no narrative surviving from Little Birch to tell us of its inhabitants' hardships but there is one very telling piece of information available to us. The rector, William Higgs, recorded in the parish register 14 burials during the 10 years 1637–1646. Five of these (36%) occurred between 7 June and 27 December 1645. Five deaths represented more than 5% of the estimated population of the parish at that date.[16]

The last time we know of Little Birch seeing any military activity was in September 1645. The Scots withdrew when the King's army reappeared at Worcester; the Scottish cavalry sent to follow him had returned to Scotland to deal with problems there. Without adequate cavalry, Leven took his army to Gloucester. The King entered Hereford on 4 September. He left for Raglan on 7 September but was back in Hereford on the 14th. On the 17th the King dined and stayed the night at Holme Lacy. It was the practice for cavalry units in the King's army to be sent to bivouac each night at a distance from where the King was staying. One of the cavalry officers, Captain Richard Symonds, kept a diary and for that day he noted: '... his Majestie marched to Ham Lacy, the seat of the Ld Viscount Scudamore ... Guards to Rolston.' This must refer to Rowlston in Little Birch; the village of that name on the way to Abergavenny would be too far away, particularly as the army was to move north the next day. Clearly Barnabas Scudamore would have felt that his own small estate only three miles away from Holme Lacy House would be a good place to locate a cavalry regiment overnight; there was a good space between Rowlston's Barn and the end of Athelstan's Wood in an elevated position with excellent views of the surrounding countryside.[17]

Something of the period can be gathered by considering the lives of two men with Little Birch connexions. One of these of course is Barnabas Scudamore, whose earlier career we have already considered. His successful defence of Hereford against the Scots in a siege lasting more than five weeks was his greatest achievement. He received a knighthood for it from the King and there was even talk of his being granted a peerage. There is no doubt that Barnabas was a brave, resourceful and extremely competent soldier. But there was another side to him. His ruthlessness in exacting contributions has been mentioned. Of the clubmen he is reported as saying that he would 'hang the dogs and drown the whelps'. He also seems to have had a gift for antagonizing his own officers and allies. By December 1645 two of his officers in Hereford, Major Howorth and Captain Alderne, had resigned their commissions after a bitter quarrel with him, and he had confined his lieutenant-governor, Sir Nicholas Throckmorton, to gaol for threatening to fight a duel with another officer. Meanwhile the hitherto loyal townspeople of Hereford were on the verge of mutiny.

Whether Sir John Bridges was ever Scudamore's potential ally is doubtful; there are indications he may not have favoured the Royalist cause. He was, however, Scudamore's nephew. He had married Mary, the daughter and heir of John Pearle of Dewsall, the owner of Aconbury. Some time in 1645, Scudamore burnt down the principal seat of the Bridges family, Wilton Castle. Whether this was to deny it as a fortified house to the Scots or because Bridges refused to allow a Royalist garrison to be stationed there is not clear. After the devastation of Wilton, Aconbury became the principal residence of the Bridges family in Herefordshire. What is certain is that Bridges took the destruction of his house very badly. He went to Gloucester and met there two Parliamentarian colonels, Thomas Morgan, who had replaced Massey as the city's governor, and John Birch. He introduced them to Alderne and Howorth who in turn seem to have been in contact with discontented officers still serving in the Hereford garrison.

The result was that on the morning of 18 December Morgan and Birch with 2,000 men captured Hereford by trickery or treachery (or a mixture of both). Scudamore escaped across the frozen Wye and made his way to Worcester intending to continue to Oxford to explain what had happened personally to the King. He fell ill, however, and before he could proceed, Sir Nicholas Throckmorton, released by Birch and Morgan, arrived in Worcester and maliciously but quite unjustifiably accused Scudamore of betraying Hereford. He was now himself imprisoned and, despite frequent pleas for a court-martial where he might exonerate himself, he remained in prison until Worcester surrendered to the Parliamentarians in July 1646.

After this Scudamore's career is mostly obscure. It is hardly surprising that when Royalist rebellion broke out in 1648, Barnabas was involved in it. However, it is interesting that he did not play any part in the rather half-hearted rising in north Herefordshire, led by his old comrade, Sir Henry Lingen. Perhaps he had made too many enemies in the county. He seems to have been active in Kent and East Anglia. He was taken prisoner in June at Newmarket attempting to raise recruits for the Royalist cause. At this stage he escaped the efficient Parliamentary machinery for fining Royalist 'delinquents' but after he was arrested again in 1651 in the presence of known Royalist conspirators, he was fined £100, twice the annual value of his property. He never succeeded in paying off this fine and died in debt in March 1652. His place of death and burial are unknown. After his death his brother, the viscount, applied successfully to have the balance of his fine remitted on the grounds that Barnabas had only a life interest in his properties.[18]

What a contrast this story of triumph and downfall is to that of Little Birch's rector during the Civil War, William Higgs. He was rector for 53 years — from 1611 to his death in 1664. At any period such a long incumbency would have been somewhat unusual, but Higgs's tenure of the living co-incided with the most turbulent period of England's ecclesiastical history since the Reformation. He lived through and apparently survived the reforms of Archbishop Laud which sought to bring enhanced ceremony and dignity to Anglican worship. Then Parliamentary victory in the Civil War brought the abolition of episcopacy and the promulgation of a Presbyterian Directory of Worship, and then the gradual growth of independent sects. In 1653 the clergy ceased to be responsible for making entries in the parish register and by 1659 the Little Birch register was being used to record parishioners' taxation payments. Finally, in 1660, the Restoration brought the re-establishment of a church with bishops and the 1662 Prayer Book.[19]

Higgs was evidently able to accommodate to these changes probably because he was an integrated member of his village community. On 29 May 1640 he witnessed the will of his neighbour, Thomas Gwillym, and 22 years later, on 14 June 1662, his own will was witnessed by Thomas's grandson, John. All this is perhaps surprising because Higgs was not a native of Little Birch or even of Herefordshire. He came apparently from Derby, gaining a degree from Balliol College, Oxford in 1601. He seems to have been born about 1580 and must therefore have been about 84 at the time of his death.[20]

The Militia Assessment of 1663 shows that Higgs was by that time one of the larger landowners in Little Birch. His will reveals how he had acquired his land. He bequeathed it to his son, also called William, and described it as consisting of two farms purchased respectively from Thomas Gynny and from members of the Gwatkin family. Both the Gynny and Gwatkin families had been resident in the village for 100 years previously. Section 8.3 below will deal further with the precise location of this land and the significance of some of the details about it in Higgs's will. It is sufficient here to say that it must have comprised at least 100 acres and that it probably included land that belonged to Lower House Farm as delineated on the tithe map of 1841. Indeed a house on the site of the present farmhouse may well have been Higgs's residence. The visitation of 1716 shows that, at that time, there was no 'parsonage house', so the rector would have had to make his own arrangements.[21]

William Higgs was buried in Little Birch on 12 June 1664. He had evidently acquired not only acceptance but also modest wealth. The inventory of his goods at death recorded a value of £103 15s 10d. His legacies included £100 for his younger son John, sums for a daughter, two grandchildren, three servants and for two friends. He also left a sum to the poor of Little Birch — the endowment of Higgs's charity (see section 11). The 53 years he spent in Little Birch had not been without tragedy. The only substantial time between 1611 and 1653 when entries in the parish register were not made by him was a period in 1619 and 1620 (though he continued to sign off the year's entries in a rather faint hand.) On 24 July 1619, in another hand and in English — Higgs made his entries in Latin — is an entry recording Higgs's marriage to a woman simply named as Joyce, wife of William Higgs. Less than six months later on 10 January is an entry recording Joyce's burial. She may not have been his first wife, for he would have been about 40 then; less than two years later, on 27 November 1621, he married again, to Maria Wells.[22]

In contrast to Barnabas Scudamore, Higgs evidently had a number of children. Apart from the two sons, William and John, mentioned in his will, he had at least two daughters. There was also another son, Thomas, born and baptized in Little Birch in 1623. Like his father he was educated at Oxford, graduating from New College in 1644, but, since he is not mentioned in Higgs's will, he probably pre-deceased his father. Barnabas Scudamore married comparatively late, in 1648, but, unlike William Higgs, he died childless as well as in debt.[23]

Fig. 6.2 The will of William Higgs. (For a transcript see Appendix 1)

7 Population and the Pattern of Settlement before the Nineteenth Century

In 1836 the Registration of Births Marriages and Deaths Act established the office of Registrar General. This office provided the direction and expertise for the collection of data needed for the censuses conducted every ten years since 1841. From that year censuses collected details of all persons by name residing in every household in a parish. Before 1841 there were four censuses — in 1801, 1811, 1821 and 1831 — conducted according to the requirements of the Population Act of 1800. These indicated the total number of persons living in each parish and analysed this total by gender and occupation, as well as stating the total number of households. The collection of data for these earlier censuses was carried out by parish officers; both the collection and the subsequent computation and printing of the data were not carried out with the same degree of accuracy that prevailed after 1836. Some parish figures from the 1801 census are particularly unreliable.[1]

There were no comprehensive censuses before the nineteenth century. However, it is possible to make more or less reliable estimates of the population of some individual parishes back as far as 1541, when parish priests were first required to record baptisms, burials and marriages within their parishes. The method for estimating the population of a parish for a particular year involves counting the baptisms from the parish register for a ten-year period around the year in question and working out the annual average. This figure is then divided by the national average annual birth rate per thousand for the same ten-year period and multiplied by 1,000. The aggregated data from parish registers together with data from nineteenth-century censuses has been statistically processed to generate estimates of the total population of England for each year since 1541 as well as the annual national rates of births, deaths and marriages per thousand.

In principle it is possible to do the same calculation with the data for burials or marriages, but the results are less reliable. There are far fewer marriages than burials or baptisms, so the results derived from these are less likely to be statistically significant; and the death rate is more volatile because of the occurrence of local epidemics. Of course this method even applied to births is subject to error. Some ministers were not diligent in making their register entries and some parishes contained inhabitants who were not members of the established church — Roman Catholics and dissenters. The Little Birch registers survive from 1557 and seem generally to have been kept reasonably well apart from the first 50 years or so and the period 1553–59. Nor apparently were there any Catholics or dissenters in the parish in the seventeenth and early eighteenth centuries. There are, however, two factors which need to be kept in mind when considering the population estimates based on parish register entries. One is that they are accurate only in proportion to the degree to which any parish conformed to the contemporary national birth, death and marriage rates. Secondly, the smaller the sample the greater the danger of statistical deviance: Little Birch is not a large parish and, particularly in the sixteenth and seventeenth centuries, it had a small population.[2]

Apart from the parish registers, there are two other sources of information. There were during the period a number of counts of members of the established church. In those days religious allegiance — at least publicly — was universal and Little Birch, until well into the eighteenth century, apparently had no religious minorities. These counts were of communicants — that is of adults — so each figure has to be appropriately increased to take account of what experts believe to have been the proportion of the population below communion age at the relevant period. There are also a number of taxation records such as that of the Hearth Tax returns, which give data about the number of households. These are fascinating documents for what they tell us about the relative wealth of households within parishes, but attributing numbers of inhabitants to different types of household is not easy.

So much for the sources of evidence, their limitations and how they can be used. What can they tell us of the population of Little Birch between the middle of the sixteenth century and the beginning of the nineteenth century? We are fortunate that in 1548 Little Birch was one of the Herefordshire parishes to have its *houselings* — i.e. its communicants — counted. There were 40 of them and, taking account of the likely number of children, this suggests a total population of 53. We thus have a baseline figure for the beginning of the modern era. To provide a link to the period where census data is available, the figure from the 1811 census has been chosen in view of the suspect figures from some of the 1801 returns (see above). Almost exactly in the middle of the intervening period there is another count of communicants, the so-called 'Compton Census' of 1676, which has again been adjusted to include the probable number of children. Finally, two estimates have been made on either side of the 1676 date from the parish register. The first, for 1641/2, uses the average annual figures for baptisms recorded between 1637 and 1646, in the middle of the long incumbency of William Higgs. The second for 1713/4, is based on the average annual baptisms recorded between 1709 and 1718; the first seven years of these were presented by the rector, Richard Treharne, for the visitation of 1716.[3]

The results are set out in the accompanying table and graph. The data has been presented to allow a comparison between the estimates for the five selected years and the figures for the same years that might have been expected, given a population of 53 in 1548, had the population trends in Little Birch been the same as in England as a whole.

What emerges is both interesting and somewhat surprising. Between 1548 and 1641/2 the population of England grew by 76%. This was almost exactly mirrored in Little Birch where the growth for the same period was 72%. But during the next 35 years, while the population of England actually fell by 2%, that of Little Birch rose by 10%. The second half of the seventeenth century is the only prolonged period of population decline in modern English history; by 1713/4 the national population had recovered by only a little under 5% from its 1676 level and was only about the same as it had been in 1658. By contrast, in Little Birch, the increase in population since the 'Compton Census' appears, by this method of estimation, to have been an astonishing 44%. In the century before the 1811 census the population of the parish continued to expand, but now at a slower rate than that of England as a whole — 62% as opposed to 89%. Even so, given the sharp and atypical increases in the late seventeenth century, there were probably about 50 more people living in the parish in 1811 than might have been projected from the 1548 *houseling* count.

Once again it must be emphasized that these figures for Little Birch are estimates necessarily based on small samples and may therefore be subject to error. However, they seem sufficiently significant to justify an attempt at explanation. The most likely cause for an increase in population between 1650 and 1710, against the national trend, was inward migration into the parish. And the most probable cause of such inward migration was the existence on the northern edge of the parish of a substantial area of common waste land not regulated by strict manorial control. The extent, nature and history of this common are described in section 8 below. What it would have offered was a place to settle for those who found themselves displaced in their native parishes.[4]

The cause of such displacement was probably enclosure of open-field arable land and the consolidation of land holdings in the wider area. Herefordshire is usually thought of as having been an 'enclosed' county. John Leland, writing in the late 1530s, described Archenfield as 'full of enclosures very (full) of corne and wood'. Yet it is obvious from archive records that there was a substantial amount of open-field arable cultivation in the area in the sixteenth century. This was not of the same type as that of the great open-field systems of the east Midlands and most of it had disappeared, probably as a result of private agreements between landowners, by the beginning of the eighteenth century. Rationalisation of this sort was bound to lead to some degree of displacement.[5]

As the common waste extended into the neighbouring parishes of Aconbury and Much Birch, one might expect to find rates of population growth in these during the same period higher than the national average, but this does not seem to have been the case. In Much Birch, judging by a comparison of the baptismal entries in the parish register for 1709–1718 with those for 1670–1679, the population appears actually to have fallen by perhaps as much as 18%. In Aconbury the population growth between 1676 and 1711 appears to have been about the same as the national average. Whilst some of this discrepancy is no doubt due to the statistical error inherently a risk in small samples, part of the reason is probably different degrees of pressure encouraging migration and opposing encroachment in each parish according to the activities of local landowners. It must also be remembered that the proportion of common waste to the total area of the parish was smaller in Much Birch and very much smaller in Aconbury. As the figures show, the population level achieved in Little Birch by the second decade of the eighteenth century was not a temporary blip and, since it was not an area of industrial growth, the attractiveness of the common to squatters seems the only explanation.[6]

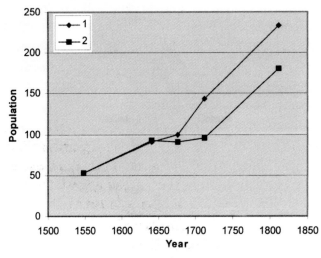

Year	Population Estimate 1	Population Estimate 2
1548	53	53
1641-42	91	93
1676	100	91
1713-14	144	96
1811	233	181

Fig. 7.1 Little Birch Population 1548–1811
Line 1 shows the population estimated for actual year as follows:
1548: Count of 'houselings' (adjusted to allow for children)
1641-42: Calculated from baptismal entries in the parish register, 1637–1646
1676: Compton Census (adjusted to allow for children)
1713–14: Calculated from baptismal entries in the parish register, 1709–1718
1811: Census
Line 2 shows the population prediction based on the 1548 figure and assuming parish had followed national population trends

60

These developments in the late seventeenth century are not merely significant in the population history of the parish; they crucially shaped its modern settlement pattern. In the Iron Age and the Roman period, as we have seen, the centre of local settlement was probably the Iron Age hill fort on the summit of Aconbury Hill. In the Middle Ages, habitation concentrated on lower ground, perhaps in places that had been subsidiary settlements in pre-historic times; these included Bromley, Rowlston/New Mill and the area around Little Birch church. The encroachments on the common moved the centre of population gravity partially back up the hill. When the common was enclosed by Act of Parliament at the beginning of the nineteenth century, the first task of the surveyor in charge of the enclosure was to lay out a pattern of roads to serve the scatter of houses and small-holdings the enclosure process regularised. Later, many of these roads were adopted and metalled, facilitating further development. Late twentieth-century planning concepts such as 'infill' and 'development envelopes' have re-inforced this pattern. Thus Little Birch would not have been as it is today without the period of change in the century or so after 1650, which was as significant as the development of *trefi* in the post-Roman period.[7]

It is impossible to say much of the population of the parish before 1540. Presumably the area, to some degree at least, would have followed the broad national trends suggested by historians for earlier periods. This would mean a comparatively high total for the late Iron Age and Roman periods, succeeded by a decline caused by epidemic disease and political instability between the departure of the Romans and Domesday. There would then have been 250 years of steady growth, shatteringly reversed by the successive epidemics of bubonic plague which afflicted the country after 1348.

Without parish registers we cannot know how many people in Little Birch succumbed to the so-called 'Black Death', but there are some interesting pointers. One means suggested for estimating the impact of the plague in a particular area is to examine the episcopal register to determine the number of institutions of clergy to vacant livings; even if, as in the diocese of Hereford, no reason is usually given for the vacancy, an abnormally high number of institutions in a given period may suggest an epidemic. In the diocese of Hereford (which of course included half of Shropshire as well as Herefordshire) there were between five and nine institutions to livings in each of the four years from 1345 to 1348; in 1349 there were 159. Archenfield seems to have been particularly hardly hit; in the parishes nearest to Little Birch new priests were instituted in Bridstow, Peterstow, Much Dewchurch (twice), Llanwarne, Llandinabo and Tretire. Little Birch did not escape; on 8 July Stephen de Castello was instituted to the living following the death of his predecessor. Since it may be assumed that priests were likely to reflect the disease patterns of their flocks, this has led one study to identify Archenfield as the 'plague-patch of the diocese'. A generation after the first outbreak of bubonic plague, the poll tax of 1377 recorded 27 taxpayers in Little Birch. If this figure reflects all the adult population and there were the same proportion of children to adults as in 1548 (when 40 adults were counted), the population of the parish after the 'Black Death' was only about two-thirds of the low level of the mid sixteenth century. Two other pieces of evidence from the later Middle Ages support the theory of a population crisis. In 1400 the accounts of Aconbury Priory show that one rent had been renegotiated downward, some had not been paid and the bailiff had dared not enforce payment, while at Caldicot there was a defect of rent because of a want of tenants. In 1428 there were apparently fewer than ten households in the parish of Saint Mary at Birches.[8]

Finally, it is worth revisiting Dr Stanford's formula for estimating the population of Iron Age hill forts. This suggested a population range for Aconbury of between 1,260 and 1,680. Of course this would reflect the total for a hinterland extending over a number of modern parishes. We can use the parish data on baptisms collected for the seven-year period 1709–15 in the Visitation of 1716 to generate a comparison. We cannot be sure how far the Aconbury hinterland stretched and, in any case, the 1716 data is not completely comprehensive. If, however, we aggregate the baptisms for the parishes of Aconbury, Ballingham, Callow, Little Birch, Little Dewchurch, Llandinabo, Much Birch and Much Dewchurch and take the annual average, we arrive at an estimated population for the eight parishes in 1712 of 945. This would certainly indicate, if Dr Stanford's hypothesis is correct, that the population in the early eighteenth century was no larger than in the late Iron Age.[9]

8   The Ownership & Use of Land from 1540 to 1840

In 1836 the Reform Parliament, which, among many other measures, legislated on Poor Law reform and the registration of births, marriages and deaths, turned its attention to the vexed question of tithes. The Tithe Act was designed to put an end to the unseemly disputes which sometimes arose over the payment of tithes. It set out the principle that tithe payments should be commuted into fixed money rent charges assessed according to the value of a land holding based on an average yield over seven years. For every parish liable to tithes the Act required an apportionment schedule and a map. The schedule listed all the fields and other pieces of land in each holding, providing the following information: owner, occupier, name, usage (i.e. grass, arable, etc), area (in acres), number on map. The map displayed all the numbered fields and buildings (differentiating between farm buildings and residences) as well as roads, tracks, ponds and watercourses.

There are no detailed maps of Little Birch (i.e. maps indicating features such as field boundaries) pre-dating 1800. This may be because Little Birch was never a part of a great estate, and, if the large estates that held parcels of land in the parish (such as those of Holme Lacy and Langstone) produced maps, these do not apparently survive. The Hereford sheet of the first Ordnance Survey map, published in 1831 at a scale of one inch to a mile, does not show great detail and has poor definition. The surveyors' drawings used to produce it, made in 1815 at two inches to a mile, contain more detail but by no means all field boundaries, and are sometimes marred by questionable draughtsmanship. An accurate map was produced to accompany the enclosure award for the common in 1824 (see 8.4 below), but this, of course, only depicts the area of the parish — about 10% — which was common waste. The tithe map of Little Birch, therefore, produced in 1841, is the first detailed and comprehensive map of the whole parish. It was prepared just as the repeal of the corn laws was about to revolutionise the economic base of English agriculture, and it thus serves both as a window into the past as well as a signpost towards the present.[1]

In some ways Little Birch is fortunate to have a tithe map which covers the whole of the parish. Not all land was liable to tithes. Land that had belonged to monastic orders before their dissolution was generally exempt, and this condition might have been expected to apply to New Mills Farm and Athelstan's Wood. Certainly the tithe map for Aconbury is a small sheet covering only the portion of Athelstan's Wood lying in the parish of Aconbury; the agent for the Guy's Hospital estate, Whaley Armitage, and his son, Arthur, had taken good care to establish that tithes would not be levied on the estate's property in Aconbury. However, long before the trustees of the will of Thomas Guy had acquired the Aconbury land, Athelstan's Wood — both the portion in Aconbury and the larger portion in Little

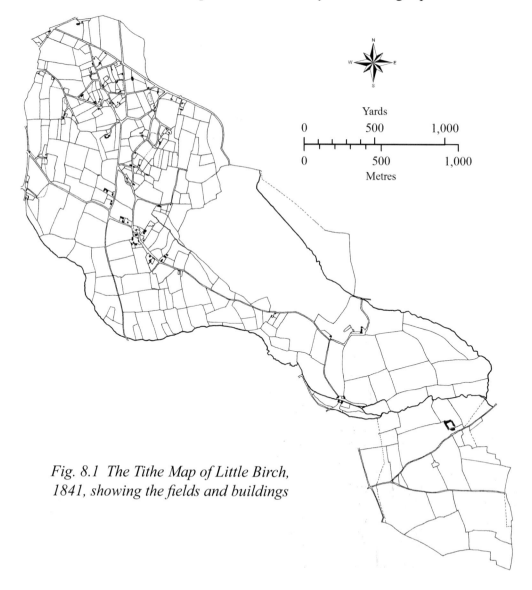

Fig. 8.1 The Tithe Map of Little Birch,
1841, showing the fields and buildings

Birch — together with the Rowlston/New Mills property, which lay wholly in Little Birch, had been sold to the Scudamores of Holme Lacy. The first Viscount Scudamore (1601–1672), who was a pious Anglican and a friend of Archbishop Laud, restored the tithes of all these properties. (A curious feature of the tithes on New Mills Farm was that a third of them was due to the rector of Llanwarne; a similar arrangement pertained in Much Birch with some fields attached to Minster Farm.) The other land in Little Birch which actually was exempt from tithes was the area enclosed from the common in 1824. According to a clause of the private Act of Parliament of 1812 which authorized this enclosure, the rector received an allocation of land from the common as glebe in lieu of any right to tithes from the enclosed land in the future. Fortunately, the enclosures from the common were included in the tithe apportionment schedule, endorsed as exempt from tithes, and were also indicated on the tithe map.[2]

According to the apportionment, the land in the parish not exempt from tithes totalled 831 acres. This comprised 580 acres of arable, 100 acres of meadow and pasture and 151 acres of woodland. These figures — and particularly that cited for woodland — may not be wholly accurate in detail, but they suggest that a far greater proportion of the farmland was under arable cultivation than is the case today. The map, however, provides in visual form a much more interesting insight. This is not immediately apparent from the original map, because its very large scale makes a panoramic overview difficult. Viewed on a smaller scale reduction — say 1:10000 (approximately six inches to a mile) — it reveals that the parish was divided into four distinctive parts:

FARM	SIZE OF FARM ACRES	ARABLE AS % OF HOLDING	NO OF ARABLE FIELDS	AVERAGE SIZE OF ARABLE FIELD (ACRES)
Green Farm	23.51	69.46	6	2.72
Sunny Bank Farm	32.3	73.59	8	2.97
Upper House Farm	23.51	53.04	4*	3.12
Lower House Farm	66.55	62.16	11	3.76
Church Farm	86.81	80.44	16	4.36
New Mills Farm	147.12	84.79	12**	10.4
Bromley Court	144.01	80.74	9	12.92

Fig. 8.2 Tithe Map 1841: Size of Arable Fields
Notes - Fields in Little Birch farmed with the above holdings in 1841
* In addition to the land he owned, John Mutlow of Upper House rented 2 pasture fields totalling 4.73 acres and 1 arable field of 4.56 acres
** In addition to New Mills Farm, rented from Sir E.F. Scudamore-Stanhope, James Bennett owned and farmed 2 arable fields totalling 15.28 acres

- Bromley Court and New Mills Farms, lying to the south-east of Athelstan's Wood, the two largest farms in the parish, with comparatively large arable fields averaging in size in excess of 10 acres;
- Athelstan's Wood, which almost completely divides the parish in two at its narrowest part, leaving a belt of small fields only two or three deep along Ruff Lane between the wood and the boundary with Much Birch along Wriggle Brook (at this time and earlier generally called Riddle Brook);
- Church Farm, Lower House Farm and the other farms in the north-western portion of the parish, all smaller than Bromley and New Mills, and characterized by smaller arable fields, often somewhat longer and narrower in shape;
- the cluster of small, irregular enclosures in the north of the parish, in the upper part of the valley formed by the small stream which rises south-east of Uplands — the area that was a common until 1824.

These four areas will be examined in turn.[3]

8.1 New Mills and Bromley

These two holdings, though they were included within the parish of Little Birch either at or shortly after its creation, were almost certainly originally separate settlements, perhaps *trefi* within a greater *mainaur* before the eleventh century (see section 4 above). Since the sixteenth century — and, at least in the case of New Mills, before this — they have been characterized by having apparently relatively stable boundaries, and single owners, with ownership remaining in one family for a comparatively long period.

By 1629, according to the deeds, Bromley was in the possession of the Kidley (or Kydley) family. In fact their ownership almost certainly dates back before this; entries relating to the family are decipherable in the Little Birch parish register from as early as 1602. The Kidleys were not, however, in Little Birch in the time of Henry VIII; in 1547 Richard Kydley was paying taxes in Fownhope. The family name may derive from Kidley Hill in Ballingham. Apart from Bromley, the Kidleys owned other properties in south Herefordshire in the seventeenth century, including land in St Weonards, Madley and Much Birch and also rented land, including, for a period, possibly Rowlston. In the eighteenth century the estate passed by marriage to the Oswald family. After Richard Oswald's death in 1746 it was purchased (in 1748) by John Roberts. He was not related to the current owners but was the owner of Pennoxstone Court in Kings Caple. In 1806 Bromley was sold on again to George Terry, the owner at the time the tithe map was compiled. By then the farm was tenanted by Thomas Preece, an example of the increasing tendency for larger farms to be rented rather than owner-occupied.[4]

As explained in section 5, the lands of Aconbury Priory in the parishes of Aconbury and Little Birch had passed via an intermediary speculator to Hugh Parry of Poston in Vowchurch during the 1540s. The histories of these properties in the two parishes differ. The history of Aconbury has, however, always been intimately connected with that of Little Birch; the ecclesiastical livings of the parishes were united and the gift of the living lay with the owner of Aconbury until the second half of the nineteenth century. The ownership of Aconbury must therefore be recounted.

The grandson of Hugh Parry, John, left no male heir; his daughter, Elizabeth, married John Pearle of Dewsall. They likewise produced no male heir, and in 1638, their daughter, Mary, married Sir John Bridges, the son of Sir Giles Bridges of Wilton Castle and the man who was to become the implacable enemy of Sir Barnabas Scudamore in 1645. John Pearle died in 1643, though his will does not seem to have been proved before 1649, and Aconbury became part of the extensive Bridges estates in the county. In the 1663 militia assessment Aconbury is noted as being held jointly by Sir James Bridges, son of Sir John, and Sir William Powell of Pengethley, who had married Lady Mary Bridges after the death of her first husband. The Herefordshire branch of the Bridges family was a cadet line, the senior line being Lords Chandos; when the senior line failed, Sir James became Lord Chandos. After his death in 1714, his son, also James, acquired enormous wealth and the title Duke of Chandos; but by 1728, financial pressures compelled the duke to put his Herefordshire estates up for sale. The purchasers were the trustees of the will of Thomas Guy, a wealthy London printer, who were seeking a suitable investment to endow the hospital provided for in Guy's will. The sale was completed in 1731, but one of its conditions was that the daughter-in-law of the duke, the Marchioness of Caernarvon, whose husband had pre-deceased the duke, had a jointure on two-thirds of the estate. Those portions, which included Aconbury, would not come under the control of the governors of Guy's Hospital until her death. This did not occur until 1754, which is why the report of that year referred to in section 2 above is the first one relating to Aconbury conducted by the governors' representatives.[5]

In 1592 the Rowlston/New Mills estate and the whole of Athelstan's Wood — in Little Birch and Aconbury parishes — were purchased from the Parry family by Sir John Scudamore of Holme Lacy. He was the grandson of the John Scudamore who had been the local receiver to the Court of Augmentation at the dissolution of the monasteries. The lands of the former Aconbury Priory in Little Birch were to remain a part of the Holme Lacy estate until it was finally sold in 1909. The interest of Barnabas Scudamore in Rowlston has already been noted. As we have seen, his brother-in-law, the first viscount, unlike Sir Walter Pye and Sir Henry Lingen, was a cautious Royalist and kept his family fortunes comparatively intact until the Restoration.[6]

The wealth of the Holme Lacy Scudamores was no protection in the eighteenth century from a series of family misfortunes. These had begun with the scandalous behaviour of the wife of the second viscount. Then in 1710 the third viscount, riding from Holme Lacy to Hereford one day, suffered a fall from his horse which occasioned injuries from which he never fully recovered. He died in 1716 at the age of 32, leaving as heir a daughter, Frances. She made an apparently good marriage to the Duke of Beaufort in 1729 but was later involved in a notorious affair with William Talbot, later Earl of Shrewsbury. Her husband divorced her, and she subsequently married Charles Fitzroy, illegitimate son of the Duke of Grafton. Once again there was only one female heir, again called Frances Scudamore; Fitzroy had taken the name Scudamore on his marriage. The instability implicit in her mother's behaviour was much more pronounced in the younger Frances. In 1771 she married Mr Charles Howard, a lineal descendant, by a cadet line, of Thomas Howard, fourth Duke of Norfolk, executed by Queen Elizabeth I in 1572. She had already attracted comment from Lady Mary Coke, who described her in 1769 as being suspected as a 'concealed roman catholic' and of being 'very particular in her temper'. Through the failure of the senior line, Howard's father became tenth Duke of Norfolk in 1777 and he himself succeeded to the title in 1786. His marriage with Frances, however, was a disaster; she became increasingly mentally ill and had to be confined, whilst he acquired a reputation as a drunkard.[7]

Unsurprisingly there were no children; the duke died in 1815 and his wife in 1820. There were then no lineal descendants from the first viscount. After 1815 a complex series of chancery proceedings began which lasted for 14 years and ended in the Scudamore possessions being divided between two families descended from the first viscount's sister, Mary. Documents referring to Scudamore holdings during this period frequently refer to the legal complexities of the estate's ownership. Ironically, Sir Edwin Francis Scudamore-Stanhope, who inherited Holme Lacy itself and, among other properties, the Scudamore lands in Little Birch, and who appears as their owner on the Little Birch tithe map, was a descendant of Sir John Bridges. Sir Edwin's tenant at New Mills in 1841 was James Bennett, whose family had apparently held the tenancy for a considerable period; Thomas Bennett is recorded as one of the poor law overseers in 1784.[8]

There was a tantalizing and unfortunate consequence of these events. As a result of the prolonged chancery proceedings, many deeds relating to the Scudamore estate were placed in the Chancery Division of the National Archives and were catalogued; these included deeds relating to the Little Birch properties between 1592 and 1633. At the end of the nineteenth century, Sir Edwin's descendant, the Earl of Chesterfield, withdrew them and lodged them with his solicitor in London in premises destroyed in an air raid during the Second World War. The destruction of these records is a great loss to students of the parish's history because they would have furnished details of how the land was organized at the end of the sixteenth century and might have helped answer one of the most difficult questions faced in describing the local landscape then: to what extent open field arable farming was practised and how long its practice survived.[9]

This question is relevant to the whole parish, and the basic principles of the open field system may conveniently be considered now. As is well known, arable agriculture in the Middle Ages was practised in many parts of England not in small enclosed fields grouped into discrete farm holdings but in large open fields, in each of which every member of the village community would hold a number of strips. In the classic examples of such arrangements in the East Midlands, where a large parish was often co-terminous with a single manor and its field-system, the fields, usually two or three in number, could be very large — 200 acres or more; complex rules were needed through the local manorial court to ensure the system was operated in a disciplined and harmonious way. The only partially surviving example of such arrangements is at Laxton in Nottinghamshire. The work of H.L. Gray at the beginning of the twentieth century demonstrated that there were many regional variations of open field agriculture. In Herefordshire, the open fields and the field systems into which they were grouped were generally smaller than in the east Midlands and there were often several distinct systems within one parish. This may well have been because of the prevalence of hamlet settlement in the county and particularly in the Welsh areas where *trefi* were usual. Unfortunately there is no agreement among experts about how, when and why open-field farming developed.[10]

When John Leland (see section 7 above) spoke of Archenfield being 'full of enclosures' he can hardly have meant that all the arable land was enclosed because there was clearly a considerable amount of open-field farming there at the time. He probably meant that open fields and enclosed arable fields were intermixed with a rather higher proportion of the latter than might have been found in some other districts. He might also have been confused by the fact that open fields in Herefordshire were generally smaller that those found further east. In the absence of the early Scudamore papers for Rowlston we have to depend on what can be learned from the records prepared at the time of the dissolution. These suggest that in Aconbury there were probably three large arable fields near to Aconbury Priory itself, Millfield, Quarrell Field and Huntley, each containing 40 acres of demesne land (i.e. that farmed directly by the priory and not leased); there may well have been additional portions of these fields leased to tenants. These field names were still preserved on the Guy's Hospital estate map of 1852. By that time the fields had obviously been partitioned though field sizes were still generally larger than at New Mills or Bromley. There can be no doubt that these fields were open in the mid-sixteenth century. There is, however, also mention of several closes.[11]

The evidence for Rowlston is a little less direct. The annual rental values given at the dissolution are £2 for the manor, £1 for the mill and five shillings for the closes or enclosures. This might imply that between 10% and 20% of the land was enclosed at this date. The picture that emerges is very like that for Aconbury — an intermingling of open arable fields with enclosures of various types.[12]

There is much speculation about exactly why and how open-field systems were broken down, just as there is about their origins. The Black Death in the fourteenth century severely reduced the population so that there were fewer people to undertake labour-intensive arable farming — as indicated in the difficulty Aconbury Priory had in finding tenants in 1400 (see section 7 above). The growth of the wool trade in the later Middle Ages encouraged mixed farming, for which open-field arable systems were insufficiently flexible. But open fields disappeared from the landscape at widely different times in different parts of the country. It has been suggested that the early enclosure of Herefordshire occurred because of the amount of assarting carried out in the county's extensive woodland. This would have produced comparatively early enclosures since the greatest pressure for assarting occurred during the three centuries of steady population growth between the Norman Conquest and the Black Death. It would account for the mixed appearance of the district in the sixteenth century but it would not wholly explain why the remaining open fields were enclosed at different times.[13]

The answer to that question is more likely to be related to the number of owners involved in any one field system. Where ownership was concentrated in one person, enclosure was comparatively easy and could be accomplished quickly. Where ownership of the parcels of land in the field system was in the hands of a small number of people, the process would take a little longer, usually proceeding incrementally by a series of private agreements. Where there were a large number of owners and complex machinery for co-ordinating farming activities, agreement might be delayed until a private Act of Parliament provided for a comprehensive allotment of land. This latter situation arose in many of the large open-field villages of the East Midlands in the late eighteenth and early nineteenth centuries. The second scenario applied, as we shall see, to the arable land of the northern part of Little Birch.

In Rowlston, there had already in 1538 been a single landowner for more than 200 years. Though in the thirteenth century, Roger Codach seems to have granted land to several parties, by the end of the century it was apparently all in the possession of Aconbury Priory. The remarkable continuity of holding and farming activity over more than five centuries can be gauged by the fact that in 1294 the Prioress of Aconbury possessed one carucate — about 120 acres of ploughland — in Rowlston: in 1841, of the land which James Bennett rented from Sir Edwin Francis Scudamore-Stanhope, just under 125 acres were under arable cultivation. It was thus easy to accomplish enclosure in Rowlston. The field shapes recorded in 1841 are of a type associated with enclosure by a single landowner in the sixteenth or early seventeenth centuries and it was probably during the ownership of the Parrys or soon after the estate was acquired by the Scudamores that enclosure took place. Though no comparable data is available for Bromley, the similar size and shape of its fields in 1841 suggest it may have had a similar enclosure history. This might possibly be connected with the fact that in 1634 Edward Kidley of Bromley had power of attorney for the manor of Rowlston from Viscount Scudamore.[14]

8.2 Athelstan's Wood

In the Middle Ages Athelstan's Wood formed part of the forest of Aconbury, though this does not mean that the whole area was one of continuous woodland. By the nineteenth century part of what had been the forest of Aconbury comprised two separate blocks of woodland. The more northerly of these included Wallbrook Wood, Holloway Bank Wood, the recently planted Aconbury Warren Wood, as well as, on the other side of the road linking Caldicot and Little Birch, Pike's Wood, and, beyond the Aconbury to Little Dewchurch road, Nether Wood. To the south, separated from Pikes Wood by only a couple of fields, lay the southerly block, made up of Lady Coppice (beyond the Aconbury-Little Dewchurch road), Rough Hill Wood and Athelstan's Wood. The boundary between the latter two woods ran in a south-south-easterly direction from a point very near the spring which is the source of the stream running through Athelstan's Wood. All of these two areas of woodland lie within Aconbury parish except for Athelstan's Wood, the major portion of which lies in Little Birch. The Little Birch tithe map estimated the acreage of the wood within the parish as just under 137 acres, whilst the Aconbury tithe map estimated the portion lying in that parish as 69 acres. This is at variance with the information on the 1904 Ordnance Survey map (scale 1:2500) which shows just over 161 acres in Little Birch and just over 42 acres in Aconbury. The Ordnance Survey map is in fact the correct one; almost certainly the tithe map surveyors included in their acreage all the woodland lying to the north-east of the stream, though as their own map shows, the Little Birch parish boundary encompasses some of this area.[15]

In 1538 all the so-called 'great timber' of these woodlands had been reserved by the crown, as had been the case at the time of the initial grants to the priory. This situation still pertained as late as 1573. Because Hereford Record Office holds the papers of the Guy's Hospital Herefordshire estates, we can gain a rather fuller picture of the part of the woodlands that came into the estate's possession. When the representatives of the hospital's governors reported on the estate in 1754 they noted that the fine timber was mostly in Nether Wood and Wallbrook Wood. They did not visit Held Wood; in 1573 this had been reported as being largely destroyed by rabbits but in 1754 things were probably better since the rabbits on the piece of land called the Warren had apparently died out. Held Wood like most of the rest was probably coppiced. Certainly the book containing the estate's timber valuations between 1810 and 1880 shows a regular cycle of coppicing in most of the estate woodlands.[16]

On most large estates the woodland was kept 'in hand' i.e. managed directly by the owner rather than leased out like the farms. This was true of Athelstan's Wood, at least for most of the time, just as it was of the woodlands on the Guy's Hospital estate. It is likely that while it was in the possession of the Scudamores much of Athelstan's Wood was coppiced. Certainly in the middle part of the seventeenth century there was a very particular reason for this. In the late 1620s a series of agreements were made between Sir John Scudamore of Holme Lacy (he did not become Viscount Scudamore until 1628), his kinsman William Scudamore of Ballingham and Sir John Kyrle of Much Marcle relating to the construction and operation of an iron forge at Carey Mill. About 400 metres to the east of where the old railway bridge crossed the Wye from Ballingham to Fawley, and near to the south bank of the river, are three small islands. The mill was situated on the south bank; the islands were linked by a wall to form a mill pond and a weir was constructed from them to the northern bank to divert water into the millpond. Though the hammers were operated by water, very large amounts of charcoal were required for the forge. An agreement of 1628 specifically included 'Ailestons Wood' as one of the sources for this charcoal; precise specification were given about the age and size of timber to be cut for the charcoal, at what time of year it was to be cut, how long it was to be left before being stacked in 'cords' and how big the cords were to be. The coppicing cycle seems to have been 15 years.[17]

The forge continued to operate for around 60 years. During the Civil War it must have been part of the vital iron industry extending from South Wales across the Forest of Dean which compensated the Royalists for the fact that the main centre of the nation's iron and heavy armaments manufacture in the Weald was firmly under Parliamentarian control. Its existence, however, was detrimental to the local population in two ways. In 1641, the eccentric writer and early advocate of inland waterways, John Taylor, made a journey by boat from London to Hereford. He travelled in what he described as a 'scullers boat' with two men and two boys to carry the boat where rivers were not available or not navigable. The main example of the former problem was the stretch from the headwaters of the Thames to a tributary of the Severn. But one of the worst examples of the latter problem occurred on the stretch of the Wye between Monmouth and Hereford where he noted seven weirs (including that at Carey Mill) which caused the river to be 'debard of all passage with boates'. He also noted that the shortage of fuel for heating made the navigation of the river desirable so that coal could be carried to Hereford. Carey Mill was not only contributing to the obstruction of river traffic on the Wye, it was contributing to the widespread over-exploitation of local woodlands which made such traffic essential. When in 1649 the viscount began erecting another forge near Holme Lacy, the citizens of Hereford vigorously protested against it to Parliament.[18]

The Wye Navigation Acts at the end of the seventeenth century provided for all the owners of weirs on the river to be compensated so that the river could be cleared for navigation. Any decline in the market for charcoal, however, would not have meant the end of coppicing in Athelstan's Wood any more than in the woods around Aconbury. There was still a great demand for coppice products used in agriculture and construction: laths for walls and ceilings, hurdles for enclosures, chestnut poles for hop-poles. This ensured that trades such as woodman and lath-cleaver were well represented in Little Birch in the early nineteenth century.

8.3 Church Farm, Lower House Farm and the farms in the north-western half of the parish

Beyond the land he rented from Sir Edwin Francis Scudamore-Stanhope in 1841, James Bennett owned a couple of fields of his own. Farther north-west again was a compact smallholding known as the Ruff, owned and farmed by John Jones in 1841 (though in 1832 it had been owned and farmed by Charles Ravenhill.) Then came some fields owned by Kedgwin Hoskins of Much Birch. This narrow strip of land runs between Athelstan's Wood and Wriggle Brook. Beyond this are the remaining farms in the parish. These farms, only a little greater in total area than New Mills and Bromley put together, are totally different in character and history. Not only are there, inevitably, changes in family ownership but there appears to have been far less continuity in the size and location of holdings. The documents to construct a complete history of this area between 1540 and 1840 are not available, but, even if they were, the history would be lengthy and immensely complex — far beyond the scope of this book. All that can usefully be done is to offer a broad overview of what apparently happened and to explore the reasons for the area's distinctive character.[19]

Two factors dominate the pattern of land ownership here: the persistence of Welsh customs of inheritance and the survival, at least in the northern portion of the area, of open field farming. If one looks at the taxpayers of Little Birch in 1547 a number of family names are apparent: they include Huggyn, Weare, Genye (or Gynny or Gyny) and Baylye. By 1600 some new names have appeared in the parish register: Gwillym, Gwatkin and Abrahall. By the time the Militia Assessment of 1663 was conducted, Huggyn, Weare and Baylye have gone and Higgs has appeared.[20]

It is best to start with the Gwillyms. In 1841 they were the only family that had been in the village before 1600 and still held land there. This enables us to pinpoint the house which was the centre of the holding: Church Farm. In 1841 Church Farm was the largest farm in the parish after New Mills and Bromley, and John Gwillym had the highest militia assessment after Viscount Scudamore and John Kidley in 1663. In 1671, John Gwillym, described as a gentleman, was taxed on four hearths, the same as John Kidley. The Gwillyms were the successors to George Baylye, one of the largest taxpayers of 1547. His daughter and heir, Elizabeth, married Thomas Gwillym of Fawley, the son of John Gwillym, the last bailiff of Aconbury Priory.[21]

The Gwillym holding in Little Birch must have originally been larger than the 87 acres of Church Farm in 1841. It had been partitioned in the seventeenth century by what looks like the operation of gavelkind. When Thomas Gwillym, the son of the Thomas who married Elizabeth Baylye, died in 1641 his will did not mention his land, but it stipulated that all his possessions should be divided equally between his sons John and Thomas including his goods and chattels, both household and agricultural implements. This implies that both sons would need equipment for farming and it may mean some division of land had already taken place or was accepted as a customary outcome of succession. Thomas Gwillym junior, living at Langstone in Llangarron, was already accumulating an estate in South Herefordshire that would eventually amount to 1,000 acres. His portion of the Gwillym lands in Little Birch was taxed at £8 in the militia assessment of 1663 while his brother John's portion was taxed at £9. Even when Thomas's descendant Robert Gwillym eventually disposed of the last of his Herefordshire estates in 1794, the Langstone Gwillyms still held nearly 60 acres of land in Little Birch.[22]

John Gwillym only survived his father by five years. When he died in 1646 his will divided his lands so that his younger son, also called John, inherited the

Little Birch lands he had from his father, whilst his eldest son, Anthony, was left a farm that had come to John as the marriage portion of his wife, Margery. This is actually named as Trewenny, a name preserved in the 1841 tithe map as Trewinny, a field just in Much Birch across Wriggle Brook beyond Cress Cottage. A comparatively modern house farther up the lane towards Minster Farm is called Trewenn. Anthony Gwillym's inheritance was evidently a farm in this part of Much Birch.[23]

The home of the Abrahall family is much more difficult to determine. Judging by the tax levied on them in 1663 they must have owned a substantial amount of land which was then in the possession of the widow Mary Abrahall. The will of William Abrahall in 1641 left land to his wife and daughters but there is an implication his son also owned land. Some of the Abrahall land can be located in one of the open fields but not their house.[24]

Something similar to the Abrahall inheritance may have happened in the case of Thomas Weaver who died in 1658 leaving land to his younger son, John, but also mentioning that an elder son, Thomas, already held land in the parish. Among the fields that John inherited was one named as Daniells Rough. Judging by other details in the will, this could have been the site of the holding later called the Ruff.[25]

The case of William Higgs, whom we have already met in section 6 is particularly interesting. His holding of land was assessed at £7 in 1663 and on the basis of comparability with the assessment of other landowners in the parish it can hardly have been less than 100 acres. Indeed in 1741, his descendent John Higgs, then described as a gentleman residing in Eaton Bishop, owned 127 acres in Little Birch, divided between two farms as had been the case in the mid-seventeenth century, by 1741 both being leased out to different occupiers. William Higgs's will states that he purchased one of these two farms (probably the larger) from Thomas Gynny. This gives us a clue to the farm's identity. According to the tithe map the field in the angle between New Road and Bannut Tree Lane was called Guineas Broom and belonged to Lower House Farm. Since the Higgs family continued to own the major part of the estate built up by William Higgs until the late eighteenth century, it is possible to track its subsequent changes of ownership from the Land Tax returns. The name of the property is not mentioned but it can be tracked through the fixed amount of tax charged each year. It remained in the possession of the Higgs family until 1783 when its owner appears to have been Peter Burton. It then passed to the Floyd family until in 1808 it is listed under the ownership of William Pugh who remained its owner in 1841 where it is identified as Lower House Farm. This would have been a useful residence for the rector of the parish since there was no parsonage house at that date.[26]

The other farm acquired by Higgs was purchased from the Gwatkin family. Identifying the farmhouse that might have belonged to this is more difficult. One of the Gwatkins, John, continued to hold some land in Little Birch (taxed at £4 in 1663). In his will William Higgs left John Gwatkin ten shillings describing him as 'my neighbour'. The nearest house to Lower House in 1841 was Upper House (to which was attached at that stage some 23 acres of land). This stood on the site of Gerald Skyrme's present home. It was still standing in the 1930s, described as derelict and probably dating from the late fifteenth century. However, the will of Thomas Weaver the elder, dated 1658 and already referred to, strongly suggests that at that time Upper House belonged to the Weavers. It is possible that the Gwatkin house was on or near the site of the present rectory. At all events it seems clear that in the mid-seventeenth century there was a concentration of at least four farms within about 250 metres of the church — exactly what we would expect in an open-field village.[27]

Finally the will of William Higgs must be considered for what it tells us about the inheritance practices of the time. When Higgs described his second farm as having been purchased from five members of one family — Richard, Thomas, John, Hugh and James Gwatkin — it is clear he has had to buy out all those with an interest in a gavelkind property. It might be assumed that as an English immigrant, Higgs would not feel bound to follow the custom. Indeed his will left all his land to his elder son (also William). His younger son, John, was left £100 and a feather bed. John was clearly under 21 at the time the will was drawn up and his older brother was additionally required to furnish £10 to put him in an apprenticeship if his father died before his 21st birthday. But there is a very significant final paragraph. £100 was a large sum, nearly as much as the entire value of the items in the will's inventory. Higgs senior stipulates that if, when John reached the age of 21, his older brother as his father's executor had not paid him the £100, he might enter all the premises and properties left to William and claim half their annual income. It looks very much like another form of gavelkind.[28]

There is one later, fuller and more remarkable instance of gavelkind in Little Birch. This relates to Green Farm or, as it was often called in earlier centuries, Upper House or Merefold Gate. Its history before the early eighteenth century is unclear. In 1841 its lands consisted of about 23 acres lying on the northern and eastern sides of the Woodfield (see below). Its position at the higher end of the Woodfield may have given the farm one if its alternative names. At some stage probably in the early eighteenth century this holding was acquired by Edward Williams and passed after his death equally to his two sons, Thomas and Jonathan. Clearly it was not a large enough holding to support two families. Jonathan became a customs official in Bristol and sold his share to his brother Thomas. Thomas left the farm again according to the custom of gavelkind to his three sons, Thomas, Jonathan and John. Jonathan junior appears to have mortgaged the property and in 1741, Thomas junior bought out the mortgage and his two brothers' shares. None of the Williams family had lived there since Edward; the farm had presumably been rented out and the income distributed among whomever had shares in it at the time. Thomas Williams junior was actually a clergyman, vicar of Vowchurch from 1750 to his death in 1785. When he died the farm again devolved according to the custom of gavelkind to his two nephews, John and Thomas. It was only because the latter died intestate and without heirs that his brother was eventually able to sell the farm to James Powell of St Devereux, ancestor of the present owner, Bill Powell, in 1803.[29]

Apart from these major farms two further types of landholding must be mentioned. Deeds show that there were clearly a number of cottages and smallholdings in the village, though probably relatively fewer in 1650 than in 1840. There were also a number of holdings of land belonging to owners outside the parish. These were not absentee landlords of the type common in the nineteenth century but rather yeomen from neighbouring parishes who probably farmed their lands in Little Birch as an integral part of their own farms. One example of this is Thomas Binkes. He is shown on the Militia Assessment of 1663 as owning land taxed at £4 in Little Birch — perhaps as much as 50 acres. He also appears as one of the raters for the assessment in Aconbury and, therefore, almost certainly a resident there. In William Higgs's will there is a legacy of ten shillings to 'Thomas Byncks of Merrifould the younger'. Clearly Binkes rented Merrivale from the Bridges family and owned land, probably reasonably adjacent to it, in Little Birch.[30]

Apart from gavelkind, and perhaps in some ways resulting from it, the other important feature of the farms in the north-west of the parish, at least until the early eighteenth century, was the survival of some degree of open field arable farming. There are indications in extant documents of at least two open fields. There may have been more, or the two that can be identified may have been bigger than can now be proved.

Between 1590 and 1622 a series of deeds indicate the existence of a field called Myndfield. The deeds relate to exchanges of land by members of the Willym family. The Willyms lived in Much Birch. They are not included in the 1663 Militia Assessment but one of the daughters of the rector of Little Birch, William Higgs, evidently married into the family because in his will he left his grandchildren William and Henry Willym ten shillings a year each. In 1707 the Willyms were the owners of Riddle Brook Farm, which lay just across Wriggle Brook in Much Birch. The description of some of the pieces of land in these deeds makes it certain that the Myndfield consisted of open strips of land often

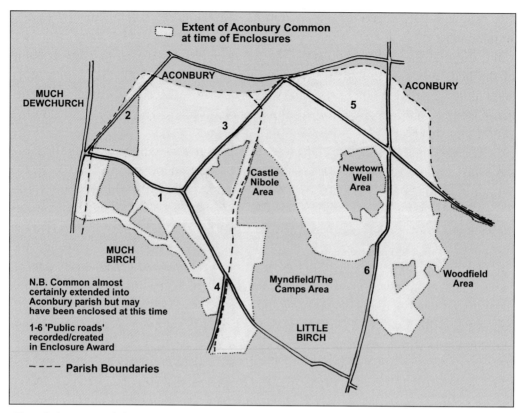

Fig. 8.3 Map of the extent of common/wasteland in Little Birch and Much Birch at the time of the Enclosures in 1824

of as little as one acre identified by their position relative to the parcels of the other owners. There are references to the proximity of Aconbury Hill (the name of the common). Since the only other land in Little Birch abutting the common, towards Athelstan's Wood, clearly had another name, and in view of the meaning of 'mynd' — mountain — it seems fairly clear that the area indicated was probably the land sloping upwards from Mesne Lane between the two arms of the common; this would also seem a natural place for a farmer based at Riddle Brook Farm to acquire land. The name 'mynd' did not survived as an element in any field name in 1841, though one or two long narrow fields, very much the size and shape of strips, survived on the tithe map near Fairview.[31]

This area might presumably have included the fields known in 1841 as the Camps, Upper Camps, Lower Camps and Far Camps. It is interesting that a lease of 1686 from William Gwillym of Langstone to his kinsman John Gwillym of Little Birch refers to 'all those ffoure severall parcels of arable being now divided with severall inclosures and commonly called the Camps', a phrase which strongly suggests that the area was then enclosed in four pieces but that a different arrangement could be remembered. Whether that arrangement was as a single enclosure or as part of an open field is impossible to say. 'Camp' as a field name often signifies an enclosure. The nature and diversity of species in some of the hedgerows in this area, including the presence of bluebells, could imply ancient enclosure, even primary enclosure from an assart. All this emphasizes the complexity of the history of the land in this part of the parish and how difficult it is to disentangle it.[32]

The evidence for the second open field is much more robust. This seems to have survived considerably longer than the Myndfield. It was referred to as the Woodfield and lay as far as can be determined roughly between Crow's Nest Lane, Green Lane, Athelstan's Wood and Ruff Lane. A glance at the tithe map furnishes many clues. For a start several farms — Lower House, Sunny Bank, Church Farm and Green Farm — are shown having individual fields in this area each one called Wood Field, suggesting that each represented the consolidated strips those farms held in the open field. Several fields have the significant name 'Tendings' meaning an enclosure, by implication of land not previously enclosed. A group of five small fields just to the east of Prospect Villa almost exactly preserve the size and shape of open-field strips. Two of them are not even fenced from each other though in different ownership. By 1904 there had been amalgamations and the five enclosures had become three. Today the easternmost one has become part of the field on the other side and the remaining four are now one. Finally there is a characteristic access lane leading into the heart of the field from the focus of the settlement around the church. This proceeds with a number of right angle turns past Higgins Well and Yew Tree Cottage. There is no purpose in its existence other than to give access to the strips; the agricultural building near where it ends was not built until after the preparation of the tithe map.[33]

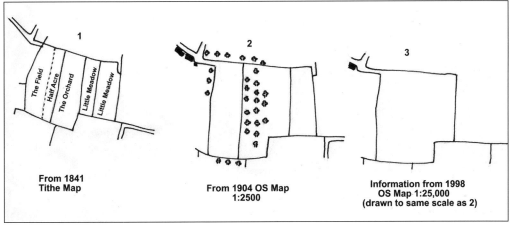

Fig. 8.4 Map of strip fields, once part of Woodfield, in 1841, 1904 and 1998

Apart from these pieces of evidence there is a plethora of references in deeds to parcels of land in the Woodfield. This is because many deeds of the Langstone branch of the Gwillym family have been preserved and the Woodfield survived long enough as an open field to feature in deeds after the division of the Gwillym lands in Little Birch in 1641. In fact the very first of these deeds — a lease — dates from that year. Thomas Gwillym of Langstone was clearly anxious to rent out land he could not farm from Llangarron. His tenant for two parcels of land, one of three acres and the other of one acre was the rector, William Higgs, who was equally anxious to increase his farming enterprise by adding rental land to the land he owned. The description of the two parcels is unmistakeable; the first is adjoined by strips belonging to Thomas Gwillym or already in the ownership of Higgs; the second adjoins parcels held by John Gwatkin, William Abrahall and Richard Weare. There are a number of similar documents dating over the next 70 years or so. A particularly lengthy one dated 1702 is a lease to Richard Weaver of Orcop. This includes an orchard and close of land adjoining and on Aconbury Hill commonly called the Old House Orchard, which sounds as if it could be Well Orchard. It also includes the so-called 'New Tendings' between Green Farm and Crow's Nest Lane, evidently already enclosed, and several other small parcels in the Woodfield that are evidently unenclosed. The 14 acres known as Wood-broke and lying between Athelstan's Wood and the stream (which in 1841 belonged to Kedgwin Hoskins), however, are described as a close.[34]

Other property of the Langstone Gwillyms in Little Birch gives the impression of enclosed land of long standing. Leases of 1670 and 1696 to Roger Hennond and his son Thomas refer to Castle Nibole as a messuage with 20 acres of land belonging to it and bounded on all or most sides by the hill called Aconbury Hill. It is interesting that these leases like the one of 1702 reserve the right to William Gwillym of the timber trees on the land or any trees likely to become timber trees: another instance of keeping timber growth 'in hand'.[35]

As the eighteenth century progressed, the financial pressures on the large Langstone estate grew. In 1738 Robert Gwillym, the great-great-grandson of the Thomas Gwillym who had received half his father's land in Little Birch in 1641, married a Lancashire heiress, Elizabeth Atherton. His Herefordshire estates were disposed of in two sales, the latter in 1794. The sale particulars show that the Little Birch property had been divided into two almost equally sized holdings each of just over 29 acres. One advertised as Castle Nibbott Farm with the Camps effectively included all the land the estate possessed from or near the old Myndfield. In the late seventeenth century the Castle Nibole land had been let to the Hennond family and the Camps to the Little Birch branch of the Gwillym family. In 1794 the whole of it was now leased to the Gwillyms of Church Farm. The other holding, rather pretentiously called Little-Burch-Land Farm, consisted of the scatter of fields the estate owned in and around Woodfield. These included Well Orchard (the farmhouse of the holding though was technically on the common), the New Tendings, various parcels in Woodfield almost certainly now enclosed as well as the old enclosures at the southern end of Woodfield. This rather scattered holding was rented to John Waters. These two farms did not remain single holdings for long after the sale. By 1841, Castle Nibole was in the hands of Henry Hampton while the Camps had become part of Sunny Bank Farm. The later history of Well Orchard will be considered further in the next subsection.[36]

The area occupied by the Woodfield cannot have been more than 60 or 70 acres and the Myndfield probably smaller. This is far smaller than the great open fields of the East Midlands but apparently not dissimilar to the open fields around Aconbury Priory at its dissolution, discussed in 8.1 above.

It remains to say something of the other cultivated area of this part of the parish, the fields lying to the south of Mesne Lane and Ruff Lane. The fact that two names appear more than once on the tithe map, Mesne Field and Port Field, belonging to different farms, and that there was an intermixture of holdings in this area suggest that the fields could have been open here at one stage; we have seen a similar repetition of the name Wood Field preserving the history of multiple ownership in an open field. There is no easily traceable documentary record to prove their existence or how they might have related to the other two fields. The fields appear bigger and squarer on the tithe map than the fields to the north of them, more like those of Bromley and New Mills, and so if ever they were open, they are likely to have been enclosed at an earlier date than the Myndfield and the Woodfield.[37]

8.4 The Common

Before examining the common, we must first clarify its name. In the surviving deeds from the sixteenth and seventeenth centuries it is referred to as Aconbury Hill, even the parts farthest away from the summit of the hill, around Well Orchard and Green Farm. On the first Ordnance Survey map of 1831 it is called Aconbury Common. It is obvious from the nature of the settlement and from Guy's Hospital estate documents that it once occupied land in the three parishes of Aconbury, Little Birch and Much Birch. The nature of land ownership in Aconbury made it possible to enclose the parts of the common in that parish by private agreement and earlier than those in Much and Little Birch. When they came to be enclosed by Act of Parliament at the beginning of the nineteenth century they were described as Much and Little Birch Common.[38]

A common or common waste was strictly an area deemed too poor to be used as arable or meadow, on which members of the village community or manor would have apportioned rights of rough grazing, the collection of fuel and so forth. In theory such rights should have been policed and enforced by the manorial authorities. The system, however, often broke down. Though it was enclosed earlier, we have a record of such a break-down on the portion of the common lying in Aconbury in 1754 — compiled as part of the first report on the area to the governors of Guy's Hospital — which is a valuable insight into what was certainly happening more widely on the common. The report noted that there were a number of cottages on the common erected without any grant of permission and paying no rent. Some had been there for 20 or even 30 years and there was a danger that they might eventually be claimed as freehold if no action were taken. Some of the cottagers were apparently willing to accept leases and pay rent but the freeholders of the manor would not accept this (presumably since it would diminish their rights of common). Each year these freeholders would beat down the cottagers' fences and ride across the enclosures to prevent the cottagers acquiring a 'prescriptive right by undisturbed possession'. The report recommended action be taken to regularize the situation.[39]

It is not quite clear who the freeholders of the manor of Wilton were — whether the Hospital's official tenants at farms like Merrivale or Caldicot, or from a wider area. It should be noted that by 1754, whilst Aconbury and Much Birch lay in the manor of Wilton, Little Birch lay in the manor of Wormelow. This might mean pressures against encroachment were lower in Little Birch than in Aconbury and Much Birch and thus explain a larger growth of population through encroachment on the common in Little Birch than in the other two parishes (as outlined in section 7). At all events, since the governors of Guy's Hospital were lords of the manor of Wilton and owned nearly all of Aconbury parish, they were able to deal with the problem. At least one lease for an encroachment had been granted in the seventeenth century, probably before a flood of encroachment aroused the freeholders' hostility. By 1800 it looks as if the whole of the Aconbury portion of the common was leased out to cottagers by private agreements.[40]

The residual common in Much and Little Birch occupied about 180 acres, roughly half or a little more of which was located in Little Birch. The Little Birch portion included the high ground extending southward from the most northerly point in the parish with one finger extending along Parish Lane, another roughly south of the Castle Inn and a third along the eastern side of the steep valley leading from Newtown towards Higgins Well. The area around Newtown Well appears as an island of enclosed land in the common but was almost certainly once part of it; the encroachment it represents was probably so ancient that it did not need to be regularised and was excluded from the common as defined in the commissioner's survey. At Well Orchard on the other hand, almost certainly another very early encroachment, the field around the house was regarded as excluded from the common but the house itself was counted as an enclosure allotment.

Because of the multiplicity of landowners, matters were not so simple in Much and Little Birch as in Aconbury. A private Act of Parliament was needed to authorize the process. This was passed in 1812 according to the guidelines governing all such Acts. The key role in the complex process of such an enclosure was that of commissioner. The man chosen for Much and Little Birch was James Cranston the elder of Kings Acre. Cranston, a nurseryman, was the proprietor of Kings Acre Nurseries — a landscaper and surveyor, and one-time gardener to Uvedale Price at Foxley. He and his son (also called James) acted as commissioners for four other enclosures within the county with awards made between 1821 and 1833 — at Bishopston and Mansell Lacy, Byford, Clehonger and Kings Pyon.[41]

The commissioner had to survey the land and to have surveyed and set out a network of carriageways and driftways (roads for driving stock) to serve the area being enclosed. He was also responsible for seeing that watercourses were regularised. In Little Birch this involved the proper regulation of the stream running from Newtown Well so that it did not incommode transport on the re-aligned carriageway known as New Road. The map accompanying the enclosure award also demonstrates a further example of the management of watercourses. On the other side of the lane north of Saddlebow, the former Wesleyan chapel, is a small spring. In very rainy weather water from this source is likely to cause waterlogging in the lane south of Saddlebow and in the field south-west of Hillcroft. The enclosure map shows a channel for water draining from this spring dug across the orchards behind Hillcroft — the house was not built at this time — and at the side of Copse Lane down to the Newtown stream at Walls Pool.

The commissioner's main task, however, was the allocation of land. Here there were certain allocations which were not related to landholdings of the existing owners' farms. These included the requirement to make an allocation of glebe in lieu of tithes. In Little Birch the glebe allotted amounted to 14½ acres. The lord of the manor, Sir Hungerford Hoskins, was allocated nearly nine acres. Cranston himself as surveyor was entitled to an allotment as a fee for his work. He chose a piece of land which would probably not have been particularly attractive to a farmer, but which to a landscaper interested in the picturesque, would be of great intrinsic value. The plot of over seven acres on which Uplands now stands has the finest panoramic view in the parish. Land was also allotted to the poor law overseer for the erection of poor cottages. The process of allotting all the land was a lengthy one, the final award not being made until 1824. It is instructive to note that when the surveyors for the first Ordnance Survey map made their drawings of the area in 1815, most of the common was marked with stippling to show it was still unenclosed. Practically the only exception was the area north of Chapel Pitch and west of Old Hill. This included Cranston's allotment and was shown as already enclosed. Cranston seems to have taken his fee up front.

Most of the larger landowners were given proportionate allocations of land, though not apparently the owner of Bromley. The allocation relating to New Mills was about 11 acres, though at the time of the award, the whole of the Holme Lacy estate was in chancery. There were, however, a large number of very small allocations to cottagers and farm labourers. This was because, under the terms of the Act, any encroachment which could be established as having existed for 20 years or more was protected. In this way John Vaughan, a labourer, was allocated about a third of an acre, the site of the present Cherry Cottage, a portion of which was probably already built. This property remained in the Vaughan family for more than 100 years and when it was sold in 1926, it had no individual title deeds. The title was effectively authorised in the award. Like all the other enclosures, the extent and location were described on a schedule which referred to a numbered plot on an attached map. The description of each allotment carefully noted who had responsibility for the surrounding boundary hedges or fences, which it was the duty of those allocated land to create and maintain.[42]

The enclosure of the common must have radically altered the appearance of the land in the north of the parish. But there were to be many adjustments in the years immediately after the enclosure as various pieces of land which were not particularly useful to those awarded them changed hands. Sir Edwin Francis Scudamore-Stanhope, for example, whose title to the Holme Lacy estate portion of the first viscount's estates had been confirmed in 1829, had 11 acres of land necessarily a long way from New Mills or Athelstan's Wood including parcels near Well Orchard and nine acres east of Old Hill and north of Green Lane now known as Australia.

The enclosure had been designed to be fair but its results had not always been convenient. This presented energetic and enterprising individuals with great opportunities. An example of this was the way Well Orchard was developed as a small but integrated unit. In 1796 the tenant of Well Orchard, John Waters, had bought a small portion of that part of the Langstone Gwillym's Little Birch estate called Little-Burch-Land Farm. It seems that this land had been sold in 1794 to Thomas Bennett, the tenant of New Mills Farm who had presumably purchased it for speculative purposes. Waters could afford to buy only a small fraction of what he had rented; this included the Tendings and the field adjacent to Well Orchard House, the house being then still technically on the common. In 1832 this land was acquired by William Griffiths and by that time included the house. The Griffiths family do not appear in the parish register before 1800; Richard, the father, is described in later register entries as a labourer; William was a timber dealer. Between them they owned or rented about 11 acres of land around Crow's Nest Lane. This included the cottage, long since vanished, owned and lived in by

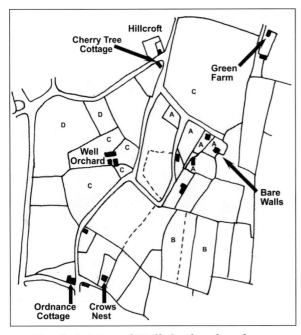

Fig. 8.5 Map of Well Orchard and area in 1841 (taken from the Tithe Map), showing ownership.
A – Owned by Richard Griffiths
B – Rented by Richard Griffiths from Elizabeth Penner
C – rented by Wiliam Griffiths from John Griffiths
D – Owned by Sir E.F. Scudamore-Stanhope

Richard which had been on the edge of the common north of Prospect Cottage and known as Bare Walls. It was, however William's younger brother, John, who was the real entrepreneur. He kept the Pack Horse Inn in Hereford on the site of the present Kerry Arms. In 1838 he purchased Well Orchard and the Tendings from William, who had evidently got into some financial difficulties. He was also able eventually to purchase the land that had been allocated to Sir Edwin Francis Scudamore-Stanhope at the enclosure. The deed conveying Australia to Griffiths is particularly interesting because it is accompanied by a bulky document outlining the circumstances of the chancery actions relating to the Holme Lacy estate and giving details of the Duchess of Norfolk's lunacy. John thus built up a compact family estate of around 22 acres, but he never lived in it. His sister Ann married William Davies, a blacksmith, in 1838. At first they lived with Richard Griffiths at Bare Walls, now renamed Smith's Folly, but later they moved to Well Orchard, which William Davies farmed for many years.[43]

In conclusion we may summarize how land ownership had changed over three centuries in Little Birch. At New Mills Farm and Bromley there had been considerable continuity, but elsewhere much had changed. In the sixteenth and early seventeenth centuries the centre of farming activity in the north-west of the parish was centred around the church. There were probably at least four farmhouses there controlling between two-thirds and three-quarters of the cultivated land west of Athelstan's Wood. By 1841 the proportion represented by Church Farm, Lower House and Upper House was probably less than one half. The deconstruction of the open fields coupled with the effects of inheritance practices had not had the effect of consolidating holdings in the north-west of the parish, indeed rather the reverse. The largest farm here was Church Farm with just over 86 acres. This was almost certainly smaller than the Baylye/Gwillym estate before its partition in 1641, and even the estate William Higgs had built up in the mid-seventeenth century. There were also almost certainly a larger number of smallholdings, many resulting from the enclosure of the common. Finally there was one change that evidenced itself in the whole of the parish. In the early seventeenth century all but one of the farms in the village had been owned by resident yeoman farmers from within the parish or from adjoining parishes. The exception was Rowlston owned by the Scudamores. By 1841 all the larger farms were owned by non-residents and rented out, a change which neatly demonstrates the process of gentrification even in a village which was not wholly owned by any powerful magnate.

9 The Development of Farms after 1840

After the enclosure of the common in the 1820s, which allocated a portion of the common to owners of property in proportion to the land they already owned, there was obviously some trading of portions and rationalisation. This resulted in some, who were tempted to make a little money, in gaining no land and others building up their acres to create what might be regarded as a farm. By the time when the Tithe Map was drawn up in 1841 (see pp.63-65) there were many small farms and some larger ones. Each of these had a number of fields and each of these was named, together with the field's use in that particular year. Much of interest is shown by these names as they often refer to local features or local traditions. Where the fields existed before the enclosures their names may have been in use for many centuries. Some names, however, were simply descriptive but dull!

Field names
Surrounding the house known as Castle Nibole is a number of fields called Castle Field or Castle Ground. Such a collection of 'castle' names raises the possibility that they were near to a castle, such as a motte and bailey. No convincing remains of one exist though it has been suggested that one may have been present in an area opposite the Castle Inn where excavation for stone has obviously occurred. However the Woolhope Club examined this site in the 1990s and decided that it was not likely to be castle remains because of its position — off the brow of the hill. They felt it more likely that a castle, if it had existed, would have been somewhere under the buildings of the present farm, Castle Nibole, whose name (often misspelt and origins unclear) might well have some connection with the original structure. It may yet be, of course, that the origins of the name 'Castle' lie in the fact that one owner had illusions of grandeur or that others alluded to it thus as some sort of joke as may have been the case in 'Crab's Castle'! For whatever reason, land awarded to the owner of Castle Nibole at the enclosures may well have acquired the field names because of belonging to a farm named 'Castle'.

Other interesting field names may also indicate previous history of the land. As suggested previously in this book there may well have been a large field known as Woodfield where strip cultivation took place in the Middle Ages. There are two fields named Woodfield in this area. On the site of another possible medieval field are fields such as The Camps and Upper Camps. Close to these is one called Stoney Acre. There has been a suggestion that these names could indicate a possible Roman encampment, maybe backed up by the farm name Walls Pool. However, Wall could have come from the old English for well or even from a local landowner. The word Camp could have come from Campus meaning open field and the word Stoney could have referred to the presence of naturally occurring stone near the surface such as the rubbly cornstone. The nearness of stone to the surface is a problem in many fields, making ploughing difficult. A field on Green Farm near to Athelstan's wood is also well known for the rubbly stone constantly turned up by the plough.

The majority of field names in the area refer simply to its use — orchard or meadow — or its size — five acres, furlong and so on — or just simply Field or Common Field (indicating it was part of the common). One name of interest is Black Pits. It is sited close to Athelstan's Wood suggesting is could be the site of a charcoal burning platform. (There are also cottages which were called Black Pits near to Castle Nibole, these could have had the same origin.) Another name of interest is Malthouse Meadow which happens to be sited right behind the Rectory! There are several Mesne fields, indicating ownership by the lord of the manor, part of his demesne or, alternatively, a corruption of Myndfield meaning hill field. There is also a Glebe field being the apportionment of the enclosed common awarded to the rector.

Down at the edge of Athelstan's Wood is a long narrow field called Saffron Meadow, named, presumably, as it was a place where wild saffron grew. The fact that wild saffron grew in the area has been confirmed by Margaret Mullins who remembers her father instructing her to go and pull up the plants below Walls Pool because of their toxicity to cattle.

Land ownership in 1841

By the time that the Tithe Map was drawn up in 1841 the ownership of land had settled down to a number of farms of varying sizes, a few 'cottage farmers' and some cottages with one or two small fields attached. In many cases much of the land owned by these had been enclosed before the Enclosure Act for the common. At the south-east end of Little Birch parish Bromley Court covered some 144 acres with some more in adjacent parishes. It was obviously enclosed a long time before and was owned in 1841 by George Terry and rented by Thomas Preece.

A farm of this size would have been a lucrative holding but seems to have had a succession of tenants during the rest of the nineteenth century. Next to this, New Mills Farm, which included Rowlston, covered a fractionally larger 147 acres. In 1841 this still remained in the ownership of Scudamore-Stanhopes and was rented by James Bennett who also owned the land previously belonging to Crab's Castle. (The cottage and garden were rented out.) Church Farm was still owned by the Gwillim Family in 1841 and rented by William Crompton. It included not only land north and south of the church but also along Mesne Lane, creating a holding of 86 acres. These are very likely to be the remnants of a much larger estate of which parts had been sold off at various times. It is obvious from the field map (Fig 9.2) that the lands of Upper and Lower House are interspersed with each other and with those of Church Farm, possibly implying that they may at some time have been owned by Church Farm. However, rather scattered ownership of land was not uncommon.

The 32-acre Sunnybank Farm was owned by the Williams family of Much Birch who was renting it to James Wheeler in 1841. Of the smaller farms existing at the time of the Enclosures, Green Farm (23 Acres), to the west of Athelstan's Wood, had obviously been in existence before the 1700s, though formerly known as Upper House. It was already in the ownership of the Powell family by 1841. The Upper House below the church also owned 23 acres and was in the ownership of John Mutlow who remained there for many years. The house has long since disappeared (now replaced by The Sycamores). Lower House (66 acres), lying beyond this had some land bordering Athelstan's Wood and elsewhere. It was owned by a William Pugh of Lower Bullingham and jointly rented by Thomas Leighton and William Williams.

Walls Pool had some land before the common was enclosed but gained some adjacent land making a total of 6 acres. It was owned by George Powell who rented out the house to James Ridgeway. Both Castle Nibole and Well Orchard had obviously both created their acreage by enclosing land in the middle of the common so increased their acreage markedly with their enclosure award. Castle Nibole, having 14 acres, was at this time owned by the Rector of Little Birch, Henry Hampton who also had use of the Glebe fields opposite Castle Nibole as compensation for tithes which could not be collected from enclosed common land. The cottage on Castle Nibole land was not inhabited in 1841, indeed was probably derelict. Henry Hampton, of course, lived in the Rectory as part of his living which was owned at this time by the Guy's estate. Whitcombe's Place, between Prospect House and Prospect Cottage, possessed a compact 4 acres before the commons were enclosed and was in the ownership of Thomas Pritchard. Shrubb Cottage (now Glenthorpe) had already enclosed a few acres from the common before the

Enclosure Award and was in the ownership of John Stallard. The Stallard family was associated with this holding well into the twentieth century. Lower Black Pitts, (now The Chestnuts), seemingly three dwellings at that time, had a few acres between them. James Cranston, the commissioner who oversaw the enclosure of the common, awarded himself seven acres and built a well-sited house (now known as Uplands). These acres have had a varied history (see below).

During the latter part of the nineteenth century these various farms changed ownership and/or tenancy and acquired or lost or exchanged land. This land was being used for a variety of purposes. A large proportion of this would have been arable, about 80% in 1841, growing, among other crops, barley — as indicated by the need for a malthouse. It is likely that some local people brewed their own beer, for hops still grow in some of the hedgerows in the area. Some of the land was meadow for sheep and cattle grazing and some was orchard. Obviously some of

Name	Owner	Tenant	Acreage[1]	Key on Fig. 9.2
Bromley[2]	George Terry	Thomas Preece	144 – 0 - 1	B
New Mills	Scudamore-Stanhope	James Bennett	147 – 0 - 18	NM
Lower House	William Pugh	Thomas Leighton and William Williams	66 – 2 - 8	LH
Upper House[3]	John Mutlow	-	23 – 2 - 2	UH
Church Farm	Thomas Gwillim	William Crompton	86 – 3 - 9	Ch
Green Farm	James Powell snr	James Powell jnr	23 – 2 - 2	G
Sunnybank	Samuel Wheeler	-	32 – 1 - 8	S
Castle Nibole[4]	Henry Hampton	-	28 – 0 - 39	CN
Walls Pool	George Powell	-	11 – 1 - 15	1.
Ruff Farm	John Jones	-	6 – 3 - 25	2.
Crab's Castle	James Bennett	-	15 – 1 - 4	3.
'Fairview'	Thomas Mellin	Thomas Davies	6 – 1 - 31	4.
Whitcombe's Place	Thomas Pritchard	-	4 – 1 - 33	5.
Well Orchard	John Griffiths	William Griffiths	8 – 2 - 4	6.

Fig. 9.1 Table of farms and 'cottage farms' in 1841-2
Notes: 1. Acreage measured in acres, roods and perches
2. Bromley had acreage in other parishes
3. John Mutlow also rented 9 acres from Kedgwin Hoskins
4. Castle Nibole house was uninhabited at this time. Henry Hampton, the rector, lived at the rectory which was owned by Guy's Hospital. The house and gardens at Walls Pool and Crab's Castle were rented out

the newly enclosed land was planted as orchard as the Ordnance Survey map of 1904 (surveyed in 1886) indicates more orchard than was registered in the tithe map. Around and before the Enclosures there was a general move on the part of wealthy estate owners to relocate some of their tenants to free up land for cultivation or stock. This relocation tended to be to poorer, uncultivated lands on commons where a cottage would be built and about an acre of common could be enclosed for orchard. Orcharding was a very valuable, multi-purpose way of using land,

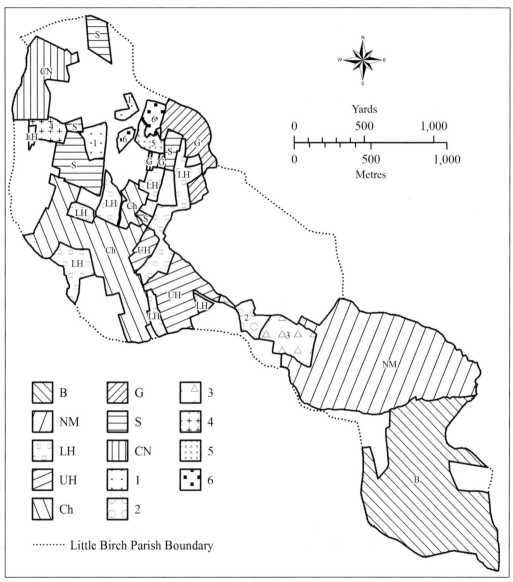

Fig. 9.2 Map of farms and smallholdings in 1841 taken from the Tithe Map.
For key see last column on Fig. 9.1 opposite

providing apples for market and, of course, for cider-making, also grazing for sheep and wood for burning and carving. It seems that Herefordshire was well known for its wood carvers — one product of which was dolls' heads which were sent off to London for assembly into complete toys. Many orchards grew wild daffodils which were picked for sale at Hereford market.

The cottagers of Little Birch, or more strictly, Aconbury Hill, attracted the attention of a group from the Woolhope Club who visited the area on 18 June 1885. The report in the *Transactions* described them as:

> ... a thrifty race, and from their well-cultivated gardens a good store of flowers, vegetables, strawberries, and other fruits are produced for Hereford market. The women and children collect in their season mosses and wild flowers for decoration, elderberries and cowslips for wine, nuts, chestnuts etc., selling them in Hereford market, thus turning an honest penny to supply household wants. Of the surplus population, not a few of the 'young men' enter the militia, while the 'maidens' find in household service the means of earning an honest livelihood. The people of Aconbury Hill may not have much book learning, but I have never met with any labouring people who have learned better than they how to earn a frugal living by honest thrifty labour.[1]

Land use and ownership in 1900s

By the beginning of the twentieth century land ownership was changing. Many of the smaller holdings gradually fell into disuse and the cottages have become ruinous or have totally disappeared. Their land was subsequently bought up by one of the larger farms. Castle Nibole, in particular, greatly built up its acreage from the 1940s. By the latter half of the twentieth century there were only six farms of any size: Bromley, New Mills, Lower House, Church Farm, Green Farm and Castle Nibole. Some detail of the changes within each of these is given below.

Bromley and New Mills

Bromley Court was in the ownership of the Terry family but farmed by tenants until the end of the nineteenth century. It was then sold to a Price and in 1911 was bought by the Roberts family. The farm consists of 210 acres some of which lies in several adjacent parishes.

Soon after purchasing Bromley, the Roberts bought New Mills Farm. This had been sold off in 1909 when the Holme Lacy estates were broken up and disposed of by the Stanhope descendents. New Mills was at that time tenanted by the Hughes family. The addition of New Mills and, later, Oakfields, increased Bromley acreage to 460 acres. The Crab's Castle land remained in separate ownership but continued to be farmed by Bromley.

A succession of tenants occupied New Mills farmhouse after its acquisition by Bromley but in 1928 the Townsends moved in. Victor and Geoff's father went to work initially for Bromley, but on moving into the then uninhabited New Mills farmhouse he farmed an increasing amount of land for himself, and became a full tenant of the Roberts at Bromley in 1936. He was also able to buy the Crab's Castle land. Geoff Townsend took over the tenancy of New Mills from his father in 1955 and remained in the farmhouse until 1991 when he moved into a bungalow he had built on Crab's Castle land. When he semi-retired, the farming of New Mills land returned to Bromley. Geoff continued to keep a small herd of cattle on the Crab's Castle land which he owned, but these have now been sold and the land let out to Altwynt Farm. New Mills farmhouse and buildings were sold by the Roberts in 2000 and holiday lets are now being developed in the barns. Bromley today farms mainly arable, with some sheep and cattle.

Crab's Castle cottages were sold, together with Athelstan's wood, in 1909[2] at the break-up of the Home Lacy estate. They were than sold on in 1923[3] when Crab's Castle was described as one dwelling house (formerly two) and having 10½ acres of arable and pasture land. By the 1930s it was lived in by a Whitworth who kept goats which ran free in the woods, and it continued to be inhabited up to at least 1952 when a Kendal was recorded as living there on the Electoral Roll for that year, but it has now completely disappeared. The site, opposite the lane up from New Mill farmhouse, is marked by a few apple trees and daffodils.

The land of The Ruff farm passed to Bigglestone Farm in Much Birch which already owned adjacent fields. Its many small fields were merged into one large one. The cottage became uninhabited before the 1920s and gradually decayed although inhabited by a tramp who kept chickens in a shed there. It finally disappeared by the 1980s. Only a front doorstep remains beside the lane opposite Athelstan's wood.

Lower House

In 1857, after William Pugh and his wife had died, the fields that lay in amongst those belonging to Church Farm were sold to George Frederick Bonner of Church Farm and the remainder, apart from one outlying field, went to the 'divisees' of the estate who then sold the balance of the farm. A James Jones was farming it in 1885, and a Mr Lydiatt in 1905 and 1917 according to Kelly's *Directories* for those years. In 1920, Upper House, described in the sale particulars[4] as a smallholding with the house and buildings in a dilapidated condition, came up for sale and its buildings and 21 acres was bought for £800 by Mr J. Innes who already owned Lower House. (One small field was sold to George Bonner of Church Farm and

Fig. 9.3 Aerial view of Lower House Farm taken in the 1950s

another, adjacent to Rectory land, to a Mr G. Marchant of Hereford.) James Innes died in 1926 but his wife, Christiana, continued at Lower House until 1938. It was then sold to the Guy's Estate. At this time of economic difficulty, many farms were sold to the Guy's Estate, who promised a fixed rent to their tenants. The Pursey family took up the resultant tenancy and used the land for a milking herd. After losing their herd in a Foot-and Mouth outbreak, they moved away in 1943.

During their time at Lower House, Vic Townsend remembers working for them and being asked to remove stone from Upper House and using it to fill a hole in the yard at Lower House. Upper House was occupied into the 1930s and still stood to first floor level at the end of that decade. In 1943, two chimneys and the back wall were still standing, as was remembered by Gerald Skyrme whose father took up the tenancy then. In 1961 the Guy's Estate sold out to Charles Clore, when the Lower House tenancy was described as possessing 65.5 acres. This now stretched from Wrigglebrook across the lane and up the side of Athelstan's Wood to Green Farm lands. At various times there had been minor alterations to field ownership. The Skyrmes farmed mixed arable and dairy herd initially but eventually converted to dairy only, with some kale. In the 1970s Gerald also took up the tenancy of Warren Farm (in Aconbury parish), increasing the acreage for grazing, and ran both farms until his retirement in 1993. Lower House was then sold for refurbishment with 16 acres stretching alongside the lane. The land north of this went to Merrivale, another (now) Duchy property and the land south of the lane was bought by Strickstenning farm in Much Birch. It is farmed by Bigglestone Farm. Gerald and Dot, his wife, now live in the house they built, The Sycamores, on the site of Upper House. When the much renovated farmhouse was sold again, the three most distant fields were sold separately, thus completing the break up of what was once a reasonable sized farm in conjunction with its neighbour, Upper House, which had been in existence for a long time.

Church Farm

Having been in the ownership of the Gwillims for four centuries, Church Farm was sold in the 1850s to George Bonner who had owned land in Little Birch for the previous fifteen years at least. According to Lascelles' *Directory* for 1851,[5] he was then farming the land but after this it was rented out to a variety of different people during the rest of the nineteenth century. It acquired some extra land from Lower House in 1857 and one or two extra fields when Upper House was sold. Kelly's *Directory* of 1891[6] records a John Lewis farming the land and those of 1905 and 1917 record a Blashill farming the land. In 1922 the farm was sold to Thomas Bowen in whose family it remained until 1987. During this time it passed to son Hugh and, in turn, to grandson, David and grandson-in-law. The farm ran a dairy herd throughout this time. In 1988 it was sold to the Langfords who farm it mainly as arable land in conjunction with their main farm at Norton Brook. Mr Langford senior continues to live in the farmhouse. The Bowens retained a field north of Mesne Lane which is rented out for horse grazing.

Green Farm

Green Farm has remained in the ownership of the Powell family since they bought it in 1803. Although in 1841 it was still only 23 acres, it has incorporated several other farms and holdings over the years. The farms have themselves had a varied history.

Well Orchard started as a smallholding enclosed within the common, the house being built on common land. The neighbouring field containing the well had already been enclosed before the Award. The owner at this time was John Griffiths (landlord of the Packhorse inn in Hereford) and was tenanted by William Griffiths. John owned a large field further north and adjacent to Green Farm land. Just south of this was a small cluster of fields and two or three cottages known as Bare Walls or The Rows (even Smith's Folly) which was owned by Richard Griffiths (see section 8, p.84). Ultimately this land was combined. The Rows was inhabited until the 1881 census but does not appear after this so presumably became derelict. (It has now completely disappeared apart from house platforms and a well with pump.) Well Orchard was lived in by Davies from the 1840s to early 1870s. From 1875 until 1915 it was rented by Powells, who then bought another property, so had no further need of it. It was then farmed by the Watkins family until 1930, the Keatings until 1939 (the sports writer Frank Keating spent his early years in Well Orchard) and Joneses until 1959. In the meantime it was owned by Monkleys, who were corn merchants, from 1938 and who sold it to Powells in 1960. During this time it has also acquired more land. Fields allotted to Scudamore Stanhope in the enclosures were bought by Well Orchard. These included a field below the house, at the bottom of School Lane and an adjacent coppice. It also included a large field at the north edge of the parish nicknamed Australia because of its distance from the rest of the farm! In addition it included two more strips in the remains of Wood Field, enabling these to be combined into one larger field. The land was farmed together with the rest of Green Farm and by the mid 1980s the house was no longer inhabited and is now derelict.

Fig. 9.4 Threshing on Green Farm in 1878/9. The threshing machine belonged to G. Matthews, Ross, and was new on 24 December 1875. Its engine was a 4456, &HP. The well dressed gentleman standing on straw is Thomas Powell; the man in the foreground in white shirtsleeves is George Powell (who later emigrated to Canada)

Whitcombe's Place was in the ownership of the Pritchards in 1841 but they had obviously sold it on by 1851. It is difficult to decipher who was living there during the next 30 years but by 1891 John Davies, a tailor, was in residence. By 1875, however, the holding had been bought by Well Orchard so presumably the house was rented out. Some time after this the house became derelict, being used as a farm building. The buildings are all now derelict and much stone has been removed. From what remains to be seen of the house, it was obviously half timbered with brick infill. With the purchase of this property and Well Orchard, 32 acres were added to Green Farm.

Green Farm also bought the two fields owned by Sunnybank which were in the middle of their land. The final acquisition in 1971 was of a collection of old orchards and a derelict cottage behind Saddlebow View and known as Jones's Orchard. It was owned by the cottage now known as Hillcrest. Green Farm land has been used for general mixed farming over the years although some of the land has been unsuitable for deep ploughing due to rock near the surface. Some arable cultivation continued until 1975 and pigs continued to be kept up to 1985. Since then only sheep have been kept. There was an exchange of fields with Merrivale Farm at the time of the break up of Lower House Farm to make more sensible arrangements and the site of The Rows was sold to Prospect Cottage. After these changes the total acreage of Green Farm is 65.5 acres.

Castle Nibole

The size of Castle Nibole's holding has increased over the years more than any other farm in the parish. It had 28 acres in 1841 but when it was sold by Rev. Henry Hampton in 1857, he retained the glebe land and only 14 acres were sold to William Waite. William Waite undertook the rebuilding of Castle Nibole house in the best Victorian style of the time. He lived there for a short while but then bought Swiss Cottage (now Hergest — rebuilt) and was recorded there in the censuses of 1871, 1881 and 1891. Castle Nibole house was rented out although the land continued to be farmed by him and his son. By 1891 his son-in-law, H.W. Southey, was living in Castle Nibole House, in fact, he was recorded as a farmer there in the 1885 Kelly's *Directory* although the land was being farmed by a relative. He was proprietor and editor of the *Merthyr Express* and was using Castle Nibole as a weekend and holiday home, although his wife took up permanent residence because of her health. Two fields were bought from Rev Dodington to add to the 14 acres. (The Glebe fields retained by Henry Hampton were passed on to Stephen Thackwell who succeeded him and then to Rev Dodington.) When H.W. Southey died in 1930 Castle Nibole passed to his son then was eventually put up for auction in April 1933 (see advert overleaf). It did not reach the reserve, being withdrawn at £1,700, but was eventually sold in October of that year to G. Wood. He rented

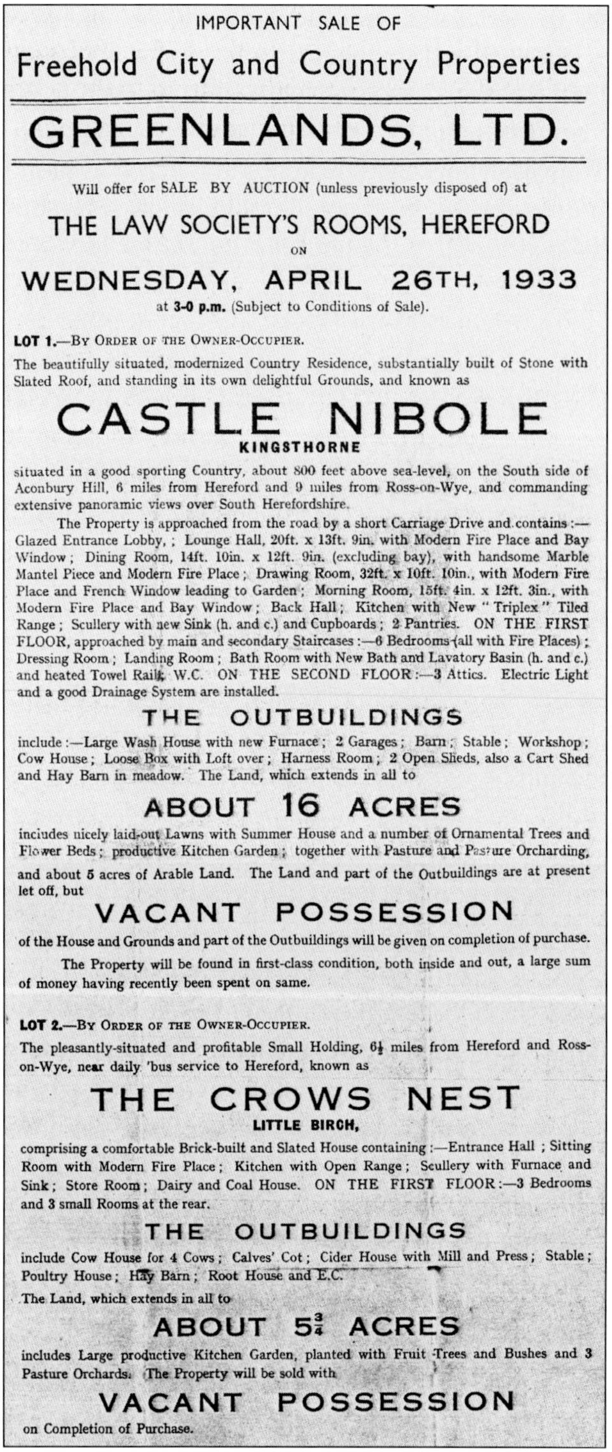

IMPORTANT SALE OF

Freehold City and Country Properties

GREENLANDS, LTD.

Will offer for SALE BY AUCTION (unless previously disposed of) at

THE LAW SOCIETY'S ROOMS, HEREFORD

ON

WEDNESDAY, APRIL 26TH, 1933

at 3-0 p.m. (Subject to Conditions of Sale).

LOT 1.—By Order of the Owner-Occupier.

The beautifully situated, modernized Country Residence, substantially built of Stone with Slated Roof, and standing in its own delightful Grounds, and known as

CASTLE NIBOLE

KINGSTHORNE

situated in a good sporting Country, about 800 feet above sea-level, on the South side of Aconbury Hill, 6 miles from Hereford and 9 miles from Ross-on-Wye, and commanding extensive panoramic views over South Herefordshire.

The Property is approached from the road by a short Carriage Drive and contains :—Glazed Entrance Lobby, ; Lounge Hall, 20ft. x 13ft. 9in. with Modern Fire Place and Bay Window ; Dining Room, 14ft. 10in. x 12ft. 9in. (excluding bay), with handsome Marble Mantel Piece and Modern Fire Place ; Drawing Room, 32ft. x 10ft. 10in., with Modern Fire Place and French Window leading to Garden ; Morning Room, 15ft. 4in. x 12ft. 3in., with Modern Fire Place and Bay Window ; Back Hall ; Kitchen with New "Triplex" Tiled Range ; Scullery with new Sink (h. and c.) and Cupboards ; 2 Pantries. ON THE FIRST FLOOR, approached by main and secondary Staircases :—6 Bedrooms (all with Fire Places) ; Dressing Room ; Landing Room ; Bath Room with New Bath and Lavatory Basin (h. and c.) and heated Towel Rail ; W.C. ON THE SECOND FLOOR :—3 Attics. Electric Light and a good Drainage System are installed.

THE OUTBUILDINGS

include :—Large Wash House with new Furnace ; 2 Garages ; Barn ; Stable ; Workshop ; Cow House ; Loose Box with Loft over ; Harness Room ; 2 Open Sheds, also a Cart Shed and Hay Barn in meadow. The Land, which extends in all to

ABOUT 16 ACRES

includes nicely laid-out Lawns with Summer House and a number of Ornamental Trees and Flower Beds ; productive Kitchen Garden ; together with Pasture and Pasture Orcharding, and about 5 acres of Arable Land. The Land and part of the Outbuildings are at present let off, but

VACANT POSSESSION

of the House and Grounds and part of the Outbuildings will be given on completion of purchase.

The Property will be found in first-class condition, both inside and out, a large sum of money having recently been spent on same.

LOT 2.—By Order of the Owner-Occupier.

The pleasantly-situated and profitable Small Holding, 6½ miles from Hereford and Ross-on-Wye, near daily 'bus service to Hereford, known as

THE CROWS NEST

LITTLE BIRCH,

comprising a comfortable Brick-built and Slated House containing :—Entrance Hall ; Sitting Room with Modern Fire Place ; Kitchen with Open Range ; Scullery with Furnace and Sink ; Store Room ; Dairy and Coal House. ON THE FIRST FLOOR :—3 Bedrooms and 3 small Rooms at the rear.

THE OUTBUILDINGS

include Cow House for 4 Cows ; Calves' Cot ; Cider House with Mill and Press ; Stable ; Poultry House ; Hay Barn ; Root House and E.C.

The Land, which extends in all to

ABOUT 5¾ ACRES

includes Large productive Kitchen Garden, planted with Fruit Trees and Bushes and 3 Pasture Orchards. The Property will be sold with

VACANT POSSESSION

on Completion of Purchase.

Fig. 9.5 Sale notice for Castle Nibole (and Crow's Nest) in 1933

it out to Mr and Mrs David Dyke formerly of Laburnam House, Parish Lane, in 1940. They eventually bought Castle Nibole and its 16 acres in 1941. The glebe fields continued in the ownership of the vicar, being rented out in the 1940s to Alan Williams of Glenview (who had a bread round in the area). The Dykes were able to buy these fields in the 1950s from the current incumbent, Rev Dyer Wright. The land adjacent to this, originally belonging to Uplands, was still owned by Monkleys of Chapel House and rented by Went of Ellerslea in Aconbury, but was bought by the Dykes in the 1960s. Several properties were bought over the succeeding years, their acreages being added to the farm and their houses being rented out. A small amount of land was retained with each cottage. One of these purchases was ***Walls Pool*** which brought 10 acres. Some of this land had been enclosed before the enclosure award although the house was built on the edge of the common. The holding was awarded quite a large acreage of common land in proportion to its size. Much of this land was orchard on the 1904 OS map and many daffodils still remain in the fields on the bank. An asset associated with this holding was its suitability for sinking a borehole and by 1947 this was achieved, supplying piped water to much of Little Birch and some of King's Thorn. In the 1950s *Fairview* was purchased. This was a holding of some 6 acres compactly situated to the south and east of Castle Nibole land, therefore making a sensible addition. The house was sold on to the Beavans with land for a garden.

In 1955 Sunnybank Farm, which had about 32 acres and a borehole, came up for sale. This was owned by John Williams of Much Birch in 1841 and rented by Samuel Wheeler who continued there until the 1870s. After this time the Pickerings lived there into the 1890s when a Mary Dance and her mother and children moved there, who appear on the 1901 census and are recorded as farmers in the 1905 Kelly's *Directory*. 1917 and 1929 *Directories* list a Brookes as farmer here and in 1941 a Rogers was listed. A Buckler was the last owner who sold to the Dykes. The purchase of Sunnybank by Castle Nibole provided useful acres between those of Fairview and Walls Pool, thereby connecting together all parts of the extended Castle Nibole holding. Its borehole was linked in with that of Walls Pool making the water supply more efficient. Sunnybank also provided a house which, with some work, became commodious accommodation for Mr. and Mrs. Dyke's daughter, Margaret, and her new husband Basil Mullins. They continued to live there until 1976 when the house, buildings and about three acres were sold off, all of which has been much renovated.

In 1961 *Crow's Nest* with nearly 6 acres was also purchased by the Dykes. This holding, which was originally owned by the Gwillim family, was an amalgamation of smaller holdings on which there had been five habitations. By 1841 three of these appear to have been built and owned by a Christopher Seir (a tailor) and rented out to various people. He himself was living in one in the 1850s. He obviously soon began to fall into financial difficulties and mortgaged his land. By 1864 he was helped out of his predicament by selling the properties he still owned to Stephen Thackwell, the Rector. Owners of the other two properties followed suit. Seir's property with three dwellings on the site of and to the north of the present Crow's Nest was sold for £245. A field of one acre was sold for £37. £160 was paid for a 'tenement', land and orchard together with cider mill and buildings, the whole amounting to about an acre. This land was on and just below the present barns adjacent to the lane. Three fields and another dwelling situated behind the present house were sold for £200. Stephen Thackwell's holding now consisted of over five acres and cost him a total of £642, (more than it was sold for in 1918!). It was rented out but during his ownership one of the houses was rebuilt and new barns were built necessitating the demolishing of two of the old cottages. The remaining ones fell into disuse and have disappeared. These cottages, as seen in the 1841 tithe map in this area, contributed to a cluster of habitations around the area of Higgins Well and the church, forming the nucleus of Little Birch. (Although

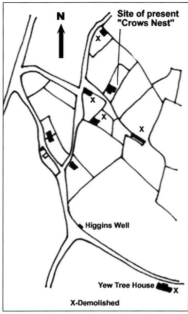

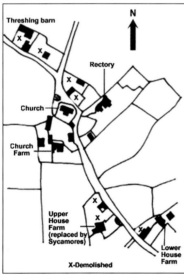

Fig 9.6a&b Maps of (top) Crow's Nest area and (lower) the church area to the immediate south as in 1841 (drawn from the 1840 Tithe Map). These show the larger number of properties at that time forming the nucleus of Little Birch 'village'

many of the cottages have been lost in this area, there have been some additions such as Greening's Acre and Hillcrest in the 1960s.)

The new house was called Laburnham Villa. It was rented by a Thomas Williams during the 1880s and 1890s though by 1883 Stephen Thackwell had died and Laburnham Villa was sold to a Hugh Junor who was in the Royal Engineers. By the 1890s Hugh Junor was an Ordnance Surveyor, obviously travelling the country, and purchased two other neighbouring properties, Ordnance Cottage together with Bannut Tree Cottage (now Bellwood) and also Prospect Villa above Laburnham Villa. Both were rented out. When Hugh Junor died in 1908, Alfred Baldwin, a carrier already living in Bannut Tree cottage, bought this in 1910 and by 1917 he was recorded as a farmer, carrier and overseer and was living in Laburnham Villa, now called Crow's Nest. This, Ordnance Cottage and Prospect were sold in 1912 for £700, then in 1918 Crow's Nest on its own was sold again for £400. In 1933 it was sold again to Thomas Bowen of Church Farm for £560 and when he died in 1961 it was sold for £2,150 to Mr and Mrs David Dyke of Castle Nibole. They farmed the land and rented out the house. It was renovated in the 1970s then lived in by the Mullins for a while before the whole was sold in the 1990s.

The Dykes, then the Mullins farmed the land owned and acquired by Castle Nibole for a dairy herd. They rented and owned other fields in the area, some outside the parish, and would have had in total well over 100 acres which was mostly down to grass with a small amount of arable. They had their own dairy and delivered milk over a wide area, incorporating other smaller rounds over the years including that of Harry Walter who then helped on the farm. When Basil Mullins retired in 1993 the rented land passed elsewhere and Crow's Nest and two other fields were sold. The remaining

90 acres are now used by daughter Kate and son-in-law John Dillon for breeding and fattening beef cattle. The building up of this farm was mainly due to the enterprise of Mrs Dyke who managed much of the day-to-day running. David Dyke continued his employment with the Electricity Board.

Fig. 9.7 Castle Nibole in 2000, built by the Waites, the extension on the left was added by H.W. Southey

Other holdings which remained independent of these farms were used variously as nurseries or smallholdings/market gardens, continuing the tradition for which 'the cottagers of Aconbury Hill' were well known. They include The Uplands, The Follies, Fernleigh, Crossways and Glenthorpe. Again, some further information about these is of interest.

Uplands

This was built in the 1820s by James Cranston of Kings Acre who, with his father, ran the English Fruit and Rose Company at Kings Acre. This possibly accounted for its original name of Rose Cottage. James Cranston was the parliamentary enclosure and tithe surveyor who was responsible for

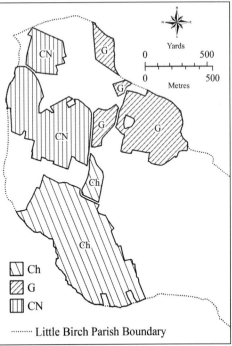

Fig. 9.8 Map of the three farms on Aconbury Common in 2006. Ch = Church Farm; G = Green Farm; CN = Castle Nibole

the enclosure of Aconbury Common in Little Birch. Along with Rose Cottage he awarded himself 7 acres from the common. This land was possibly used for growing for the nursery. By 1841 he had acquired another 3 acres. The house at this time was lived in by Martha Hodges who ran a school or day nursery which the census shows had 11 pupils aged from 2 to 7 years old. None of the names were those of other people living in the parish. It is not clear whether the land

Fig. 9.9 Uplands in 1988. Built by James Cranston before 1824 with subsequent additions of two bays and an extension on the left

continued to be used for Cranston's nursery but the 1861 census records Mansel Maddy as a farmer of 28 acres, though that for 1871 records a Maria Moseley as farming 12 acres. No mention is made in the 1881 census of the use of the land but by 1891 the census records seven gardeners/nurserymen including Thomas Yapp who was then living at Rose Cottage. The land was obviously now being used as a nursery and in 1899 it was sold by the Cranstons to Kings Acre Nursery. By 1901 George Yapp was Foreman and living at Rose Cottage; five nurserymen were recorded in the census. There are still a few old-fashioned garden shrubs growing in the hedges alongside the green lane (Chapel Pitch) such as Snowberry, possibly escapees from the nursery of this period. Kings Acre Nurseries sold the property and 11 acres to Alice Monkley from King's Thorn for £1,000 in 1920, who renamed it The Cedars. It was then sold on in 1929 to the Maddocks and renamed again — Prysowen — but the fields adjacent to the glebe fields were retained. It is not clear what the land was being used for at this stage. In 1936 it was sold and gained the name by which it is now known — Uplands. During the next ten years it changed hands another four times, its price increasing from £1,250 to £5,500. The last of these purchasers was the Guy's Hospital Estate who, with Charles Clore who bought this estate, owned it for 20 years with a succession of tenants. The land was mostly farmed. In 1965 it was bought for £7,000 by Margaret Richards who owned it until it was bought by the Morleys in 1988. The house has a large, well laid-out garden but the rest of the land was rented out to Castle Nibole and later to Merrivale Farm.

The Follies

In 1841 this house which was formerly on common land was divided into at least two dwellings and was occupied by four different people. The land amounting to over four acres was equally divided into four fields. Throughout the rest of the 1800s and early 1900s it was farmed as smallholdings, probably as two properties. It was bought by the Bibbys in 1930, and developed as a nursery and market garden. Large glasshouses were erected, numbering eight at one time. Tomatoes were grown and the maximum crop produced was two and a half tons in one year. Early daffodils were also brought on in these greenhouses and other flowers too. A large variety of vegetable crops were grown on the land together with fruit bushes and more flowers for cutting. In the early days there was a shop selling the produce but the Bibbys, who had moved up from Abergavenny, had connections with Tredegar and the bulk of the produce was transported by them to Tredegar market where they had two stalls, one for the top quality produce and the other for the rest. The four acres did not suffice for the level of productivity they required so the upper part of the field below The View was also rented (The lower part was used by the school). At maximum output during the war the Uplands land was also used. The house remained as two dwellings, the Bibbys living in one half and the other latterly lived in by Mrs. Bibby's sister, Mrs. Cutter, and her husband. The nursery continued up to the late 1960s, when it was brought to a close due to Jack Bibby's ill health. Mrs. Bibby continued to live there until 1983 when it was sold for renovation and was converted into one property. The land was returned to fields for grazing. Before renovation, one of the cottages had a barred window and there is anecdotal evidence that when prisoners were marched from the Magistrates Court (at Harewood End) to Hereford gaol they would reach this house and spend the night here, marching on the following day.

Crossways (formerly Sunnybank)

This had been a smallholding from 1841 to the end of the nineteenth century and well into the twentieth century. It is well remembered as the home of Charley Iles who had a lorry business. He also kept a few cows. The adjacent field was a cider orchard and the field on the opposite side of the road provided rough grazing for cattle. In the late 1940s the then tenant cleared the orchard and erected some greenhouses. He attempted to establish a market garden, also using parts of the field on the opposite side of the road, but without much success. In 1953 the Rowans acquired it and made a somewhat more organised attempt, resulting in a much more successful establishment. Initially they had a few Guernsey cattle, grew feed for them and, at one point, had 1,000 laying hens. They also cultivated market crops such as lettuce and cauliflowers. After a few years the livestock was disposed of and they concentrated on market crops, acquiring more land to increase their output. As a borehole was sunk and water was more freely available for irrigation a three-crop rotation of celery, lettuce and brassicas was set up, and this continued until the Rowans gave up market gardening in the 1980s.[7] They built a house on the adjacent land, and Crossways and the fields opposite were sold and are currently used for horses.

Fernleigh

This is a holding which now consists of nearly three acres. Although there was a dwelling, probably divided into two, there in 1841, this was obviously replaced in the late 1800s or early 1900s with a more substantial house.

The dwelling in the field where Fern View now stands must have come into its owner-ship when the dwelling was abandoned. With more land available, a somewhat larger smallholding was established. By 1936 a Beavis

Fig. 9.10 Fernleigh in 2000

was recorded on the electoral roll as living at Fern Lea and in 1952 a Smith was there. It was very overgrown when the Lloyds bought it in the early 1950s. After clearing the ground with horse and plough they established a smallholding growing vegetables for sale at market. They also had pigs, cattle and a few sheep. Swill for the pigs was collected over a wide area. As time went on the sheep and cattle were disposed of and they concentrated on vegetable growing. Later, goats replaced the pigs and these were bred and shown for many years; the milk was supplied to children with allergies. The goat sheds also accommodated a pigeon loft for racing pigeons. Eventually the goats were sold and vegetable growing ceased in the 1980s then finally the pigeons were sold. The Lloyds' daughter Susan uses the land for ponies apart from the patch on which Fern View was built for their other daughter, Diane.

Glenthorpe

This was already in the ownership of the Stallards by 1841. The house became known as Shrubb Cottage and at this time it owned fields below it and opposite Fernleigh and also adjacent to Fern View. The Enclosure Award gave them the field on the opposite side of School Lane. The Stallards used the land as an efficient smallholding, in due course acquiring Glenview with the field by School Lane and Sunnyside, now Newtown Cottage. The Stallard family continued at Shrubb Cottage throughout the rest of the 1800s and up to the 1930s when a female Stallard married a Creed. The Creeds did not live at the renamed Glenthorpe for long. By 1952 the Joneses were living there and they established a shop on the site. The Grundys took this over in the late 1950s but it did not last long after the closure of the school in 1959. The land was used for cattle grazing and some vegetable growing. Sometime during the 1970s the Creeds sold Newtown Cottage and Glenview, the latter with about five acres. Both cottages have undergone extensive renovation. In the 1990s Glenthorpe was bought by the Headleys and an organic smallholding together with a box delivery scheme was established which still continues.

Although the area of King's Thorn has not been studied in such depth as the parish of Little Birch, some reference to land-holding is of relevance. The pattern was much the same as in Little Birch, where there was a multitude of small fields. Many of these were along Little Birch road and along Wrigglebrook, an area which appeared to have been enclosed before the Commons Enclosure Award. On the 1842 Tithe Map for Much Birch these fields are shown as mostly belonging to different people. This could well have been a legacy of squatting. A few larger fields existed on the more level ground. The holdings of any size included Upper Wrigglebrook Cottage and Ladywell. The Brookes family became owners of this later in the century and owned many fields scattered round the area. They still own fields adjacent to Barrack Hill, an area of common land until the Enclosures. Warren Farm in Aconbury parish has land which stretches over to Barrack Hill. The land belonged to Guy's Hospital and now The Duchy of Cornwall but the house has been sold. At the top of the hill, land once belonging to Lower House (in Aconbury) and Greenways now belongs to Merrivale Farm, another Duchy property. West of Wrigglebrook the fields on the bank mostly belong to Minster Farm in Much Birch.

The use of the farmland has shown a substantial change during this period, most notably from mainly arable to much more grassland. There was, however, a large amount of arable cultivation during and just after the Second World War. This shows clearly on aerial photographs taken by the RAF in 1947. Castle Nibole and Lower House both supported large milking herds during much of the latter half of the period and Green Farm was turned over largely to sheep.

Most of the smallholdings have now disappeared either by being amalgamated into larger holdings or by being used as gardens or fields for grazing. Inevitably, the changes on farms and smaller holdings were inextricably connected with social and economic changes in the area and, indeed, over the country as a whole. This will be explored in section 10.

A final property in Little Birch parish which deserves mention because of its large acreage is that of ***Athelstan's Wood***. In 1841 it was still in the possession of the Scudamore-Stanhopes of Holme Lacy. When this estate was broken up Athelstan's Wood, together with Crab's Castle, was sold in 1909.[8] The wood was described then as being 161 acres (in Little Birch parish) and 'being densely Timbered chiefly with Oak and Ash and a good stock of Tellers [tillers/suckers] and Underwoods, and capable of holding a large head of game. There are several charming sites in and adjoining the wood suitable for the erection of a good residence'. (This suggestion was obviously not followed through!)

By 1923, the wood was again on the market together with Crab's Castle when the wood was described as containing 'Ash, Oak, Larch and Chestnut Trees, with Underwood'.[9] So, presumably the larch and chestnut had been planted since 1909. The shooting was still described as good, 'there being Pheasants, Woodcock and other game'. At some point after this the wood was bought by a Mr Little, a timber merchant from the Forest of Dean, who maximised his assets with a great deal of felling. He subcontracted to a number of people to clear the smaller less useful timber, much of which was sold as firewood. Some of the present conifers may have been planted then in the felled areas. However, the wood was sold on again to a London solicitor and the woodland then became managed by Economic Forestry. During the 1960s and 1970s, a lot more of the mixed woodland was felled and replaced with conifers such that there is now only a relatively small proportion of natural woodland remaining. With such a large conifer cover, there is very little in the way of undergrowth apart from alongside the rides. The wood has been managed for pheasant shooting for many years.

10   Social and Economic Development of the Parish

Population from 1811

As mentioned before, towards the end of the 1700s and into the 1800s people were moving onto unenclosed areas and 'squatting' as they were turned off the better land on the large estates. This is reflected in the 1811, 1821 and 1831 censuses[1] where although, initially, the population is apparently falling, the number of houses is increasing. Then after a short period the population increases dramatically. This is probably due to the large number of births in the parish as the parents become settled and, indeed, felt more secure as their ownership of their holdings was ratified by the Enclosure Award. It is interesting to note that the population peaked in 1851, the decline thereafter being a combination of a declining birth rate and emigration. This is mirrored by a decline in the number of houses as holdings were abandoned and their land was taken over by larger farms. However, both population and number of houses have increased slowly in the latter part of the 1900s though, typically, with fewer people per household, reflecting the national trend for smaller families and a local increase in retired couples (see Fig. 10.1 overleaf).

The decline in population after 1851 is probably, in common with other areas, the reflection of a move away from the country into towns where greater earnings were possible. It may also have been the case that rented fields were sold or rented out to someone who could pay more, thus making poorer people's livelihoods unviable in a period of agricultural financial hardship. This appeared to have an effect during the 1860s and 1870s when the number of children per household was falling. It is interesting to note that as a more stable economic period ensued in the 1880s, the average family size increased again before a gradual decline in the 1900s which occurred for social rather than economic reasons. Indeed, the highest percentage of children under 15 was reached in 1891 (40%), but as the total population was falling at this time, this implies there must have been emigration to jobs elsewhere. During the 1900s the building of a few larger houses partially reversed

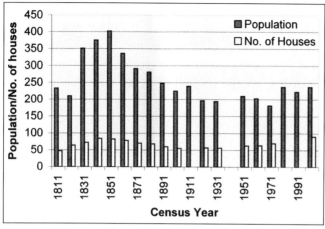

Census date	Population size	No. of dwellings
1811	233	47
1821	210	64
1831	351	72
1841	375	84
1851	402	82
1861	336	78
1871	291	70
1881	281	68
1891	248	60
1901	225	55
1911	239	
1921	196	57
1931	194	56
1941		
1951	210	63
1961	203	64
1971	182	70
1981	237	
1991	223	
2001	237	90

Fig. 10.1 Little Birch Population 1811–2001

the outflow. The decline in the 1960s and '70s was due to young people moving away and many houses being occupied by elderly people. At this time there were very few children in the village. However, from the 1980s onwards there was more building and refurbishment which brought more families, resulting in an increase in the population to a level not seen since the beginning of the 1900s.

It is interesting to note that the rises and falls in population are affected as much by emigration and immigration as they are by births and deaths. The censuses from 1841 make it clear that there are new names appearing and old names disappearing at the ten-yearly intervals. The influx of new people was particularly noticeable in 1851 when the census showed that 48% of heads of households were not there ten years before. After this the percentage of new names on each census fell to an average of around 30% until the end of the century, but nevertheless shows a surprisingly mobile population. In the 1901 census the number of incomers had risen again to 41% and it is reasonable to assume that this was the trend throughout the 1900s, except, perhaps, at war times. From 1841 until 1901, ten families appeared consistently in the censuses. They included Powell, Stallard, Vaughan, Higgins, Whitcombe and Watkins. Of these, Stallards continued up to the 1930s and Powells have continued to this day.

Employment

Little Birch and the surrounding parishes have never been a very wealthy area, having been by-passed by the Industrial Revolution. The inhabitants made their living from the land, either as farmers or woodsmen. The poorest people would have been smallholders, subsisting on their own plots carved out of the commons, and gaining some income from the larger farms when extra labour was required at times of ploughing and harvesting. Others earned money as outdoor or indoor servants of the larger farmers and landowners. Then there were those who would have been involved with agriculturally connected trades. In the 1801 census, 56 of the 247 inhabitants were recorded as working in agriculture (23%). This percentage was more or less maintained until the 1830s. It is not entirely clear which occupations were classified as agricultural during these earlier censuses. When occupations were detailed from the 1841 census onwards, it appears that the agriculturally-linked ones declined; this may have been due to different definitions. However it becomes obvious that by 1891 there is a definite decline, falling further in 1901. This would have been due to some introduction of mechanisation and the amalgamation of smaller farms, also the reduction in arable farming.

The census of 1841 records 10 men calling themselves farmers but 48 farm labourers. There were also a blacksmith, two thatchers (at this time many properties would have been thatched — Buddlia was still thatched in living memory) and many more trades. Some trades related to house building and maintenance: seven carpenters and two lath cleavers (for lath and plaster walls) were represented as well as 11 stonemasons. This large number of masons, many of whom were lodgers, may have been due to the fact that the church was being rebuilt at this time. Apart from these, most appeared to be working for themselves, although there was one person described as a journeyman, a qualified artisan working for someone else. Most of the women worked in the home, either in their own or someone else's as 'female servants'. There was a notable exception: Martha Hodges aged 40 was running a boarding school with 11 pupils and was described as a schoolmistress (see p.102). It is interesting to speculate who these infants were and why they were not living at home; their surnames are different from those listed as other inhabitants of the parish.

By 1851, however, there was a doubling in the number of farm labourers shown in the census which might suggest more intensive use of the land. However, the description which people gave themselves may have changed as only six farmers were recorded. The trades were still represented. The number of scholars had increased. Where exactly the school was at this time is unclear but Jane Jones, wife of the census enumerator James Jones (who styled himself schoolmaster in 1841 but obviously was no longer), is recorded as schoolmistress. A James Jones was recorded in the Apportionment of the Tithe Map to be living in Higgins Well Cottage. Anecdotal evidence states that there was a school up the lane to Yew Tree Croft where there are the ruins of a building. A house called Yew Tree House stood on this site on the 1904 OS map, and maybe this was the early school. However, there is more anecdotal evidence suggesting the school was sited in the large threshing barn since demolished in the field opposite Sunnybank. Schools in barns were not unknown, there was such an arrangement in Orcop, for example. By 1861 there was a substantial increase in the number of scholars, presumably due to a new school built in 1859 and maybe due to better and more regulated educational standards. During the earlier part of the century there were at least ten servants recorded — often young girls lodging in the house where they served. It was a common feature of country areas where the teenage daughters of labourers were sent off to work as they were too expensive to keep at home. Children in Victorian times were expected to grow up early. The 1841 census records a 10-year-old John Preece working as a servant. Later in the century the numbers of servants steadily declined, probably due to better paid jobs elsewhere. The establishment which boasted the largest number of servants was the Rectory where Stephen Thackwell, rector from 1857 to 1883, enjoyed a very comfortable lifestyle to which he was presumably accustomed from his privileged birth (see biography in section 15).

During the 1800s the population would have been largely self-sufficient, able to grow and rear much of their own food and indeed there was a butcher, who would have been used for slaughtering animals, living in the parish for most of the time; one was recorded at Lower Black Pitts. For those little extras which could not be grown there was a shopkeeper/grocer also throughout this period. Its location is not clear and, indeed, may have changed. In 1881 it was recorded as being in Chapel Cottage — adjacent to the Methodist Chapel. Interestingly, there was also a shop here in the early 1900s. To fulfil the needs of the thirsty agricultural workers the Castle Inn pulled pints throughout this time and at one point it may also have been the site of the village blacksmith. The clothing needs of the ladies and the men were supplied by tailors, drapers, dressmakers, shoemakers and glovemakers and there was also a laundress! There was always a carrier/carter for transport of people or goods to and from, probably, Hereford. This service and the farms would have required the expertise of the carpenter for making carts and the spoke cutter and wheelwright for the wheels. As mentioned previously, most people with orchards would be making their own cider and barrels required for this and other storage needs were made by the resident cooper. There was also a hoop-maker providing wooden hoops for the barrels (and for ladies' dresses?!). There were, of course, those involved in timber felling, carrying and charcoal burning.

During the 1800s it was rare for anyone living in the parish or, indeed, in the surrounding area, to be employed in anything other than agriculture or trade. The exceptions were the rector, the minister and the schoolteacher, along with the occasional barrister, accountant, and retired policeman who made their homes here for a short while, but there were few houses of sufficient standard to attract them without spending money on improvements. Prospect House/Villa was one of these, presumably much enlarged at the end of the 1800s to accommodate

Robberts (accountant) who had a family of ten including children and relations — as recorded in the census of 1901.

The censuses during the 1800s make it possible to link some members of the population with their trades and where they lived. Notable amongst those who remained in the area carrying out their trade for many years is Christopher Seir who, in 1841, was a tailor living in one of the cottages associated with the Crow's Nest site. This he later sold to Stephen Thackwell, the rector, but by 1861 he was still a tailor; then in his seventies and living with his niece at Walls Pool. A Watkins, father and son, were carpenters living at Poplar Cottage for at least 30 years. Another carpenter, Charles Monkley turned up at Model Cottage (no. 2) in 1881. William and George Fencott, father and son, were coopers for up to 20 years around 1861–71. They lived at the Crab's Castle/Rowlston barn area. A Thomas Williams, also a cooper, lived in Higgins Well Cottage in 1871 moving up to Crow's Nest in 1881. William Beavan, living at Newtown Cottage from before 1851 until the end of the century, was a hoop maker although he was first recorded as a labourer. He brought up a large family here and one of his sons also took up the trade. There were butchers in the parish before 1891 but it is not clear where they lived. There were three in 1901: Stallard at Shrubb Cottage now Glenthorpe, Rooke at Townsend Place now Cherry Tree Cottage, and Jones at Black Pits.

In common with other parts of the country, it was rare for anyone to survive beyond the age of 70 but it is interesting to note that even the older people were still recorded as in employment and all would have been using their patches of land to grow and sell produce. There was, of course, no welfare state then. In 1908 when the Old Age Pension was first paid, the pressure on older people to continue to earn their living was lifted. However, growing then selling goods at Hereford market would have been a way of life for many so it is reasonable to assume that older people continued to do this well into the 1900s. Younger people, though, were no longer inclined to work on the land nor were they needed for it. Yet there were odd jobs such as hedge maintenance. In the 1930s a resident remembers that the hedge had to be scythed, the ditch dug and banked and all the rubbish collected afterwards. For this the pay was 4d per chain (22 yards).

At certain times of year all the cottagers needed the help of anyone available for such jobs as apple picking in preparation for cider making. This was a very important drink at least up until the Second World War. Large quantities were consumed by those carrying out heavy physical labour, drinking two gallons a day was not unusual and older residents remember waggoners taking theirs with them and 'as long as they'd plenty they'd do anything'! Water from the ponds was often used to dilute the cider as 'it worked better'. At the end of the day's work bread and cheese and a jug of cider was a common supper for local people.

Fig. 10.2 Guy's estate wood yard on Macklin's Lane in 1908–10. Power was still provided by a steam engine. The pantile-roofed building on the right is still there; Waterloo Cottage, now House, is top left

For men who were not involved with trades locally there was limited employment in the hard years of the 1920s. Some even worked on the dam being built at Llanfihangel, cycling there every day. After the Second World War, people worked at Wiggins, Bulmers, the jam factories or the tile factories, in fact there were many opportunities in Hereford if they could get there. Many moved into town or, later, took advantage of workers' buses which collected them. Women were also tempted by work in the jam factories and, during the World Wars, by work in the munitions factory in Rotherwas.

Work in the woods and with wood products had been available for many years; this included stripping bark off felled timber and taking it to Hereford to sell to the tanning factory. After Aconbury Wood came into the ownership of Guy's Hospital, work in the woods is likely to have increased. Planting of new trees in the first part of the nineteenth century would have required labour, and their management afterwards. The Guy's Estate Yard on Macklins Lane employed a number of people preparing wood and wood products to sell.

Memories of those living in the area after the installation of electric saws were of a great deal of noise during working hours. The yard ceased to function (and peace descended!) in 1961 when the estate was sold and contractors employed to do the work. However, the present owners, The Duchy of Cornwall, have plans for the yard.

Stonemasons continued to work in the village up to the 1930s when the last local quarrying site on Mesne Lane was finally abandoned. Skills in stonemasonry have continued to flourish locally. We are also fortunate in still having a number of other excellent and very busy tradesmen living and working in the area.

Property ownership

At the time the Tithe Map was drawn up in 1841 about 60% of the householders owned their own property. Although many of these were small with only enough land to support the family, it gave the people pride in ownership and they were independent of employers as they did not live in tied cottages. They were able to move from working on the land into trade and 'better themselves'. Both men and women could work on their own patches of land growing and picking produce which they could sell at market. Although incomes would be small, most food was grown or reared. The population could be regarded as poor but their independence gave them pride. Indeed, a saying among the locals in the past has been 'Little Birch people — poor but proud'.

As fortunes fluctuated through the rest of the 1800s and into the 1900s, some property owners sold out to larger landowners, some of whom lived in adjacent parishes or even further afield, and the properties were then rented out to local people. However, in common with other areas in the later 1900s, there was a tendency for rented property to be sold when the sitting tenants had no further need of it and for the houses to become owner-occupied. There are now very few rented properties in the parish.

In the latter part of the 1900s the people buying houses in the parish have, almost exclusively, been people who are not working on the land and who often have employment elsewhere. With increasing transport, particularly car owner-ship, Hereford has become within easy commutable distance and, latterly, people commute much greater distances. With these varied forms of employment come increased incomes and the means to improve houses which has been very notice-able from the 1970s onwards.

Shops in the area

In common with other country areas, the self-sufficiency of the population declined as their desire for a wider range of commodities increased. There were shops in the 1800s providing groceries but fruit and vegetables were mostly grown, and animals reared, to be killed by the butchers in the village. This situation continued into the 1930s and around then a number of establishments existed to provide for increasing demands:

Fig. 10.3 Manchester House, Lower Wrigglebrook, in 2000. The brick section on the right was a shop until the 1960s

Monkleys ran a grocery shop for some years at Chapel House.

Bibbys ran their nursery at The Follies and sold vegetables which they grew.

Preeces had a bakery at Nevermore.

George Parry then Bill Davies at Manchester House in King's Thorn ran a reasonable sized shop up to the 1960s.

Bowens of Church Farm built a wooden butchers shop opposite Sunnybank in the 1940s which lasted until the 1960s.

Jones and then Grundys ran a small shop at Glenthorpe selling sweets in particular to the schoolchildren from the 1930s until the 1950s.

Windswept Cottage on Parish Lane was also a shop at one time.

A cobbler, Chris Preece, continued at Chances Cottage into the 1950s.

Phillips ran a shop at Bannutree (now Bellwood) in the 1930s which sold paraffin, they also ran a bus which could be hired.

In 1841 a blacksmith was recorded living at The Rows and in 1851 at The Castle Inn. In 1861 one lived at Green Cottage. In 1871, none was recorded. By 1881 there was one at The Ruff and by 1891 a Samuel Whitcombe who was obviously learning the trade at the age of 19. It is unlikely that these people were all working from home but the site of their work is unclear, although it could have been at the Castle Inn for some of the time. What appears to be waste from a blacksmith's has been found during excavation at Shirley Cottage at the bottom of Pendant Pitch.

A blacksmith (a Mr Cooke at the beginning of the 1900s and later Sam Sirrell) provided services in King's Thorn from the late 1800s until at least the 1930s when its services were no longer needed; it was replaced in 1957 by Taylor's Garage, now Jabiru. There was also a blacksmith, latterly Amos Weale, up until 1948 in Hollybush Lane, Much Birch, at the Broughton Cross crossroads, which was much used by Little Birch people. Another one was run for a short while in the 1960s/'70s by Watts at Rosebank, Barrack Hill.

There has also been a selection of travelling shops over the years, some until recently, selling such items as hardware, groceries and fish. Some remember the horse and cart selling hardware which could always be heard approaching from

Fig. 10.4 King's Thorn shop and Post Office in the early 1900s.
Pictured are Mrs Williams and daughters, also Reg Cooke

some distance as its wares jangled on the rough roads. Ron Evans from Little Dewchurch delivered bread and Goldings of Hereford, paraffin.

When fewer and fewer people owned their own cows several milk delivery rounds developed over the years — latterly only Castle Nibole provided this service which continued up until the early 1990s. One of the delivery men, Sid Hitching, delivered in the area from after the war (during which he arrived as an evacuee) for over 40 years. Mona Crum also delivered for some years.

By the 1960s, the ownership of cars was such that the need for this range of shops was declining. Easier bus transport into Hereford made a much wider range of shops available. The convenience of a variety of travelling shops was still enjoyed, however, and provided for the older people who found public transport difficult. The major shop in the area was King's Thorn Post Office and Stores. This began in the 1840s when the Post Office was opened and a bakery was established here which lasted for many years. This and other commodities were delivered over a wide area.

The shop was enlarged and updated to self-service in the 1970s and continued providing invaluable service including delivery of orders, paper and milk delivery and a taxi service until it, sadly, closed in 2002.

The Castle Inn
From the time of the enclosures and probably back in to the 1700s there has been a public house in Little Birch. Its situation is interesting. It would, prior to the enclosures, have been on the open common, close to the cluster of dwellings round Newtown Well. It was some distance from the early centre of Little Birch village.

One can only speculate as to its siting; maybe it was positioned for travellers along the original tracks across the common but it was not particularly close to any of them. It was quite close to one of the open field systems but most people working on their strips would take their weak alcoholic refreshment with them. Whatever the reason for its position, it would certainly have been an important venue for the community. In the early days it would have been privately owned, brewing its own beer. There was plenty of barley grown locally and maltsters are recorded in the census, while a Malthouse Meadow is referred to in the Tithe Map. Hops were also grown locally and are still to be found in the hedgerows.

Since 1841 and probably before this the inn has been called the Castle Inn. The origin of this name is most likely to be the proximity of the inn to Castle Nibole whose name dates back to at least the 1600s.

From 1841, when the first detailed censuses were made, the licensees were recorded. Although others may have come and gone in the intervening nine years, those mentioned are:

1841 – Edward Bucklee.

1851 – Ann Arnold (her husband George was registered as a blacksmith and their son, aged 13, as his apprentice).

1861 – Thomas Layton. During the 1850s and '60s there appeared to be a rival establishment called Little Castle which was probably located at what is now

Fig. 10.5 The Castle Inn in 2000

Wye Cottage. A James Matthews ran this, recorded as a shop in 1851 but he was described as a beer retailer in 1861. By then he was aged 80 so must have died soon after as he did not appear in the 1871 census.

In 1871 and for the next 30 years the pub was owned by the Mason family. Joseph Mason was recorded as Innkeeper up to the 1891 census then in 1901 a Mrs Mason (widow), aged 26, presumably a daughter-in-law was the licensed victualler.

During this lengthy period of ownership the inn was presumably proud of the fact that it remained independent and did not become a brewery tied house. It is claimed locally that the nickname ''Pendent' or 'Pendant' originated from this and thus the naming of the hill below as Pendant Pitch.

Sometime between 1901 and 1924, this independence was brought to an end when the inn was bought by Wintle's Forest Brewery.[2] The building was obviously modernised during this period, maybe by the brewery. The modernisation must have provided accommodation similar to that seen today.

When the inn was put up for sale in 1924, at a time when the Brewery was undergoing difficulties, it was described as the Castle Hotel! Indeed, it boasted four bedrooms and a sitting room upstairs and a cosy front bar, smoke room and licenced dining room (facing the back) downstairs, as well as a modern kitchen and a multitude of outside buildings. Whether or not the inn sold is unclear. It may have been withdrawn from sale as Wintle's was rescued and then taken over by Cheltenham Original Brewery Co. in 1930. A succession of brewery takeovers ensued over the next 30 years during which ownership of the Castle passed to Cheltenham and Hereford Brewery (1945), West Country Breweries (1958) — the plaque is still inserted in the wall by the front door — and Whitbread Breweries in 1963.[3]

During this period there was also a succession of well remembered licensees: Dent in the 1930s, Probert from 1937 to 1950 and Worsfield from 1950 to 1960. During this time the Castle was immortalised on television when the assembled company was filmed on Twelfth Night before walking down the lane to see the Holy Thorn flowering at midnight, which was captured on film, proving it was not a figment of inebriated imagination! The film, sadly, could not be viewed on television in Little Birch then but it was repeated in the 1960s on *Name this Day* and a recording of this is now preserved in the village. (Buses ran from Hereford to view the thorn in bloom!) During this period a local family, the Verrys would meet together in the inn every New Year's Day, with members of their large, extended family coming from far and wide.

From 1960 to 1965 the licensee was Meredith, (during the 1960s the inn was well known for its huge sales of cigarettes and tobacco), from 1965 to 1972 it was Hill, from 1972 to 1976, Morris, and from 1976 to 1994, Gerald Prior. He bought the Castle from Whitbread Breweries thus returning it to an independent free house. It was sold to the Walker family in 1994 who ran in until 2005 when it was sold again. After a period of closure and refurbishment it re-opened in August 2006 — a welcome return of a village asset at a time when so many other villages are losing theirs.

Throughout its life the Castle has been a venue for a wide variety of activities including pub games. Over the last half century it has been the home of teams such as those playing darts, dominoes, cribbage, and pool, frequently hosting teams from other local pubs. It has also, at times, hosted hunt meets of the South Hereford foxhounds (based at Wormelow) and the Ross Harriers.

The Coming of the Utilities

Water supply
The daily requirement of water for animals and domestic use was always a problem in Little Birch. There were, of course, ponds on some of the farms and there were three ponds available for village use, both for animals and soaking cartwheels in dry weather. One was located beside the entrance to Church Farm, opposite the church, another was opposite Castlefields, near Castle Nibole and the third was Walls Pool. The first two were filled in during the 1950s. Walls Pool silted up and remained a damp area. Attempts to restore it in the 1990s were frustrated by further silting up.

The porosity of the underlying rock means that at times of lower rainfall the water in the soil will drain down to a low level. This meant that water was not generally available from the many wells higher up the hill unless they were dug very deep. (The one at Green Farm is over 30 feet deep.) During the nineteenth century a number of people had wells on their land but they were often not reliable. If supply failed then they, together with those who had no well, would have to rely on one of the communal wells. Newtown well, at the bottom of Pendant Pitch, supplied a number of people in the immediate neighbourhood. A beautifully constructed well, it would have originally been open but this exposed it to possible pollution. At some point in the twentieth century it was covered over and a hand-pump erected above it. It is remembered by some of the older inhabitants. As mentioned before, this well probably accounts for the development of a cluster of houses and enclosed land in the middle of the unenclosed common. Newtown Well did fail in dry summers leaving only one well still running which was Higgins Well. This is situated at the bottom of a valley north of the church and, as also mentioned before, probably accounts for the cluster of houses round the church. Older residents still remember having to collect water from Higgins Well in dry summers and, of course, it always had to be carried back uphill. Higgins Well had obviously been supplying local needs for several hundred years. Originally, it seems, it was not in its present position. Instead, a spring emerged in the meadow at the top of the bank to the north of the well so people collecting water had to walk across enclosed land. Legend has it that a Mr Higgins who possibly lived in Higgins Well Cottage (maybe as far back as the 1600s or even earlier) and whose land this was

> became so annoyed at the trespasses of the villagers across his land to the well that he had it filled up. However, shortly afterwards, while smoking his pipe in the great chimney corner of his house, he was startled by a sudden eruption of water under his feet. The spring had forced a new outlet at a spot which seemed to indicate to his untutored mind that there was a guardian spirit of some sort in existence quite equal to the emergency of protecting popular rights ...[4]

The above is an extract from a letter sent in 1900 to the *Hereford Times* by Mr H.W. Southey of Castle Nibole. He was repeating the well-known local legend which a reader requested to hear again. To continue the legend, Mr Higgins was determined not to reopen the well but, to appease the spirit, he moved down to the present site and started to dig. In due course water began to bubble up through the underlying rock and, miraculously, the 'inrush in the chimney corner disappeared'. The spirit was obviously satisfied that water was once again available to the people. This 'act of contrition' resulted in local immortality for Mr Higgins. Mr Southey's letter tells us

Fig. 10.6 Higgins Well in 1995, after refurbishment. Under the arch, accessible from a platform, is a protected area from which drinking water can be collected (when tested in 1994 it was shown to be still fit to drink). The large basin was for watering, or collecting water for, livestock.
Above is the inscription seen above the arch

that he was told of a lady who enclosed the well around 1800, covering it with a slab and building a walled basin for the overflow. This was done at her expense presumably because she was concerned about the condition of the open well. This, in turn, implies that the well was in its present position in the 1700s. When exactly Mr Higgins moved it is unclear. Maybe the land he took over had only been recently enclosed and before this people could collect their water freely. The good lady's work fell into disrepair after she died and the well once again became exposed and overgrown. Mr Southey motivated the people of Little Birch and further afield to contribute to a fund to restore the well in honour of Queen Victoria's Diamond Jubilee in 1897. They built the structure seen today, the dipping well covered over and enclosed on three sides, accessible by an arch, a platform to stand on and a large basin for watering animals. The whole is surrounded by stone walls and accessible by a wrought iron gate.

There were two other wells available to the local people. One was on Well Orchard land, but easily became polluted. The other was enclosed with a pump and was located just outside the Chapel. The difficulties of water supply were obviously causing some concern by 1913 when it was investigated by the Medical Officer to Hereford Rural District Council. He reported to the Parish Council (who recorded it in their minutes)[5] that for a population of 239 living in 59 houses, all collected rainwater and 18 had wells on the premises. The remainder relied on Chapel Well (5 houses), Newtown Well (15 houses), Higgins Well (13 houses), Orchard Well (3 houses) and an open spring at Wrigglebrook (7 houses). The distances water had to be carried from the nearest well were: 3 houses – less than 50 yards; 6 houses – 100 yards; 11 houses – 200 yards; 5 houses – 300 yards; 4 houses – 400 yards; 9 houses – 500 yards and 2 houses – half a mile

These distances bring home to us the incredibly time-consuming and arduous work water collection both for home use and for animals involved. Ways of reducing this were obviously employed by ingenious rainwater collection. The Schoolhouse built in 1857 had a huge tank dug under the building into which all rainwater ran. An indoor pump brought up water from this. Some other buildings of similar age had similar arrangements. In the neighbouring King's Thorn area the situation was no better. They had to rely on wells at Ladywell (below Diamond Cottage) or the well at the bottom of Wrigglebrook hill or Bull's well (just off the Thorn). Many used the well by the chapel or one on the common below the bus shelter. This was Captain's Well, a very reliable source. A story relating to water collection by Douglas Manning was of brothers from a house at the bottom of Barrack Hill constructing a bath on wheels which they dragged up the hill to Chapel Well. They then leapt aboard for the trip back home and were once seen overtaking the old Greenlands lorry!

Water supply continued to be a problem well into the twentieth century and probably held back development of the area. Various methods such as damming streams or using wind pumps were employed. The inadequacy of the supply was recorded by the local Medical Officer of Health in 1913 but ensuing delays which included the Wars meant that nothing was done. Frustration resulted in an agreement being drawn up between Captain Cope of Hergest, Mr Peake of Highbury and David Dyke of Castle Nibole in 1945. They set out to develop a good water source for themselves and the village. A water diviner named Greening from Kington advised that a well should be sunk at the gates of Castle Nibole. When no water was found at a depth of 50 feet, digging was abandoned, and a new diviner from Birmingham was employed who found an abundant supply at Walls Pool. A water tank that had seen wartime service in High Town, Hereford, was purchased for a nominal sum and installed next to Glebe field to provide a reservoir for the new supply. (A new larger one in the Glebe was installed in 1982 which continued to serve until 2004 when it was replaced.) Residents of Little Birch and King's Thorn who were prepared to lay their own pipes were allowed to connect up to this supply. They then paid a yearly rate. This borehole was linked with the Sunnybank borehole and provided a reliable supply of water which, though rather hard, makes an excellent cup of tea. This piped water allowed the building of many new homes, particularly in the Wrigglebrook area. Although this new supply was a great advance on what went before, it was not without its problems. The pumps were not reliable and leaks were not always detected and repaired promptly. There were also some disputes about rights of access where pipes crossed private land. One landowner had the habit of turning off the supply where it crossed his property and had to be threatened with violence by an angry group of residents before the supply was restored.

Piped mains water finally arrived in the 1970s and a number of properties transferred to it. Although it is more expensive and of inferior taste, the pressure is higher as it comes from a reservoir behind Acontree House at the top of Barrack Hill. This is, in turn, fed by pumping from the larger reservoir on Ridge Hill which receives its water from the Broomy Hill works.

Only when piped water was available could bathrooms and toilets be installed and the tin bath in front of the fire and the bucket in the shed down the garden abandoned for good. These 'mod cons', however, were expensive to install and so were not to be found in all the dwellings. Those who lived in rented property depended on their landlords to install these conveniences but all were not prepared to pay the extra rent which would result. Indeed, some cottages lived in until the 1990s still did not have these. Only when they were sold were they installed.

Mains sewerage, of course, still does not exist in the area, properties relying on the services of septic tanks. (This is an effective way to ensure that river water removed for water treatment does not eventually run away to the sea but soaks down into the soil!)

Electricity

It is almost impossible to imagine life without electricity and all the labour-saving devices and entertainments it has made available, to say nothing of computers. It is therefore somewhat surprising to think that the people of Little Birch and area were still managing without it well into the 1960s. Electricity arrived much earlier in Much Birch and in most of King's Thorn in the 1950s. A few houses near the Guy's estate yard were able to connect to their supply which was installed as early as the 1930s and there is a report that the Castle Inn also had it then. (Certainly there was a pole near to the present notice Board labelled SWS [South Wales Switchgear] until 2001.) Cooking was managed as it had been for centuries by using wood or coal. Multipurpose ranges were common which heated a tank of water as well as having an oven and open fire. Lighting was by a combination of candles and paraffin or oil lamps. The latter could be quite sophisticated, either standing or hanging. Cleaning involved rug-beating or possibly a hand operated carpet sweeper. Washing would obviously be done by hand, probably with the aid of a mangle, dolly and scrubbing board.

In an era when people living in towns and cities had long been enjoying the benefits of electricity and the household appliances now available to them, the wealthier people living in the area were not prepared to wait for the electricity supply but invested in generators. However, although they could now have lighting and appliances, they were unlikely to have the generator running for long periods because of the expense. This involved a certain amount of organisation, many being timed to stop when the last light was turned off in the house. The peace descending on the neighbourhood when the last light went off at night was apparently very noticeable.

When electricity cables were brought to the area, residents were able to receive a supply only if they could get together five neighbouring properties all of whom were prepared to pay the link-up costs. This made it difficult for many who were anxious to take advantage of this if their neighbours' houses were rented and the owner was not prepared to pay. After a time this scheme was seen to be unworkable and the number reduced to three then to a single house. With all houses connected within a fairly short time, people felt they had finally arrived in the twentieth century.

Lack of electricity did not prevent the keenest from acquiring a television. A few even had it for the Coronation in 1953! Ivor Crum claimed to have had the first television a few months earlier — for the FA Cup Final when Blackpool beat Bolton Wanderers. These early televisions had to be operated from car batteries which could be re-charged at King's Thorn garage.

Telephone

Though something of a luxury when it became available, some telephones appeared in the area in the 1930s, well before the other utilities arrived. A few properties were connected as soon as the Wormelow telephone exchange was up and running; Church Farm and the Castle Inn were amongst the first, being connected by 1934. The Follies had to pay for poles from the pub before they were connected. Locals have fond memories of the old manual exchange at Wormelow where people to whom telegrams were sent were often rung by the operator to see if they could have the contents read to them instead of delivering it. They would then receive it with the post next morning. One caller was apparently told by the operator that 'she's gone to her sister's and won't be back today'.

There was greater uptake of telephones after the war when the telephone boxes were also installed, one outside the village hall and the other near the old Post Office. The traditional red boxes still remain and function even though they do look rather unloved.

There is no mains gas supply in the area although some rely on bottled gas for cooking and heating.

Housing

As Little Birch was always a poor area with no large houses, the earlier dwellings, most likely of timber, wattle and daub and thatched, have all disappeared. As mentioned before, the Hearth Tax return in 1664 recorded 27 properties. Of these, only one had four hearths, seven had two hearths and seven had one hearth. The remaining 12 were considered poor enough to be exempt. There is no way the identity of these houses can be discovered but the Militia Assessments of 1663[6] give some clue by naming those to be charged and who must have been considered sufficiently well-off to pay. Kidley of Bromley and Gwillim of Church Farm may well have been included as living in houses large enough to have two or more hearths. The Royal Commission for Historic Monuments carried out a survey in 1931, but only recorded properties pre-1710, and selected just four properties to mention in Little Birch.[7]

The oldest of these, estimated to date from the late fifteenth century, was Upper House described as being timber-framed with plaster walls and two storeys with attic. In 1841 this was a farm with 23 acres so one of the wealthier properties in the parish. In 1931 it was in a derelict state (although may have still been inhabited) but rapidly deteriorated from then. Some walls were still standing in the 1970s but it has, sadly, now completely disappeared. The Sycamores is built on the site (see also p.89).

New Mills Farm is, happily, still in existence, and dates from the seventeenth century. It was a mill into the nineteenth century but the wheel and mill leat have now gone. Its history is recorded on pp.92-93.

Of the other two properties, one is part of a barn at Church Farm which was, presumably, once half-timbered. It was thought to date from late seventeenth century. Again, the farm's history is covered on p.95.

The fourth property recorded was a timber-framed barn lying in a field north-west of the church, estimated as being of seventeenth-century date. In 1931 it had a 'modern iron roof' and was in a reasonable condition. It was a substantial threshing barn lying parallel to the road to the church and had a smaller open barn (fold) at right angles to it, arranged around a yard. The field was recorded as belonging to Lower House Farm in 1841 although was later bought by Church Farm. It is some way from Lower House so the reason for its building is not clear. It is possible that the rector of Little Birch, who was not always resident in the parish, may have built it for his tithes. The main barn deteriorated after the loss

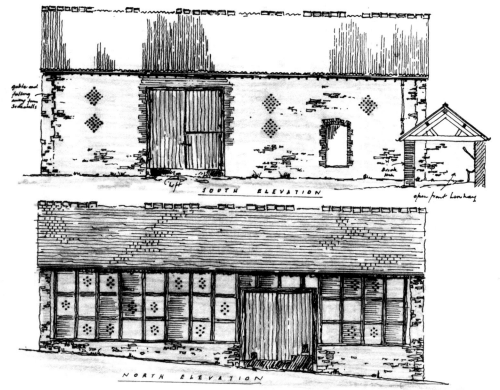

Fig. 10.7 Drawing of Rowlston's Barn by Dennis Hands from his survey in 1986

of its roof and the walls have now totally disappeared. The fold, still roofed in the 1970s, has now fallen down to the one remaining wall we see today (Fig. 13.13).

Another barn of similar age and construction was Rowlston's Barn which was half timbered on one side but stone or brick on the other three (see Fig. 10.7). It was a very substantial barn which survived up until the late 1980s when, sadly, it collapsed.

During the eighteenth century the majority of housing was, presumably, still of timber, wattle and daub with thatch. However, it is likely that some of the larger houses were being rebuilt in the fashion of the day. In several cases, deeds date from a time earlier than the age of the existing building. Although the Old Rectory deeds date from 1640 the existing building is probably later although a little of the earlier building may have been incorporated. Part of the Old Rectory may well date from the earlier part of the eighteenth century with brickwork of Flemish Garden design. Church Farm house may well incorporate building of sixteenth or seventeenth century at the eastern end but the western end is of early nineteenth century and typically Regency. The fine windows indicate that some money was spent on this which would be likely if the Gwillim family were paying for it. The back part of Castle Nibole house, although incorporated into and altered by the Victorian improvements, still shows indications of a late eighteenth- or early nineteenth-century building, if not earlier. The barn by the road, now altered into a holiday cottage, has roof timbers probably dating from sixteenth or seventeenth century. This whole site obviously has early origins with land enclosed from the common long before the Enclosure Award. Mention of a Castle Nibole occurs in the seventeenth century and the earliest deeds date from then.

Fig. 10.8 The Old Cottage in 2006, showing the steep-sided roof typical of one which was once thatched

Towards the end of the eighteenth century, settlement on common areas was beginning and some of the cottages which remain today were being built. Squatters' dwellings were being erected consisting of stone chimney and timber, wattle and daub walls with a thatched roof. Three which probably started life like this were Buddlia and The Old Cottage and Cherry Tree Cottage. The timbers used in these were, typically, unworked remaining rounded as from the original trunk; this indicates a poor dwelling. Of these, The Old Cottage is the only one retaining the steep roof typical of a thatched cottage.

The hearths in these dwellings often included a bread oven but in the case of Cherry Tree Cottage, a smaller oven was also included, possibly for drying hops.

One or two of these squatters' cottages had land enclosed from the common and so became smallholdings. With this greater security some of the cottages were rebuilt in more permanent stone. This would seem to be the case with Walls Pool and Well Orchard which probably date from the early nineteenth century, just before the Enclosure.

The majority of the older housing in the area is typical of Enclosure cottages. They are built of stone (readily available in the area) and with slate roofs — considered superior to pantiles which were reserved for the outbuildings. The roof pitch is shallow and the windows small and square. A typical example of an unaltered cottage of this type is the, now derelict, Well Orchard although it did precede the enclosures by a few years.

The accommodation of these would be one, or possibly two rooms, up and down and, maybe as a later addition, a lean-to at the back.

Dating from this time but somewhat larger was Uplands, built for Cranston who oversaw the Enclosures.

Even by the latter part of the nineteenth century these cottages were not modern enough for some people and those who could afford it were enlarging and improving. A style which was in favour at the time involved stone with brick surrounds to sash windows together with slate roofs. Typical of this are Fernleigh and Sunnybank Farm, also the Castle Inn. The same style was adopted by Stephen

Fig. 10.9 Well Orchard farmhouse and buildings in 2000

*Fig. 10.10 The Old Rectory in 2000. The right-hand side was added by
Stephen Thackwell in the second part of the 1800s*

Thackwell when he built the school and schoolhouse. Stephen Thackwell was also altering the Rectory for his own comfort at this time. The eastern end was extended in brick using the English bond pattern which was enjoying a renaissance in the 1850s. The shuttered windows were surrounded by carefully and expensively dressed stone including vermiculation. A coach-house was added dated 1855, also with dressed stone.

Castle Nibole was re-built and greatly extended at this time with a new western front in the style of Strawberry Hill Gothic. At the end of the nineteenth century another wing was added and the wealth of H.W. Southey provided some most interesting and varied stained glass and also tooled and painted leather panels.

In the latter half of the nineteenth century brick was being used as the main building material in some properties such as The Glen (formerly Newtown Villa). Stephen Thackwell built Model Cottages of brick and render, a couple of back-to-back semi-detached houses with a slightly ecclesiastical flavour and well appointed for labourers' cottages (see Fig. 15.1).

At this time there was some emigration from the parish and quite a number of these squatters' and Enclosure cottages were no longer inhabited. These have gradually fallen into disrepair and many have totally disappeared. The remains of a few are still visible.

A small number of wealthier people moved into the area at the beginning of the twentieth century and Edwardian-style houses such as Hergest and Highbury were built. However, there was very little building at this time as the area did not enjoy the facilities which were increasingly common in suburban areas.

Hardly any building took place during the times of the World Wars and the 1920s' recession. There was a scattering of new buildings in the 1950s. A police house was built next to the village hall in 1953 (Ross View), the village hall having, itself, been built in 1951 (see section 14). Just below it Lady Hull, widow

Fig. 10.11 A ruined cottage in Jones's Orchard in 2006, uninhabited for many years. The orchard still contains a number of old varieties of apple trees

of Sir Percy Hull, organist at Hereford cathedral, built a bungalow in 1953 (now Chevin House). However, with the arrival of electricity, there was sufficient call for the development of some parcels of land around the village in the early 1960s and some houses and bungalows were built. One or two had to rely on generators until the arrival of the electricity. People moving into these came from elsewhere and were working outside the village. They therefore had the money to afford the comfortable modern facilities. Buildings included the houses on Mesne Lane and the bungalows down Pendant Pitch and, later, those below The Glen.

Since the 1970s, planning regulations have been stricter and very few new houses have been built since then. However, with mains water now available and the improving economic climate, the era of refurbishment and enlargement began. There are now very few buildings which have not been greatly extended, given new windows and, in many cases, been whitewashed. Such are the changes that very little of the original cottages can be seen.

With these piecemeal improvements and the scattering of newer buildings, Little Birch has little identifying or unifying style. However, these individually developed styles bring variety matched only by the different interests and backgrounds of the inhabitants over the last few years. There are now very few people who have been born and brought up here and lived here all their lives.

11   Poverty in the Parish

As mentioned above, Little Birch and the surrounding parishes have never been very wealthy. However, by the seventeenth century some inhabitants were relatively well-off as can be seen from the Hearth Tax which was levied on Lady Day, 1664.[1] In Little Birch one house had four hearths, seven had two and seven dwellings had only one, but 12 houses were exempt altogether, presumably because they were too poor to pay.

In neighbouring Aconbury the gap between rich and poor was more marked. There one house had nine hearths — presumably this was Aconbury Court because the present Victorian farmhouse was built around an earlier dwelling and C.J. Robinson notes in his *Mansions and Manors of Herefordshire* that: 'It was probably by James Pearle that the Conventual Buildings were converted into a Mansion House, which was sufficiently commodius to form the occasional residence of the Lords of Chandos.'[2] In the pecking order below Aconbury Court, there was a substantial drop to the next level, again of a single house but with just three hearths, then came another single property with two hearths and ten that were exempt.

Living conditions could be basic, even at the standards of the day. In the 1851 census, two agricultural labourers were noted as 'sleeping in outbuildings'. The older of the two was James Pinch who was 78.[3] People who had homes of their own were often not much better off. In September 1856, tenements on Aconbury commons and wastelands were valued by Mr John Higgins for Guy's Hospital which owned the land, in order for new rents to be set.[4] Arthur Armitage, probably the agent, wrote to the governors in March 1857 detailing the valuations 'together with the remarks of the several tenants, when informed thereof. These several tenants have been informed that they will receive Notice to quit their Holdings at Micks next, and will in the mean time have the opportunity of making offers to the Governors for retaking the same.'

Armitage was not afraid of expressing his own opinion as to the suitability of the various tenants, in particular '[John Seal] is in arrear £4-10s which he says he will pay shortly. He is an idle man, working occasionally on the turnpike road. I told him that he wd have notice to quit and wd be required to give up the Holding'. The Seal family had other misfortunes, as John's sister was married to Henry George Watts who rented another tenement. He was a 'Sergeant in the 3rd Battalion of Grenadier Guards & was through the whole Crimean Campaign — deserted his wife, who lives with her brother John Seal mentioned above. In arrear two years at Lady Day 1856 & must have Notice to quit served on him at Wellington Barracks, London'.

Although Armitage could be quite judgemental about tenants he disapproved of, he was obviously touched by the plight of some of the people who lived on Aconbury Hill. He describes Richard Davis as: 'a bed ridden old man of eighty nine years of age, in a wretched tenement which ought to be pulled down when he is gone', and appears to have been in favour of leaving the old man to live out his remaining months or years without being disturbed.

Life seems to have been particularly precarious for women, who may have depended on a male wage earner. For example there were Esther and Mary Preece: '2 elderly single women living in a nearly ruinous cottage in a state of extreme poverty. They are the daughters of one of the Hospital Woodwards who has been dead many years, their brother Benjamin now holding his place : he contributes to their support by paying the rent and also £1 for a piece of land which stands in his name. They would give up the land if they might be allowed to remain in the old cottage to which they cling with great attachment.'

Two other women were living in wretched conditions: Mary Harris, 'a widow in a poor cottage with son sleeping at home. The land would let with James Preece's holding which would answer better than repairing the cottage'. Margaret Watkins, who was also a widow, lived in a 'cottage in very bad repair, and the same remark applies to this as the holding above. The tenants would doubtless raise a cry against being turned out, but it would [be] better for the governors to give them a gratuity on quitting than to suffer them to remain'.

Although the Welfare State is an invention of the twentieth century, provision of a kind had been made for the poor from as early as the fourteenth century. The Statute of Cambridge in 1388 established the precedent of each administrative area, in this case the hundred, being responsible for its own poor. In the Vagabonds and Beggars Act of 1494 people who were too infirm to work were allowed to beg, but only in their own hundred. Until the suppression of the monasteries, the Church dispensed charity through its almshouses and hospitals, but afterwards, in order to compensate for the lack of facilities, the parishes, supervised by the justices of the peace, were made responsible for the collection of alms, (at first voluntary). During the 1500s a raft of legislation was passed to try and manage the obvious problem of the sick and workless.[5] In 1552 each parish was to appoint two collectors of alms to assist the churchwardens after service on Trinity Sunday to 'gently ask and demand of every man or woman what they of their charity will be contented to give weekly towards the relief of the poor'. Ten years later it was obvious that this voluntary system wasn't working because the 1562 (Poor Law) Act stated that those who refused to give voluntarily may be taxed by justices of the peace, and if still refusing to pay may be imprisoned. In 1572 overseers of the poor were appointed and a compulsory poor rate was introduced.

Over the next two centuries, more laws were passed, some piecemeal and some in an attempt to consolidate what had gone before, but the description of these is not within the scope of a local history. Suffice it to say that various acts affirmed the mutual liability of parents and children to support each other, empowered local officials to remove any stranger likely to require relief within 40 days of his arrival in their parish unless he could show that he would never need to call upon poor relief, and required that parishioners in receipt of poor relief should be registered. By great good fortune the Little Birch Parish Overseers account book for 1784–1792 survives and gives a fascinating insight into the management of poor relief in the village.[6]

There seems to have been a very enterprising system of producing hurden cloth, a strong coarse cloth made of inferior hemp or flax, for distribution to the needy. Mary Barrel was given '1 stone of Hurden yarn to clothe her daughter' and Elizabeth Poyner '½ a stone to clothe her son'. Women's clothes obviously used more material. The yarn was spun and woven in the parish and any surplus cloth was taken to market to be sold. On 16 October 1788 William Kemmis was paid

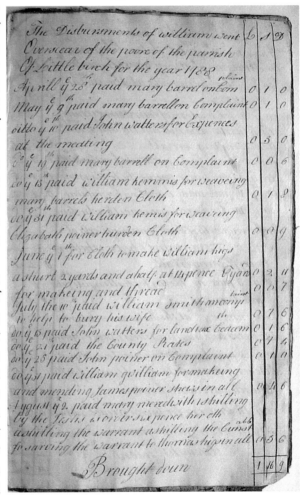

Fig. 11.1 Extract from the Overseers Account Book 1784-1792. Notice the references to hurden cloth, woven for distribution to the poor

5s 2d for weaving 31 yards of hurden cloth and on 20 October Ann Greane was paid 1s for selling it.

Although money was sometimes paid out 'on complaint', much of the relief was distributed in the form of food or clothes. On 24 May 1784 James Howells, the overseer, paid Elizabeth Poyner 1s 'on complt.', but on 14 June the same year she received one peck of wheat which cost 1s 10d. This was obviously more economical. In August Mary Gwatkin received 1s 'on complt.' and also half a bushel of wheat costing 4s.

Not only was cloth made in the village but also clothes and shoes. On 1 June 1788 2s 11d was paid out for cloth 'to make William higs a shurt 2 yards and a half at 14 pence a yard' and they didn't forget to itemise 7d 'for makeing and thread'. From 1789–90 Thomas Gwillym was the overseer and he recorded that on 4 July 1789 he paid William Gwillym 1s 7d for mending William Higgs' shoes. Whether William was a relative of Thomas we don't know, but William was certainly a shoemaker because previously he had been paid 4s 6d for 'makeing and mending James poiner shews'.

The Poyner family was the recipient of parish money for a number of years. The first mention of them was in 1784 when Elizabeth was given 6d on Christmas Eve and a rather more generous 3s 6d for a petticoat on 28 December. The following year Elizabeth was paid 2s 4d for herself and 2s 4d for her son, also 'For cloth for a waistcoat 2s 3d making 1s Trimmings 6d, Shoos 2s 6d Stocking 6d in all 0-6-9'. In 1788 Elizabeth Poyner was still receiving help from the parish to clothe her son. She was allowed ½ a stone of hurden yarn at 4s and 3s for a pair of shoes, 1s 4d for two pairs of stockings and 9d for making a pair of breeches. It's interesting that the cost of shoes and stockings had gone up, perhaps because he had grown!

The account book gives us some idea of the scale of production of hurden cloth in Little Birch. In 1788, 12 stone and 4lb of hurds (raw flax or hemp) was purchased for £2 9s 4d. This was then spun for the same price and then Mr Kemmis was paid £1 3s 6d for 'whitning winding weaving 60 yards of Hurden cloth. On 7 July, 60 yards of cloth was sold at 11d per yard for £2 15s. The account book doesn't make it clear how much yarn Mr Kemmis was given to weave, presumably not all that had been spun because otherwise the finished product would have been sold at a considerable loss.

Occasionally house rent was paid for and buildings were repaired with the help of the parish. In 1790 Thomas Gwillym paid George Evans 7s for repairing Margaret Eustance's chimney. Not long afterwards the new overseer William Mullon found that he had to give Mr Kemmis 2s 6d for 'repairing Margt Eustans house' so it must have been in a bad way.

Parishes had enough indigent people of their own to look after, so when immigrants from other areas fell on hard times, removal orders were instituted.

Thus, parish relief was used to return people to their place of birth for support. For example, on 3 November 1788, 3s was noted as the cost of 'takeing Gurge preace to his parish a hors to ride and paid William kemis 1 shilling for coming along'. Presumably this was to make sure that George went where he was supposed to go. Similarly in June 1789 John Smith was returned to Madley. This involved a cost of 6s in all:

June 6	Pd for an order for John Smith 4s and gave him	0 -5 – 0
July 4	Pd James Nickol Horse hire taking J. Smith to Madley	0 -1 – 0

By the nineteenth century these removal orders were still being carried out. In 1852 the Parish Record for neighbouring Aconbury reports that there was a removal order for the family of Samuel and Ann Cordy and their eight children from Aconbury to Cam, in Gloucestershire. The Parish Overseers' Papers for Cam reveal more details of this unfortunate family: 'On 12 June, Samuel Cordy, wife Ann and 8 children, Daniel 14, Jane 12, Caled 10, Cornelius 7, Obed 6, Selina 4, Joshua 2, and infant boy aged 1 day (to be removed) from Aconbury, Herefordshire to Cam'. There was a later entry in the papers which simply said: 25 June 1853 Samuel Cordy died and family to be removed'.[7] It seems terribly harsh to serve a removal order on a family where the mother had just given birth. One can only hope that the overseers allowed her sufficient time to recover before the family was moved on.

Overseers did co-operate with each other, as can be seen from an entry in the Little Birch account book: 'Reimbursed to Sellack Overseer who relievd Wm Williams 2 – 9 – 6'.[8]

Parish money could be used for a number of purposes, for example, firewood, stone for the churchyard wall, destroying a fox and legal matters. In 1788 Mary Meredwith was paid '1 shilling by the Jestis is order six pence her oth a shilling the cunstable fo sarving the warrant to Thomas higs in all 0 – 3 – 6.' One can only speculate. Could this have been a way of getting maintenance for an illegitimate child, of which there were many in country districts at this time? Sarah Barrol had to make four journeys to Hereford on account of her bastard child and was given 6s.

Ultimately Poor Relief was given for an expense which could not be avoided. On 10 July 1788 William Smith was granted 7s 6d to 'help to bury his wife'. When Mary Barrel died, sometime between May 1791 to April 1792 the cost of her burial was itemised: 'for a coffin 0 – 7 – 0' and 'the Clark for making Mary Barrels grave 0 – 2 – 6'. This compares with 19s 6d for 'Callender's Inft.' in 1784, 16s 6d for William Williams in 1785 and 17s for Jane Smith also in 1785.[9]

The Poor Law Amendment Act, 1834

An alternative method of dealing with people who couldn't support themselves was for parishes to send them to the workhouse, if one were available. There was one in Hereford prior to 1834 but that was just to serve the six town parishes. After 1834 all parishes elected Guardians who were encouraged to join together in Unions to build new workhouses. Hereford Poor Law Union was formed in 1836; with 53 Guardians representing 45 parishes, which included Aconbury, Little Birch, Much Birch, Callow, Little Dewchurch and Much Dewchurch.[10]

Interestingly, in the 1881 census[9], there was only one person from Little Birch listed as living in the workhouse. This was Isaac Davies, aged 14, described as a scholar and tailor. At the same time, several people with the name of Dobbins were recorded as being inmates. They originated from Little Dewchurch and Hoarwithy and it is only supposition that they were related, but it is significant that the only adult female of that name was Elizabeth Dobbins, age 26, unmarried, a domestic servant and blind. William Dobbins, age 62, was a miller from Little Dewchurch and all the others were children: George Dobbins, age 13, a scholar, born in Little Dewchurch; Thomas Dobbins, age 11, a scholar, born in Hoarwithy; Matilda Dobbins, age 5, a scholar, born in Hoarwithy; Mary Ann Dobbins, age 3, born in Hereford; and Walter Dobbins, age three months, also born in Hereford. As the miller, William, is described as married and not widowed, one wonders where his wife was.

Also listed in the same census were three boys from Much Birch: George Gale, age 10, scholar; William Gale, age 13, scholar and tailor; and Thomas Powell, age 12, scholar. Other local people were from Little Dewchurch: Harriet Harris, unmarried, age 17, domestic servant; Edward Jones, widower, age 83, a stonemason; Annie Vaughan, unmarried, age 16, a domestic servant; and Ann Walters, unmarried, age 24, also a domestic servant.

The new workhouse was designed by John Plowman and was finished in the autumn of 1837. Its impressive building eventually became Hereford County Hospital, at the rear of which is still situated Union Walk. The inmates were fed and clothed and if they were able, had to work to earn their keep. This work was manual and extremely tedious. It included oakum picking, stone breaking, pounding bones and cleaning hair.[11] No-one would be encouraged to think of the workhouse as an easy option. Indeed, Disraeli expressed the view that the Poor Law Amendment Act was 'announcing to the world that in England poverty was a crime'.[12]

Parish Minute Book

Meanwhile the Parish Council and various Overseers of the Poor in Little Birch did their best to manage any problems on their own patch. In 1852 the Parish Minute Book recorded that Mr Bonner, Overseer of the Poor asked: 'what they suppose best to be done with a pauper name of Norman'. At the next meeting, 'guardian be requested to take in hand the matter of the pauper Norman — to take steps to ascertain to what parish he belongs and be empowered to draw on the Road Surveyor to the accounts of the Parish for the requisite sum for thoroughly investigating the said matter of the pauper Norman'.[13]

One might well wonder why the Road Surveyor should be involved, but, as parishes were responsible for the upkeep of roads in their area and the Surveyor of Roads, (unpaid), had the unenviable task of organising this work, he worked closely with the other parish officers and often unemployed people were set to work on the roads. Highway rates were levied on qualifying parishioners but sometimes, if it wasn't worth while to levy a highway rate, the amounts would be included in the poor rate. It seems as if the various parish funds were not kept strictly separate, for in the Parish Overseers Account Book it is clear that money which was levied for the destruction of vermin was included in the accounts of the distribution of poor relief.[14]

In 1853 it was decided that landowners should henceforward themselves pay their cottagers' poor rates.

It is clear that members of the Parish Council took their duties seriously, as they made sure that the accounts were up to date and accurate. In 1854 'after several cases of application from parish relief ... the accounts of the expenditure on the poor were examined and it appears that the Parish is at present in debt to the Overseer to the amount £5.1.0.' The minutes don't make it clear as to how they solved that problem! In 1855 '... Ann Colcombe, widow, attended and was required to give information as to her Parish. List of nil- dom relief was examined, the Union payment settled.' The Union payment would have been the parish's contribution to the workhouse in Hereford, but the meaning of nil-dom relief can only be guessed at.

In 1863 the Parish Council was obviously thrown into disarray by the requirement '... to take into consideration the reassessment of the Parish under the recent Act, the Overseers declined the responsibility and it was resolved by a majority to petition the Poor Law Board to order the revaluation of the Parish by a competent and approved valuer.' However by the next meeting they had resolved the problem by agreeing a typically English solution: they 'decided to form a committee for making reassessment'.

The Parish Council's job was important, they not only dealt with poor relief but also in collecting money for the running of the school. In 1887 they decided that '... collection of the school rate should form part of the duties of the assistant Overseer for the future'. Usually the election of the Overseer and assistant Overseer took place without controversy and nominees were elected unopposed. However, in 1894, there was a contested election of Assistant Overseer. The son of Joseph

Mason, the previous officer, was proposed, along with two others. The Parish Minute Book records what happened: '... there were stormy discussions and a vast deal of animus'! The parishioners then voted over a period of a week, an hour each day at the school and Lewis Mason was voted in.

More decisions regarding the school were needed in 1895 and there was a public meeting of ratepayers. The following resolution was carried: 'it is resolved that the School be continued as heretofor on the voluntary system, that the Managers be authorised so far as this meeting can sanction the procedure, to undertake the proposed extension required by the Education Department according to their discretion, and that the ratepayers present pledge themselves to the payment of a voluntary special rate to provide funds which it may be necessary to raise by such means to meet the expenditure incurred.'

Charities

We know that there were ancient charities in Little Birch because from 1819–1837 Commissioners were appointed by Parliament to look into the existence and condition of charities in England and Wales.[15] The ones that they found for Little Birch were as follows:

Webb's Charity

From a Parliamentary return of 1786 it was discovered that in 1612 Thomas Webb died and his will stipulated that £10 should be given to the parish, vested in the parish officers. This produced an income of 10s a year which was paid until about 1803 when the principal was used to build two parish houses. These houses were subsequently sold several times and 'now do not belong to the parish'. It is possible, however to pinpoint where they were. In the Enclosure Award of 1824 a piece of land, nine perches in area, was allocated to the Overseers of the Poor for Little Birch on Little Birch Common.[16] This piece of land was situated roughly where Greenlea Cottage is now. There is probably no trace of the houses left, except perhaps a few stones. It seems likely that the parish houses were sold after the building of the Hereford Workhouse in 1837.

Higgs' Charity

The same Parliamentary return stated that 'Higgs' left £2 to the parish in his will, vested in the parish officers and this produced 2s a year. A loose leaf of paper in the parish register states that this interest was paid until 1773 when Edward Addis, to whom it was lent, 'failed' and the money was lost.[17] This Higgs is William Higgs, who was rector of the parish from 1611 to 1664. His will, dated 1662, which is quite difficult to decipher, can be seen in the Hereford Record Office.[18]

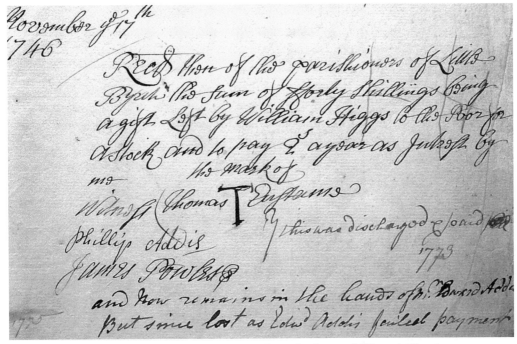

Fig. 11.2 Parish register entry recording the loss of Higgs' Charity money

Wall's Charity

The same Parliamentary return of 1786 stated that a person named Wall gave to the poor a rent-charge of 3s 4d which was vested in a Mr Quick. The Commissioners reported: 'It is not known when this rent-charge was last paid; we were unable to find any satisfactory information respecting the identity of the property on which it was paid.'

Wilcox's Charity

Someone named Wilcox gave land to the poor, which was then vested in John Bennett. It produced 3s 4d yearly. Again the Commissioners' investigations were unable to turn up much information. They reported: 'We could learn nothing which was likely to lead to the recovery of the property, which would seem to have been lost to the poor for many years.'

Although no proper records seem to have been kept about Wall's and Wilcox's charities, we cannot assume that they were improperly administered. Certainly the other charities discovered were. Webb's Charity produced 10s a year for nearly 200 years and Higgs' Charity which was instituted by the rector William Higgs, lasted for over 100 years. It is a pity that we cannot discover how Edward Addis lost the money. He must have been a trusted member of the community in order to have borrowed it. Perhaps it was a business venture which went wrong.

Throughout the nineteenth century the government passed many laws in an attempt to improve the health and living standards of the working class. In 1897, the year of Queen Victoria's Diamond Jubilee, an editorial in *Public Health* stated that 'of all the achievements of the Victorian Era ... history will find none worthier of record than the efforts made to ameliorate the lives of the poor, to curb the ravages of disease, and to secure for all pure air, food and water.'[19] However it is likely that society's main efforts were concentrated on the industrial towns. People who lived in the countryside were assumed to be better off, especially in terms of clean air and more wholesome food. Nevertheless, in Little Birch, as elsewhere, poverty was never far away and even a reliable water supply to all residents was a long time coming. It is significant that even in Little Birch the national mood was caught and Higgins Well was improved in 1897, the year of the Queen's Diamond Jubilee. However, there would always be individuals, particularly the old, who would need assistance when they fell on hard times.

Bessie Southey Charity

After 1895, when District and new Parish Councils were formed, the Parish was no longer responsible for poor law administration, but luckily for Little Birch, pillars of the community were more than willing to plug any gaps. As mentioned in section 15 Bessie Southey, 'a household word in the parish',[20] threw herself into good works, which benefited both young and old. It is quite touching to see that when her husband H.W. died, he stipulated in his will[21] that 'as a memorial to my beloved wife' a sum of £500 should be given to the Parish of Little Birch 'to form a fund in perpetuity to be called the Southey Benevolent Fund the income from which is to be used for the relief of suffering and distress amongst aged and infirm poor persons inhabitants of the said parish of Little Birch.' In a codicil dated 17 October 1928, he changed the name of his charity slightly to the Bessie Southey Memorial Fund. In accordance with his principles, his will stated 'that no applicant for the benefit of the fund shall either profit or suffer by reason of his or her religious opinions', further amended in the codicil by the words: 'membership of the Church of England is not necessarily a qualification for this benefit.' It makes one wonder if he had been aware of religious discrimination throughout his life. He also directed that his funeral should be 'as simple as possible', and gave further bequests to the London Spiritualists Association Limited, the Merthyr Tydfil Spiritualists Society, Dr Barnardos Homes, John Grooms Flower Girls Mission, the Merthyr Tydfil Branch of the Salvation Army and Herefordshire General Hospital.

I'm sure that he would have been gratified to know that the charity which he set up in memory of his wife, still exists today and is still helping people in the village which he took to his heart.

12 Roads, Tracks and Transport

The earliest inhabitants of the area would have had little need for trackways but as soon as a network of communities, such as those living in association with the Iron Age hill forts, became established then trade routes between them would have developed. As mentioned by Alfred Watkins in *The Old Straight Track*,[1] the need would have been for such commodities as salt, flint and metals. It is being increasingly shown that there was a surprising amount of long-distance trade in these early days. Watkins suggested, though controversially, that these tracks were straight with sighting points to enable people to find their way. It seems obvious, however, that if there are no obstructions, it would be much easier to walk in a straight line! These ancient ways survive in places in Little Birch and their antiquity is particularly noticeable by the fact that they are extremely sunken. One, commented on by Heather Hurley in *The Old Roads of South Herefordshire*,[2] is the track which runs from Broughton Cross (Hollybush Lane) in Much Birch, past the drive to Strickstenning, then over the Wrigglebrook and up towards Little Birch church. Depths of six feet below the adjacent fields have been cut though exposed rock in places.

The action of feet and weather on the rather crumbly rock surface has, over time, achieved this. During winter water drains into the track and a stream runs down it, further eroding the surface down to flat bedrock in places. Known as Conigre Lane, it continued to be an important route well into the twentieth century, providing access from Little Birch to the blacksmith at Broughton Cross, and still remains a Public Right of Way. This track is part of a long straight route leading in a north-south direction which will be commented on later.

Another track continues past the church in a south-easterly direction towards Rowlston's Barn. This is also very sunken in places. Although no longer accessible to motorised vehicles, this has been an important route to horsedrawn vehicles, providing access to the several cottages along here and the settlement at Rowlston. In former times, it is conceivable that it may have continued in the

Fig 12.1a Conigre Lane. Note the exposed rock face and depth of the lane compared to the figure. The lane was used by wheeled transport in living memory

Fig. 12.1b Ruff Lane, a lane well used by horse-drawn and motor vehicles in the past. The depth can be judged by comparison with the dog

same direction to Prothither, linking with the road to Hoarwithy and a possible river crossing.

A third track, very sunken in places, runs from Green Farm to Athelstan's Wood. It is possible that this continued to Little Dewchurch. Although these tracks can be recognised for their antiquity because of their sunken nature, it is quite possible that there are others which are equally old but have not weathered in the same way.

At least one of the ancient tracks may have formed the basis of a possible Roman road through the parish.

Roman roads

One road (more properly, today, it is in some places a metalled road and in others a green lane) has attracted speculation it might be Roman in origin. It enters the parish below Yapp's Turn on the eastern boundary of Priory Stone, and follows a straight southerly line, crossing Chapel Pitch and passing the School House. Where it is joined by the green lane known as Copse Lane, its present course turns sharply south-west as far as New Road. The southward section of the latter resumes the generally southerly alignment past the junction with Bannut Tree Lane (leading to Higgins Well) past Sunnybank and past the junction with Mesne Lane. It follows the course of the road to the church until that bends eastwards and then continues as the green lane called Conigre Lane; the alignment here moves a few degrees to the south-east and then runs straight to the parish boundary at Wriggle Brook.

There are some suggestive, though not conclusive, facts to support the hypothesis of Roman origin. The road lies next to or near a number of fields or places with names or part-names that are sometimes associated with Roman activity; these include the Camps, Upper Camps, Far Camps, Lower Camps, Castle Ground, Castle Field and Castle Meadow, Walls Pool, Stoney Acre, Priory Stone and, at a greater distance — about 1.5 km, Caldicot. It must be said that, with the exception of Caldicot, none of these names is evidenced before the seventeenth century and the lack of early forms means that they are susceptible to different etymological interpretations.

The alignment of the route continues, at least briefly, beyond the parish boundaries. To the north a line of tracks and paths leads over the eastern shoulder of Aconbury Hill, across the Kings Pitts to Aconbury road at The Cots and thence to Twyford Common, south-west of Dinedor Hill. Beyond this the alignment is not clear, but, if Roman, it must have led to a crossing of the Wye somewhere. South of Wriggle Brook the route crosses Hollybush Lane and reaches the A49 opposite the Axe and Cleaver. Once again, beyond this point, there are a number of possible continuations, but none indicating a straight alignment on a modern map. Finally it may be noted that, though no agger or ditch has been found, the width of the road between Priory Stone and Copse Lane — the stretch known as School Lane — is consistent with the practice of Roman engineers; this could, however, be the result of the requirements of the commissioner for the enclosure of Much and Little Birch Common (sometimes known as Aconbury Common) between 1812 and 1824.

The alignment of the road outside the parish is an important piece of evidence because within the parish the whole question of Roman origin is bedevilled by the effects of the enclosure of the common. For much of its course in Little Birch, the road that has been described in detail above led across, or along the edge of, the common. One of the tasks of the enclosure commissioner was to lay out a system of carriage roads and driftways (tracks for driving livestock) across land to be enclosed. Into this system he incorporated a number of pre-existing old roads and tracks as well as establishing new ones. Unfortunately, the award schedule and the map accompanying it, dated 1824 and now in Herefordshire Record Office,[3] do not make it precisely clear which was which. The present pattern of roads where the common was suggests two or three dominating straight roads enabling maximum access and probably created at the enclosure, with older, minor roads linking to them. The putative Roman alignment (marked VI on the enclosure map) would at first sight appear to be one of the new access roads. This impression is reinforced by the fact that the central section of it is today known as New Road and it is described in the enclosure award as leading into an 'old road', probably before the hill that climbs to Sunny Bank.

In theory the first edition of the Ordnance Survey map should clarify these uncertainties since the survey for it in this area was conducted in 1815 when very little of the enclosure had been accomplished. However the first edition was not printed until 1831 and incorporated revisions taking account of the changes which had occurred in the intervening 16 years. Thus although the name Aconbury Common survived on the map, the new system of roads set out at the enclosure has been super-imposed.

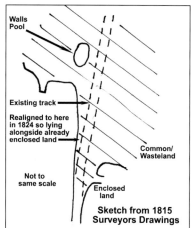

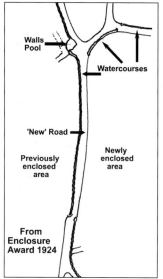

Fig. 12.2 Sketch from OS Surveyor's drawings of 1815 and from the 1904 OS map comparing the position of the track/ lane now known as New Road

It is fortunate that the original surveyor's drawing dating from 1815 survives in the British Library[4] because this tells a subtly different story.

Unlike some of the other roads, carriage road VI is clearly present in 1815, except that in the case of one section it has a very slightly different course from that established at the enclosure and persisting today. At the junction with Copse Lane, rather than turning abruptly south-west towards Walls Pool, it appears to continue straight on across the lower part of the field below Well Orchard, which was then part of the common. It is easy to see, looking at the 1815 drawing, why the enclosure commissioner might have decided to alter the course of the road. The original course left a long, thin and narrowing sliver of common land between it and the enclosed fields on the other side of the valley (Banky Field, Lower Meadow and Lower Camps). This would have been expensive and awkward to enclose, and, once enclosed, largely valueless to whomever it was allocated. It made much more sense to move the road so that it abutted the three old fields, making provision for the regulating of the little stream that ran from Walls Pool to Higgins Well along the west side of the re-sited road. This rejoined its original course — the 'old road' referred to in the enclosure award — at the point where it met the lane up to Ordnance Cottage and Bannut Tree Lane, and it was quite logically called 'New Road'.

There is, of course, an element of speculation in this argument. It does not prove that the School Lane — New Road — Conigre Lane alignment is definitely Roman, but it does suggest it is not entirely the creation of a tidy-minded nineteenth-century surveyor. Final proof one way or the other would depend on further detailed study. It would be helpful if there were a regional study of Roman roads such as that carried out in the south-east Midlands by the Viatores (see section 3), this would provide information about the road system into which Little Birch alignment might fit. Finally, this alignment itself would need the scrutiny of aerial photography and judiciously focused excavation.

Tracks remaining from Roman and prehistoric times would, if convenient, have continued to be used through the Dark Ages and medieval periods. Others would have developed as required by trade, stock movements, or other reasons.

Turnpike roads

In the eighteenth century road improvement took place for the main routes in the county. These roads were improved and maintained by the Turnpike Trusts which levied tolls for their upkeep. Although none of these roads actually ran through Little Birch parish, they ran either side of it. The King's Thorn road was then the main route between Hereford and Ross and the turnpike road was built along this line in 1726. (The present A49 between the school and the top of the Callow was built in the 1830s). There was a tollhouse at the top of the Callow, by Cross-in-Hand Farm (named because it was a cross-roads where roads to Monmouth and Aconbury and Dewsall left the Hereford to Ross road). This tollhouse survived until the 1960s when it was a casualty of a road-straightening/widening scheme. Local people still remember the last resident who always wore a black trilby hat in an unusual fashion and who displayed a notice 'No Water', showing little consideration for boiling radiators at the top of the Callow. The proximity of this turnpike road to the King's Thorn area and parts of Little Birch would have greatly improved access to Hereford and Ross. It possibly ran through Broughton Cross, i.e. down Hollybush Lane, and would therefore have been easily accessible from Little Birch church.

The other turnpike road ran along the Hereford to Ross road which passes through Little Dewchurch and Hoarwithy. This was constructed in 1730. It would have provided improved access to those living at the south-east end of the parish. There was a tollhouse on this road opposite the road from Little Birch at the junction still known as Caldicot Pike. This was still standing, an attractive building with wide eaves, up to the early 1970s although it was derelict. It was demolished to improve vision at this crossroads (though improvement due to its removal is debatable). The verges adjacent to this site are very wide, a legacy of the time when animals being driven would collect while the dues were paid. A monthly account for 'Aconbury Gate' survives for part of 1801 for James Hereford Esq.[5] This shows that his men were obviously regular users, passing through most days. For each passage he was charged 1s 7d for 19 horses and 1s 6d for a wagon and four horses. His total bill for May was something over £1 16s. This was probably not a great deal to a gentleman such as James Hereford, but would have seemed a lot to the common man and more than some people were prepared to pay, so the driving of animals to market may have involved other routes. One such from Little Birch and King's Thorn may have been along Ridge Hill. There is anecdotal evidence that, at some stage in its construction or re-construction, the stone for Hereford cathedral was transported via this route from a quarry near Much Birch.

In the eighteenth century there was still a substantial unenclosed common area known as Aconbury Common, but tracks obviously existed across this for access. As parts of the common were enclosed by squatters, routes would have become more restricted. The surveyors' drawings produced in 1815 for the first Ordnance Survey map show the situation at that time, with the well-used tracks across the common denoted by a double dotted line. These included Barrack Hill, Chapel Pitch extending to Green Farm, and a track past the school towards Sunnybank Farm. The latter two were leading towards the sunken routes which then continued to Little Dewchurch and Broughton Cross. As mentioned in a previous section, much of the original common had already been enclosed by this time so routes such as Parish/Laburnam Lane and Little Birch Road were already enclosed routes.

Enclosure tracks

The Enclosure Award lists all the existing tracks and those to be created giving some idea of the status and history of them. This has been responsible for the resultant complicated network of roads and tracks, which were then mostly given names by local people for ease of describing the neighbourhood. Some names were descriptive but others related to people then living in the cottages nearby, names which feature in the censuses at times from the 1850s onwards. This type of local naming obviously evolves, although it does seem to have stagnated in these days of house names, postcodes and a more mobile population. The map below labels these lanes as remembered from the early 1900s. They are labelled by Roman numerals on the Enclosure map dated 1824[6] but will be referred to by name in the information given after the map.

A road leading from the top of the Thorn along Little Birch Road and Mesne Lane to Little Birch Church is described as:

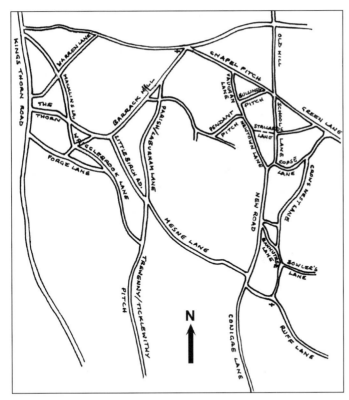

A public carriage road and driftway [for driving animals], thirty feet, branching out of the turnpike road leading from the City of Hereford ... in a south easterly direction then and over said common or waste land of said parishes of Much Birch and Little Birch unto and uniting with a Common King's Highway in the said parish of Little Birch which leads towards and unto the parish church of Little Birch.

Fig. 12.3 Map giving the local names of all the lanes in Little Birch and King's Thorn

This implies a well recognised thoroughfare along Little Birch Road and its continuation as Mesne Lane.

Another description of interest is the track which leads from the chapel to Green Farm:

> A public carriage road and driftway of thirty feet leading from the parish of Aconbury alongside and over the said common or waste land of the parish of Little Birch beginning near or adjacent to the said public carriageway No. III [Barrack Hill] at the confines of the parish of Aconbury and continues from thence in a south easterly direction unto and uniting with a common road in the said parish of Little Birch, leading from thence towards the turnpike road from Hereford to Ross at a place called Hoarwithy.

It is not clear from this where the track joined the turnpike road although an arrow on the map points to Hoarwithy along the track from Green Farm to Merrivale Farm. This would seem a less than direct route.

A third description of interest is of the track which runs from the top of the Barrack Hill down Old Hill, past the school and then continues from Walls Pool along New Road:

A public carriage road and driftway of thirty feet also from the parish of Aconbury in a southerly direction crossing the said public carriage road V [as described above] unto an ancient road in the said parish of Little Birch leading to the village of Little Birch.

As mentioned previously, this reference to an ancient road implies some recognition of the fact that this track must have existed for a very long time. The reference to the road leading to the village of Little Birch shows that the area around the church, much more inhabited then than now, constituted the village. The nucleus of housing which grew up on the common round the well thus became known as Newtown. The name New Road may refer to the fact that it led to Newtown or, alternatively, that it was created anew at the enclosures. It is undoubtedly built up and drained well on either side, the creation of the watercourse on the western side being mentioned in the enclosure details. The track in this area on the OS surveyor's drawing shows no 'kink' at the bottom of School Lane, (in fact it appears to run on a line further east than at present) but this 'kink' has been created by the enclosures — possibly to take account of the new watercourses and to create more convenient boundaries for new fields.

The other tracks created were all provided for access to property from, or provide links between, the above tracks. They were all described as 'private carriage roads' and many referred to the name of a person owning the allotment. Some reference is made of roads passing 'between old enclosures' implying, as shown on the surveyors' drawings, that many little pockets of land were already enclosed on the common or surrounding it. One track in particular, which leads past Prospect House and on into a field, refers to 'an old inclosure belonging to ... Gilbert and others'. This road would have led to the strip fields which were once part of an open system and clearly each enclosed strip still belonged to someone different.

When these roads were created, responsibility for maintenance fell on the parish. They would have only been able to afford to maintain the more important routes and the private carriage roads would be left to the occupants of the nearby houses. Maintenance would only have consisted of drainage, where possible, and stone surfacing. The road down to Higgins Well was a problem to maintain as mentioned in the Parish Council minutes.[7] Conigre Lane, so called because it runs alongside two fields called Upper and Lower Conigre which were the site of a rabbit warren, was obviously causing trouble earlier. It was mentioned in the Parish Minute Book in 1840 when a meeting was called:

... for purpose of considering the best means of repairing Conniger Lane so as to make it a proper Teaul Road [(we have been unable to find out what this is). The meeting resolves to ask that]... voluntary subscription be entered into for purpose of defraying the expenses of erecting an arch over the brook and widening the road leading and stoning it ...[8]

There is no further mention of this in subsequent minutes so it is unclear whether any work was done. The lane is still very narrow, barely wide enough for a cart in most places but people remember horses and carts using it in the first half of the 1900s so the surface must have been much better then than now.

In 1862 the inhabitants of the Parish of Much Birch requested that the inhabitants of the Parish of Little Birch would 'meet them as they ought to do by Subscribing Something towards it', 'it' being the alteration of the King's Thorn Pitch to make it less steep. This was carried out by a Joseph Cooke who charged upwards of £70 which 'falls heavily on the rate payers of Much Birch [who] consider that the parish of Little Birch will benefit the most by the alteration'.[9] Donations were received from three people: Rev Stephen Thackwell gave £10, G.H. Bonner (Church Farm), £1 and Mrs Bonner, £5. It would seem that Much Birch was rather out of pocket! However, the work done would certainly have reduced the steepness of the pitch for those with horses and carts or carriages.

After the 1890s, when councils were created, most roads became the responsibility of the Rural District Council. (Coniger Lane obviously did not.) Road maintenance then involved the laying down of bluestone, which is very hard, which was then covered with crushed stone to provide a smoother surface. The ditches, officially the responsibility of the adjacent landowner, were also maintained. As transport progressed from horsedrawn, solid-wheeled vehicles to those with pneumatic tyres, the comfort of travel must have improved enormously. Further improvement came with the laying down of tarmac in the late 1930s. The decision as to which of the roads should benefit from tarmacing and which not, appears largely haphazard. There was undoubtedly some influence brought to bear in the appropriate quarters, which although giving a comfortable ride to certain people at the time, has made it necessary for drivers to make lengthy detours nowadays.

Some formerly important routes have reverted to footpaths, such as Chapel Pitch, whilst others have become upgraded, such as Barrack Hill, now a far too busy through route for those trying to avoid Hereford's traffic jams. Two notably important routes which were not selected were, firstly, the top of School Lane leading into Old Hill, an obvious direct route up to Barrack Hill but which is now mostly a grass track and registered as a byway. The second is the lane past the church known as Ruff Lane. This would be another route to New Mills, Rowlston's Barn and ultimately to Little Dewchurch. The Rural District Council obviously realised the omission in the 1950s and attempted to make it more passable for wheeled traffic by laying down large quantities of bricks from the destruction of Harewood House. Only occasionally used, the lane has gradually deteriorated to be only fit for horses and walkers, although it remains an unclassified, unmaintained highway.

Transport

In early times there would, of course, have been very little in the way of transport. Horses would certainly have been here in the Iron Age, not so much for riding but as beasts of burden. Primitive carts were also used later in the period. The Romans who, almost certainly, would have been travelling in this area rode horses and had efficient chariots. The width of a Roman road was, of course, a suitable width for a chariot together with sunken edges for drainage.

During the Dark Ages and medieval periods, tracks would have accommodated both horses and carts but the majority of transport of goods would still have been on foot and the distances travelled in a day limited by this. In this area the tracks were often in very poor condition meaning that walking or horseback was the only sensible option. Even though carts of various types did exist it is unlikely that there were many around here. The small population and the simplicity of their requirements at this time would have meant that there was little need for transport apart from the wealthier people and those involved in military activities. Increasingly, oxen and heavy horses would become used for heavy transport of such things as timber and would also be used on the land and for transporting crops.

With the rise in the wealth of the upper classes after the Civil War, the development of a wide range of carriages took place. Again, it would have been unlikely that many, if any used the tracks on Aconbury Common. With so few people living in houses of any size, the wealth of the area was insufficient to support such extravagances. In addition, the tracks would have been in a poor state. The only people likely to have owned a carriage would have been the Gwillim family who had relatives scattered over South Herefordshire.

With the building of the turnpike roads in the eighteenth century, carriage and cart transport would have become easier outside the immediate area. The use of pack horses would also have been less arduous. At this time it is likely that transport for people in and out of Hereford or Ross became more of a reality. Indeed, by the second half of the nineteenth century carters, carriers and hauliers were appearing in the censuses[10] meaning that trade was obviously lucrative enough for them to earn their living in this way. By 1871, Stephen Thackwell employed a coachman and had already built a coach house in the 1850s so there was at least one coach on the roads of Little Birch by then.

By the twentieth century deliveries were being made on a regular basis in the area using horse and cart. King's Thorn shop, in particular, had its own cart with the name proudly displayed, and later progressed to a van.

Some of the older residents remember their parents talking of a horse bus. A problem for people returning from Hereford in such a contrivance would have

*Fig. 12.4 The horse and cart owned by King's Thorn shop pre-1914
and used for deliveries*

been the steep hill up the Callow and then the King's Thorn road. This journey, however, was made less arduous than previously by the realignment of the turnpike road in the late 1830s thus avoiding the very steep hill up to Callow village but also, sadly missing the old hostelrie there called the Guy's Head (previously the Duke of Chandos' Head, reflecting the change of ownership of the estate).[11] This is now Callow Farm. There was by then, however, The Angel Inn at the bottom of the new road so thirst could be quenched here before the climb which, for many passengers, would have been on foot to lighten the load for the horses. (The Angel is now also closed).

Fig. 12.5 The van used by the shop in the 1930s

Railways were, of course, becoming available for longer distances by the mid 1850s but the nearest stations were Holme Lacy (more than four miles distant) or Fawley for Gloucester and London trains and Tram Inn (slightly further away) for the Welsh trains. The latter was much used by H.W. Southey of Castle Nibole who would frequently travel down to Merthyr Tydfil to edit his paper. He relied on local carriers to transport him to and from the station (see section 15).

The coming of the bicycle was obviously an important advance allowing poorer people to travel greater distances to work, whereas previously they had relied on walking. It enabled some to ride to the dam being built at Llanfiangel then cycle home again afterwards — an exhausting day's work. The richer people, however, were acquiring cars by the 1920s/30s. One well-remembered car was the Rolls Royce owned by the Parishes at The Old Rectory. On election days local people were offered lifts in it to the polling station as long as they said they voted Conservative! The car was, allegedly, fumigated afterwards. The Morgan brothers of Mount Pleasant and Model Cottage both bought Morris 8s in 1937, being the proud possessors of cars in an area where most working men did not own them. The Bibbys of The Follies also owned a car and later a lorry.

During the Second World War petrol rationing reduced car travel and horses and carts became the general mode of transport again. A few cars were pressed into service on the land.

Motor bikes became a popular form of transport after the war, particularly amongst the younger men of the area.

Regular bus services began in the 1930s by Wye Valley Motors from Hereford supplemented by local enterprise (see section 14).

By the 1970s bus transport had dwindled due to the inexorable rise of car ownership. Although an hourly service continues to run along the King's Thorn road, a bus only travels round Little Birch on Wednesdays. Though invaluable for a few people, it is little used. Almost all households now own at least one car and they are a necessity for many older residents, in particular.

Despite the proximity of the A49, the roads remain quiet and the area peaceful. Speeding on the twisty lanes is not easy and consideration is shown to people on foot or horseback, often with a cheery wave. There are, of course, exceptions which tend to be associated with travel to and from work or school. Problems do occur when large delivery lorries attempt to negotiate the lanes, most firms either not possessing or not sending smaller vehicles. It is amazing, however, what large vehicles can negotiate and a well-remembered occasion occurred in 1991 when a large cedar tree fell across the A49 causing lorries and double decker buses to be diverted down Trewenny Pitch and Wrigglebrook Pitch to get to the King's Thorn road.

It is interesting to be able to still see the legacy of the common and enclosures in the form of the maze of lanes and tracks in the area.

13 Church, Chapels and Schools

Church

The history of the Church cannot be treated in isolation as it is intimately connected to that of Aconbury. At this moment in time, Aconbury Church is all that remains of what was an important Augustinian Priory founded by Margery de Lacy in the time of King John (1199–1216). Until the Reformation, Little Birch Church was known as a 'chapelry' of Aconbury but after the Reformation, the incumbent was described as 'Rector of Little Birch with Aconbury' and lived in Little Birch.

The first reference to the church is in the *Liber Landavensis*[1] or Book of Llandaff, under the name of *Birches Beata Maria* or St. Mary's, Little Birch. For centuries, both churches were in the district called Irchenfield, frequently mentioned in Welsh writings as Ergyng, anciently governed by independent Welsh princes and listed as being a subsidiary of Gwent. There was a dispute as to which bishop was responsible for Archenfield. Hereford had laid claim to certain parishes and Llandaff sought clarification from Rome. A bulletin of Pope Honorius enumerated the churches of Archenfield and confirmed that they were under 'the Jurisdiction of Bishop Urban of Llandaff. This bulletin of 1254 listed 24 churches including *Birches Beata Maria*.

The recorded list of incumbents dates from 1304 but many of these were vicars or rectors who were often 'absentees', the real work being done by curates. That first mention appears in one of the Court Rolls of the manors of Aconbury and Caldicot dated the 'Sunday after the feast of St. Andrew [30 Nov] in the 32nd Year of the reign of Edward I [1304], when 'John, the chaplain of the Birches and two brothers ... being attached for a trespass ...'.

In the *History of the Deanery of Archenfield*, it is stated that Little Birch is one of the few parishes in the Hundred of Wormelow for which a list of Church Goods is preserved from an inventory carried out in 1550. The list is very meagre, representing the few articles of metal and needlework which had escaped the earlier spoliation of the Church under King Henry VIII:

A chalice and paten of silver parcel gilt, weighing 8 oz

Two bells

A corse bell, rung about the parish on the news of a parishioner's death and
carried at the head of the funeral procession

A cross of brass

A censer and a 'tinnacle' of brass (probably meaning a sacring bell that was
swung at the elevation of the elements in the Eucharist)

A chasuble of blue satin with an alb to the same

Three altar cloths of plain cloth, with a towel

A cope of black saye

A painted cloth before the high altar[3]

In the Hereford Record Office there are presentments for the Bishop's
Visitation to the parishes and the following extracts are shown for Little Birch
in 1716.[4] The document lists 39 questions with spaces for the incumbent to give
answers. The questions covered the state of the fabric of the church, its appurte-
nances, how worship is conducted, the moral state of the parish, where the incumbent lives and much besides. The answers report that the roof of the church was
well covered, the windows were well glazed, the floor was paved and even, and
the inside walls were white and kept clean. There was a reading desk but no pulpit
— 'It has always been so'; a communion table kept suitably covered; a chalice, a
flagon and two patens kept exclusively for the use of the church; a decent font; a
comely surplice; and a large Bible 'in the last translation' and a Book of Common
Prayer in good condition. The churchyard was well fenced. There was a parish
register and yearly returns were made to the Register Office as the law required.
Entries in the register for the previous 7 years (1709–1715) were as follows: 1
marriage, 28 christenings and 12 burials. On the Lord's Day, there were prayers
twice a day and a sermon or homily every fortnight, the times for the prayers being
at 10 in the morning and 3 in the afternoon. There were no (attached) chapels. The
service was always read entire as prescribed in the Book of Common Prayer.

To the questions 'How often and at what times doth he chatechize in the
church? Do parishioners send their children and servants for instruction?' came
the answers 'In Lent and as often as children are brought to him.' Baptism was
always in church except in cases of necessity (illness); in such cases, if the child
recovered, he/she was presented in church as the law required. The sacrament of
the Lord's Supper was administered four times a year. As for visiting the sick,
preparing them for Holy Communion and for their departure into the other world,
came the response ' He doth carefully to his knowledge'.

No school, hospital, or charity school was reported for the parish. It was
recorded that churchwardens were chosen every year by joint consent of the minis-

ters and the parishioners, and that they had always handed over their accounts, money etc. to their successors. The parish clerk/sexton was noted as performing his duties, particularly that of keeping the church clean.

The list of questions continued. Regarding that concerning fornicating, incest, adultery and blasphemy in the parish came the answer 'None to my knowledge'. As for people working on the Lord's Day?, 'None'. Likewise there were no dissenters or meetings of dissenters in the parish, nor any who refused to pay rates for the repair of the church etc. As to whether there was any ecclesiastical officer who had exacted more than the legal fees — 'We know not'; and as regards any of them who had accepted a bribe to dismiss or excuse an offender who has been presented — 'We know of none'. No public penances had been performed.

To the questions, 'Hath the minister [at that date, Richard Traherne] a parsonage house? Doth he reside personally upon his cure? If not, where and at what distance?', Traherne's responses stated that there was no parsonage house either in Aconbury or Little Birch, and that he lived in Hereford which he rather optimistically describes as being within 2 miles of Aconbury and within 3 miles of Little Birch. He did, however, state that there was a curate residing within about a mile of Aconbury and within a half mile of Little Birch.

Other information about the church can be drawn from the early Parish Registers which are held in the Hereford Record Office.[5] The first contains entries of baptisms, burials and marriages from 1557, and those for the first 40 years may well have been entered from loose papers at the end of the sixteenth century. The early pages are particularly difficult to read as they have darkened with age and the entries on them, making allowances for palaeographic differences, are in poor handwriting whilst the ink has often faded.

Matters improved in 1611 with the induction of William Higgs as rector. His handwriting is clear and he set out to give the register status by making the entries in Latin. At the end of most years he signed off the register with his own name and the names of the churchwardens for that year which at that time, before the reform of the calendar, began on 25 March. Higgs, who was rector for 53 years until 1664, kept the register in this manner for more than 40 years until 1653. In that year, his entries ceased because an Act of the Commonwealth government removed the task of keeping the register from the minister and placed it in the hands of locally chosen laymen. Normal entries by the minister were resumed in 1660. In 1742, a new general register was begun which was used until 1812. From 1775, a separate register was kept to record marriages under new government legislation. Parish marriage registers are held for 1755–1812, 1813–1837 and 1837–1893. There is a separate register for baptisms from 1813–1884.

The Parish Minute Book from 1840[6] is held in the church safe and gives a good background to the functioning of the parish at that time, recording the

Annual Public Vestry Meetings for Ratepayers of the Parish at which elections for the posts noted in the table below were held.

In the nineteenth century, the system of local government developed haphazardly until the Municipal Reform Act of 1835, which established the rule of elected councils although their actual powers remained small. In country areas, local government remained in the hands of the Justices of the Peace who assembled in Quarter Sessions until the Local Government Act of 1888 which set up County Councils. Little Birch Parish Council was established in 1894. *The Parish Chest* by W.E. Tate[7] outlines the duties of the various Parish Officers and extracts of their duties given in the following table are taken from this book.

Officer	Origin	Appointment	Duty
Churchwarden	At least as early as the 12th century	In various ways – at the annual Vestry Meeting or by agreement of minister and parish. Traditionally, often one is vicar's warden and one is parish warden	To act as guardians of the parish church, its fabric, contents, churchyard etc.
Constable	At least as early as the 13th century	Appointed originally by manorial courts, later by Justices of the Peace from nominees at Vestry Meeting	Maintaining law and order; duties relating to militia musters, collection of rates and taxes
Overseer of the Poor	By Acts of 1572, 1597 and 1601	Appointed by Justices of the Peace from nominees of Vestry Meeting. Act of 1601 required at least 2 in addition to the Wardens who were deemed ex officio.	Relief of the poor through the operation of the various Poor Law Acts
Waywarden (Surveyor of Highways)	Act of 1555	Before 1691, chosen by constables and wardens advised by a meeting of parishioners. After 1691, by the Justices from a list of nominees prepared by the above	Supervision of maintenance of highways through the labour of parishioners or via commuted cash payments

The Annual Meeting also agreed the parish rate for the ensuing year and approved the Churchwardens Accounts for the past year. The churchwardens were responsible for collecting 'the rates' — not always an enviable task. References to parish expenditure on roads are very few but the Conigre Lane leading from near the end of the Mesne Lane down to the Wrigglebrook stream, past Strickstenning and up to the forge at Broughton Cross and on to the Axe and Cleaver and the main road, was often mentioned for repair as it carried a good number of heavy horse wagons bound for Little Birch and Aconbury. The lane from the church down to Higgins Well (sometimes referred to as Bowdlers Lane) also had to be kept in

Fig. 13.1 Sketch of the first Little Birch church, drawn in 1838. Much smaller than the present one, it had 13 box pews, a pulpit among them, a small gallery and large porch and entrance on the south side

good repair as the well provided a constant supply of good spring water and was used by many of the parishioners for drinking and domestic needs and for farm animals. The rates were also used for the relief of the poorer people, widows, orphans, burial expenses, the support of occasional vagrants and the upkeep of the church premises and the churchyard.

The present church building is thought to be the third stone building on the site. The first stone building which existed in 1838 and shown above, had a small square tower at the west end and was probably a development of an earlier building. At the Annual Parish Meeting in 1840, it was decided to form a committee for the 'Purpose of raising funds to build a new and larger church'. The chairman was the rector, the Rev Henry Hampton, together with the Rural Dean of Archenfield, the churchwardens named as James Bennett of New Mills and Thomas Preece of Bromley, Sir E.F.S Stanhope Bart. and Mrs Pugh of Ballingham.

In August 1840, the plan for the new building submitted by the architect, Mr. Henry Adams, was chosen and an agreement was made with Mr Pugh of Ballingham to raise sufficient stone from his quarry at 3d per cubic yard. The land quarried was probably situated at Lower House Farm and had to be left in a level state and the road to it in good condition. Tenders for the building were considered on 23 November and that of Mr George Follett of Hereford was accepted. The architect was instructed to draw up a contract between the committee and Mr Follett.

It seems that progress by the builder was very slow and at a meeting in November 1841, it was decided to give Mr Follett an ultimatum that if the building was not 'covered in' by 6 December 1841, the contract would be terminated. No further reference to the building was made in the Parish Minute Book but it was in use for worship in 1842. The entrance porch was situated at the west end of the nave under the tower.

Fig. 13.2 Sketch of the second Little Birch church drawn in 1858. Somewhat larger than the first with 44 box pews in three rows, a large gallery on a side wall and entrance under the tower at the west end

In 1855, the Rev Stephen Thackwell was appointed rector. He enlarged the rectory (opposite the church) and built a new school in 1857 and the two Model Cottages situated above it, all at his own expense. In 1868, he obtained a faculty for the necessary works to restore the church building. One item was to erect a spire on the tower, the cost to be defrayed by the rector. The project was aban-

*Fig. 13.3 The third, present, Little Birch church in the 1920s.
Note the pond next to the driveway to Church Farm*

doned in favour of a complete rebuild. This building had only been used for 27 years and the sketch above shows a tall square tower with a nave and chancel. There was also a gallery on the north side. The reason given for building a new church was that 'the present building no longer met the needs of the people', but it seems likely that there had also been some Jerry-building' in the early 1840s.

The present church, the third stone building on the site, was built in 1868 at a cost of £3,500, paid for by the Rev Thackwell. The architect was Mr W. Chick of Hereford and the builders were Messrs. Coleman of Churchill, near Gloucester. The carving throughout the church was carried out by Mr Welsh junior, of Hereford, and the building is paved with 'encaustic' tiles from the factory of Mr William Godwin. The Clerk of Works was Mr Lewis Powell and the foreman was a Mr Halliday.[8]

The new building was to be slightly larger than the existing by lengthening the chancel and by adding a 10 feet wide north aisle, which compares to the nave's width of 18 feet. Both are 49 feet long. The chancel, which is formed by a polygonal apse, measures 18 feet by 15 feet and has on the north side a small vestry. The style of architecture is 'Early Decorated'. The principal entrance is by way of a porch on the north side. The nave is lighted by two cinquefoil and two quatrefoil windows built alternately for architectural effect and all filled with painted glass by Messrs. Hartland and Fisher of London. There is a west gable window, the circular centre of which was replaced with a new design in 1986 following gale damage. This design and the installation was carried out free of charge by Mr H.J. Hobbs, a local craftsman, erstwhile of Tump Lane, Much Birch. In the north aisle, there are four small two-light windows. The chancel has five traceried windows, similar to the nave except that they are more highly cusped. The west gable is surrounded by a bell-tower in which is hung a bell weighing over 4 cwt., cast by Messrs. Taylor of Leicester. The whole of the external stone dressing, beyond that which could be re-used from the previous building, was supplied by Mr John Trask, from the Ham Hill Quarries in Somerset. The internal dressings are worked alternately with Ham Hill and Bath Stone, and throughout the building the mouldings are undercut, so as to produce the effect of light and shade. The seating and woodwork generally are of deal but the chancel, stalls and upper portion of the pulpit are executed in oak. The roofs are all open timbered, with boarding on the back of the rafters and a layer of asphalt placed between that and the tiles. The whole of the timber exposed to view is stained and varnished. The principals of the roof are supported by corbels on each side. The altar and reredos were a gift to the church made anonymously in 1899.

A new wall was built round the churchyard using Ham Stone for the piers, copings and a 'string' course towards the base. The church was opened in 1869 when the building was consecrated by the Bishop of Hereford. The organ was built by Graham-Davidson of London and installed later that year. It had one manual only but an upper manual was added by W.G. Vowles of Bristol in 1910 when the organ was rebuilt. It was hand pumped until 1963, when electricity was brought into this village and an electric pump was installed.

The oldest object now in the church is the stone font. In Jakeman and Carver's 1890 *Directory* it states that among relics from the old church were the Norman font dated 1260 (which has been carefully restored), communion table and a funeral bier of 1557.[9] In Thomas Coombe's

Fig. 13.4 The Norman font (the plinth is much later). The oak cover was made by Roger Wilkins in the 1990s in memory of Christopher Marshall

Illustrations of baptismal fonts of 1844,[10] many Norman examples are illustrated, some with the cable moulding found at Little Birch, but there is none so simple as this one which may therefore predate the earliest references to this site. Prior to the building of the present church, it was said to be found in a neighbouring cottage (Yew Tree Croft) where it apparently fulfilled a number of secular functions, including washing potatoes!

The church possessions include an Elizabethan chalice and cover paten. In *The Church Plate of the County of Hereford* by Scudamore, Stanhope and Moffat,[11] the chalice is described as an Elizabethan cup with the bowl having straight sides but the upper part having been roughly hammered out and the shape quite spoilt. The base appears to be the original. The cover paten is quite plain with a rather slender handle. On the face of the handle is inscribed 'Letvl Bvrche, 1576' within two circles. On the under side are distinct traces of the old pre-Reformation paten. This is the only case found in Herefordshire of the re-use of the old plate in the time of Elizabeth to make the new. A letter from the Rev H.P. Marriot Dodington, rector in 1884, states that an old inhabitant informed him that the chalice was originally used in the belfry for the bell-ringers' cider, at which time its stem was broken.

A funeral bier hung above the church entrance door for many years, but at a PCC meeting in 1971, the rector, Rev. John Pitchford, said that it had been removed. No explanation was given.

Fig. 13.5 The Chalice and ciborium (right) with the inscription on the top of the ciborium (above)

A memorial in granite to the men of the parish who lost their lives in the First World War stands on the roadside area of the churchyard. The names of the men recorded are: Frank Cooke, Osmund Creed, Thomas Day, Thomas Nash, George Rooke, Hubert Rooke, Richard Small, Harry Southey (son of H.W. Southey) and Gabriel Townsend. No men from Little Birch were lost in the Second World War, but Clifford (Tony) Morgan (brother of Percy Verry) was sadly killed.

Several items have been donated to the church in memory of former members. These include the lectern light in the pulpit in memory of Mr David Dyke, a churchwarden for many years; an Altar Copy of Series 2 Orders of Service in memory of Mr Robert Dyke; the oak carved lid to the font in memory of Christopher Marshall an erstwhile treasurer and churchwarden; a chalice given in memory of Mr Reginald Cooper in 1972, an erstwhile church member; a wooden bench in memory of Miss Frances Rose Lawrence, sometime sacristan here and erstwhile head teacher at Much Birch school; a wooden seat given in memory of Vida M. Kirk of Greenlea in 1965 now situated on the south side of the church; and, at the west end of the church, a bed of roses planted in memory of Mrs Ellen Kitchener.

Under the Town and Country Planning Act 1971, the church building was listed as Grade Two Star and the part of the churchyard wall with Ham Stone copings previously mentioned was given a Grade Two rating. This means that any proposed alterations have to be approved by English Heritage and are likely to be very expensive!

Fig. 13.6 Aerial view of the church and Church Farm in the early 1990s

Recent Vicars

Reference is made elsewhere in this book to the philanthropic and energetic ministry of the Rev Stephen Thackwell. He was buried in the churchyard in a grave marked by a granite plinth near to the vestry door, which he used almost every day in coming from and returning to the Rectory.

Rev Walter Fitzwarine Smith was rector from 1890 for 25 years and he too was a fastidious priest and chairman of the school managers. For some reason he lived at Much Birch, and died in 1915.

The next rector was Rev William L. Groves who was an excellent priest and who made friends with all parishioners. In turn, the residents felt they could always turn to him for help and advice. At the time of his ministry Little Birch separated from Aconbury and was joined to Much Birch. The vicarage at Much Birch was situated where the Pilgrim Hotel now stands and Little Birch Rectory was sold. The Rev Groves was ably assisted by his curate, Rev C.E. Ind, who officiated at Little Birch for 13 years. He lodged with the Badham family at Walnut Cottage, situated in what is known locally as Page's Pitch, just along from the bottom of the Barrack Hill. Under his leadership, there was a very good choir whose members included the three Bowen sisters from Church Farm — Lena, Ethel and Peggy, together with brothers Hugh and Ron. Mrs Dyke and Frank Cooke were also members. Rev Groves also ran a successful Sunday School. From his vantage point in the choir, Frank Cooke remembers that Mr William Powell used sign language so that Mr Tommy Yapp, who was profoundly deaf, never missed the sermon.

The Rev G.H. Dyer-Wright began his ministry in 1941. By 1952 he was in poor health and found that the big vicarage and garden, not to mention his parish work, was becoming too much for him and he became something of a recluse. He died in 1956 and was succeeded by Rev Albert Butterworth, known affectionately as 'Bertie'. He was a bluff genial character and was well liked in the two parishes. He lived at Birch Lodge, adjacent to Much Birch Church, formerly the home of the late Dr Maurice McGinn, and he gave part of his garden for an extension to the churchyard. In one of his Sunday sermons, he spoke in favour of corporal punishment and this was found to be very amusing by one of the congregation, being spoken from Much Birch pulpit. The story even made the national press.

Rev Butterworth retired to Weston-super-Mare and was succeeded by a young curate and his family from the St Martins team. Following the sale of Birch Lodge, Rev John Pitchford and his family first lived in Hollybush Lane while a new rectory was built in a field purchased from the Old Cedars.

In 1968, Mr Bill Mattingley was appointed organist and choirmaster at Little Birch and with his wife, Marjorie, kept this choir together for five years or so. Marjorie made 10 cassocks in 'Madonna blue'; keeping them at home and well pressed for every service. Marjorie and Bill transported the choristers to and from home each week after having played the organ for morning service at St Martins in Hereford, such was their dedication. The choir members included the Manning sisters — Gail, Stella and Jill, Sarah, and Kate Mullins, Sharon Kirby, Rosamund Atkinson, Stephen Turner and Jonathan Atkinson. Bill was presented with a silver dish inscribed 'With grateful thanks from Little Birch Church' on his 'retirement', which was caused by the alteration in times of the service. Mr Mattingley was still going strong at the age of 97 but had to move into a retirement home in North Wales near to his daughter, Joy. Sadly Marjorie passed away in 2005 and Bill died just 13 months after.

In 1972, a new benefice was formed by joining the parishes of Much Birch and Little Birch with Much Dewchurch, Llanwarne and Llandinabo and Rev. Pitchford was made the first Priest in Charge. At this time, the annual fête was organised by Much and Little Birch PCCs and was usually held at Much Birch school. Alterations were made to the interior of Much Birch Church but the parishioners of Little Birch resisted any changes being made to their church with its stained glass windows, wrought iron candelabra and screen.

The Rev Leslie Rhodes who had retired from Urmston, Manchester, became assistant to Rev Pitchford and was typical of a clergyman who had worked in industry for many years before taking up Holy Orders. He was very much in tune with people and brought a wealth of experience with him. He lived with his wife Mary, in Llanwarne and was very popular in all five parishes. At Little Birch he was instrumental in the formation of a Sunday School which flourished for some ten years. He 'retired' for a second time in 1979.

Rev Peter Newby succeeded Rev John Pitchford in 1980 and he again was a very popular priest. He was assisted by Rev Frank Morley from 1981 to 1986 and this gave Paul Wilson, who had retired from BBC films and trained as a non stipendiary priest, the opportunity to assist Peter Newby. Paul is fondly remembered for his work in the community with his wife, Anne, taking over the running of the Scouts and Cubs which flourished, forming the 'Pop in Club' and being an industrious visitor to the sick and elderly in all five parishes. Anne and Paul 'retired' to Staunton on Wye in 1994.

Christopher Hollowood's tenure as priest in charge only lasted three years during which David Enoch, who had also retired from the BBC, trained for Holy Orders and was ordained as a priest in 1992. He assisted in the benefice as a non-stipendiary priest for several years and in 1994 was appointed priest in charge of the Kings Caple group of parishes which he served for six years as a well loved and respected priest with great help from his wife, Mary. He retired in 2000 but sadly died in 2002.

Alan Jevons was appointed priest in charge of the five parishes in 1992. Alan and his wife, Susan, who was also a Methodist preacher, worked extremely hard in the benefice and soon after their arrival, their second son, Lewis, was born, a brother for Owain. Alan was also made Rural Dean of Ross and Archenfield Deanery during which time a reorganization of the Deanery took place. As a result of that process, Kings Caple and Sellack parishes were joined to the Birch Group and Hentland and Hoarwithy joined the St Weonards group of parishes. Alan was moved to the Tenbury Wells group of parishes in August 2002.

Kay Garlick, who was one of the first women to be ordained in Hereford Cathedral, had spent a number of years as chaplain to the Hereford Sixth Form College, resigned that post and was installed as priest in charge of the Birch Group in January 2003. She has brought an energetic enthusiasm, her musical talents and an empathy with all age groups. The Birch Group was renamed 'The Parishes of the Wormelow Hundred' in 2004. Kay was appointed to the Archbishops Council in 2006. For a full list of incumbents, see Appendix 2.

Chapels

The Methodist Movement was founded by John Wesley in 1739 within the Church of England but became a separate body in 1795. A series of doctrinal divisions in the early 1800s caused a split into Wesleyan, Primitive and United Methodists. These divisions were healed in 1932, uniting the three into the Methodist Church.

In Little Birch, there were two Methodist chapels in existence for some 70 years: the Primitive Methodist Chapel at the top of Barrack Hill (still an active place of worship) and the Wesleyan chapel at the far end of the 'green lane' leading from Model Cottages towards Green Farm. The date at which the Wesleyan chapel was established has not been found but in the sale details, reference is made to deeds dated 1851 and 1867 and the building is recorded in the 1861 census. It was closed about 1910, being described as a single-storey chapel with a stable adjoining that had been served by 'itinerant preachers'. Consent for the sale was given by the Wesleyan Church Committee based in Manchester and included the following: '... taking all possible means to secure the premises against being used for the manufacture or sale of intoxicating liquor or as a theatre or dancing or music hall.'[12] It was sold to a William Parlby of Castle Cliffe, Hereford in 1911 for the sum of £20 and the following year he obtained an estimate to convert the chapel into a two-storey house and this was duly followed through. Parlby then approached the Stallards of Shrub Cottage with a view to buying adjacent land on which was an orchard with a ruined cottage. After protracted negotiations, a sale was agreed. The dwelling is now known as Saddlebow View and has been altered

Fig. 13.7 The eastern end of the former Wesleyan Chapel, now Saddlebow View

and enlarged in recent years.

The origins of the Primitive Methodist Chapel are well recorded in documents kept by the Hereford Methodist Circuit.[13] In 1834, there was an Assignment of a plot of land from Mr W. Robins and his mortgagee to Mr John Morton and others as Trustees, for the erection of a chapel for the use of the Primitive Methodist Connexion. A building was erected later that year but no details of its construction are given. Chapel Cottage was shown to be in the occupation of John Morgan, a sawyer and Primitive

163

Fig. 13.8 The Sunday School members in 1946. Those pictured include:
Back left, Bet Jones (Geoff Jones' mother) who played the organ at chapel,
then Mrs. Bellamy. Back right, Peggy Davies, below her Colin Davies.
First row left 'Happy' Andrews, seated left Tony Andrews. Others include three
Verry girls, Iris and Beryl Ruck also, possibly, Brenda Ruck, Ken Powell, Gillian
Field, David Hart, Thelma Davies – apologies for any omissions or mistakes

Methodist preacher in the census for both 1851 and 1861, but in 1871 and 1881 it was occupied by a John Cordy, described as a shopkeeper. The first chapel is likely to have been a mainly wooden building but a new and larger stone chapel was built in 1858 and, in 1859, new Trustees were appointed. The chapel has been served by preachers in the Hereford Methodist Circuit after the departure of John Morgan. In 1879, it was registered for the Solemnisation of Marriages.

There was a thriving Sunday School here from at least the 1900s and more recently the records[14] show 19 scholars in 1937, 27 scholars in 1948 and 20 in 1965.The teachers were Mr Sid Watkins, Miss Watkins, Miss M. Dyke, Miss Austin, Mrs Williams, Mr Trevor and Mrs Doreen Roberts (née Skyrme).

Scholars named in the registers include:

1937	1948	1965
Pearl Barrell	Joan Andrews	Rosemary Bishop
Irene Crum	Tony Andrews	Wendy Brown
Mary Crum	George Ashburner	Brian Gardner

Enid Davies	Patrick Davies	Carol Gardner
Joyce Devereux	Lilian Gwynne	Janet Matthews
Linda Gwilliam	Nell Gwynne	Mary Morgan
Constance Hirons	Beatrice Jones	Neville Morgan
Beatrice Jones	Peter Longworth	Daniel Price
Lily Morris	William Martin	David Price
Amy Powell	William Oliver	Gwyn Price
Dulcie Powell	Gordon Owen	Clive Roberts
Edith Powell	Michael Parry	Elwyn Roberts
Irene Sirrell	Dorothy Powell	Jennifer Roberts
Iris Sirrell	George Powell	Margaret Roberts
Doris Verry	Jimmy Price	Kevin Townsend
Edith Verry	Beryl Ruck	Peter Townsend
Eileen Verry	Brenda Ruck	Susan Townsend
Jean Verry	Michael Ruck	Timothy Townsend
Phyllis Verry	Kenneth Sant	Anne Wooles
	Valerie Sant	John Wooles
	Derek Taylor	
	Colin Verry	
	David Verry	
	Evelyn Verry	
	Olive Verry	
	Thelma Verry	
	Sandra Waite	

Keith Newman reopened the Sunday School in 1976 and kept it going until 1986. Scholars included:

Jackie Baker
Mark Blossett
Ben and Rebecca Danks
The Hancock girls
Tanya and Tony Lewis
Diane Lloyd
Sarah Mason
Nicola and Paul Newman
Lorna and Lee Standen
Roxanna, Kate and Ian Walker
Helen Wrigley and the Pritchard girls

Mary Newman took over as organist from Elvira (Vi) Baldwin on her demise in 1984 and the harmonium was replaced in 1993 with an electric organ given by the Doody family in memory of their parents, Ken and Sheila, who were stalwarts of the chapel for many years. Keith Newman has kept the building in very good order, both inside and out, and the electric tubular heating has been upgraded in recent years together with double-glazed windows. A new stone entrance porch and doors were constructed by Stephen Turner and Roger Wilkins.

Fig. 13.9 *The Methodist chapel in 2000*

The Rev D.A. Hewitt was minister from 1962–1967, in 1984–1989 Rev William Bethel, 1989–1992 Rev Susan Spencer, 1992–1995 Rev Rosie Coulter, 1995–2000 Rev Andrew Renshaw, 2000–2002 Mr John Wells, 2002–2005 Rev Liz Morris and from 2005 Mr Paul Dawson. Since 2000, links between the chapel and church have grown stronger thanks to the energy and enthusiasm of John Wells and Ken Compton and, at present, joint services are held on the second and fourth Sundays of each month.

The Gospel Hall on the Barrack Hill started sometime in the late 1880s. The services were evangelical and 'Believers' baptism' was performed by total immersion of the candidate. Open air services took place on King's Thorn Common (a well-grazed area where the bus shelter now stands) on fine summer evenings from the early 1900s and the hymns were accompanied by a harmonium. Services were led by Mr. Leonard Cox of The View and the Gillander family who were also prominent members. The building ceased to be a place of worship in the late 1930s and was converted to a house. It is now known as The Hall.

Fig. 13.10 *The former Gospel Hall in 2000, now known simply as The Hall*

166

The Schools of Little Birch

The National Society for Promoting the Education of the Poor in the Principles of the Established Church (1811) set up schools in which basic literacy and numeracy as well as religious knowledge were taught.

The Rev. Henry Hampton was named as the sole Manager of the school in 1841 and it is reasonable to assume that he was the founder of Little Birch and Aconbury School in 1840. It had one schoolroom with 35 boys and 28 girls on the register. James and Jane Jones were the Master and Mistress with an annual salary of £20. Reference is made to the school in the Terms of Union with the National School dated 23 April 1841;[15] a copy of which is shown overleaf. No records of the site of this first school have yet been found but local tradition refers to two possible sites, one at Yew Tree House and a more probable one in a barn (see map alongside) in a field 80 yards north-west of the church. At the time, this property

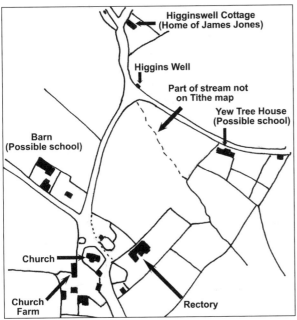

Fig. 13.11 Map showing possible sites of the first school in 1841 (based on the Tithe Map of 1841)

Fig. 13.12 Date stone removed from the demolished barn, the possible site of the first school

Fig. 13.13 Sketch showing all that remains of the first possible school building

was part of Lower House Farm but possession of the field later passed to Church Farm. The Bowen family who farmed Church Farm from 1922 to 1988 found spoil from a boiler fire when tidying around the barn and also a large cobbled area. The barn was pulled down over 30 years ago and only one wall of a fold, which was built at right angles to the barn, can be seen at the present time. In the 1841 census, James Jones was listed as a schoolmaster, and in 1851 his wife, Jane, was still shown as the schoolmistress whilst James was listed as a mason and Parish Clerk. No other information has been found about the running of the school.

Coincidentally, the 1841 census lists a Miss Martha Hodges of Rose Cottage (now Uplands) as a schoolmistress (see p.102), but this is likely to have been a private school which had closed before the 1851 census was taken as at that date Rose Cottage was the home of a William Smith, Barrister at Law, with his wife and four children.

The first reference to the building of a 'New School' for the parishes of Little Birch and Aconbury is found in the Parish Minute Book[16] on 7 August 1857 when at a Vestry Meeting 'A Copy

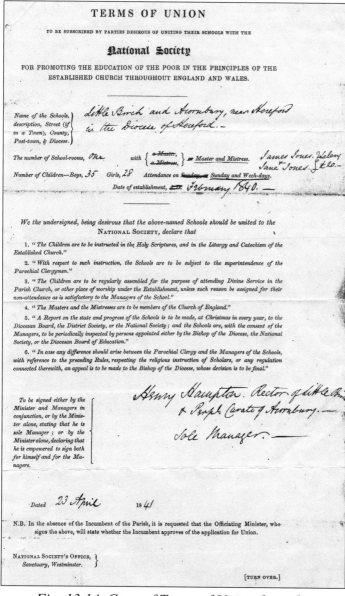

Fig. 13.14 Copy of Terms of Union from the National Society dated 1841 for the first school at Little Birch

of a Deed of Gift of Land' for the proposed school was read, discussed and ordered to be placed in the Parish Chest. Those present were Stephen Thackwell, rector and chairman (who had donated the land); John Lawrence, churchwarden; William Green, churchwarden; William Paine and James Jones, Parish Clerk.

The Church of England Education Foundations in the Diocese of Hereford records[17] that the Little Birch Church of England School was comprised in a deed dated 12 February 1857. No record of the building of the school has been found but it was paid for personally by Rev Stephen Thackwell and his initials were stamped on the weathervane, still to be seen on the east gable of the building. It was situated here as the midway point between the extremities of the two parishes and had accommodation for 81 children. The Trustees were the rector, the Archdeacon of Hereford, the churchwardens and the nominated

Fig. 13.15 The bell-tower on the former Little Birch School. Note the initials 'S T' on the weathervane (Stephen Thackwell)

managers. It was set up as a Voluntary C of E School governed by the managers who appointed the teachers and who were responsible for the day to day running, with the syllabus set by the Diocesan Education Committee.

According to Arthur Armitage, the land agent, in his report[18] to Thomas Turner Esq., Treasurer of Guy's Hospital, on 16 March 1857, 'As Incumbent of Aconbury, Mr. Thackwell has from the Govs. a donative stipend of £40 per annum and from Queen Ann's Bounty £12. He happens to be a man of ample means that built at his own cost an excellent school and house in Little Birch for the united parishes which he maintains with the aid of the govs. who give him £5 per annum and the Govt. grant earned by the school.'

The *History and Directory of Herefordshire*, 1858[19] shows that a National School for boys and girls was in existence with a Mr John Preece as master. He was followed in 1861 by a William Baker who in turn was succeeded by James Liddington in 1871 with his sister, Elizabeth as assistant.

The school was closed in January 1882 due to the building lapsing into disrepair. There is a Minute Book of the meetings of the School Managers from 1882 to

1939[20] and at a meeting on 17 August 1882, it was agreed to notify the Education Department of the Managers' intentions to carry on the school as a voluntary one under a Certificated Master. It was also decided that an advertisement for a master be put in the *School Guardian*, requiring someone who was married or had a sister living with him who could teach sewing. The salary would be £40, half the 'weekly pence' and house and garden rent free. It was also decided that the Treasurer should obtain estimates for the necessary repairs to the house and school. The preferred applicant declined to take up the post and so a Mr Bridgland and his wife from Birmingham were appointed and they took up their duties on 9 October, when the School was reopened.

Each of the first two children in any family had to pay 2d per week and any further children from the same family were charged 1d per week. To put this into context, the cost to a family sending three children to school would be 5d out of an average income of 96d per week, so that it is not surprising that some children were often sent home because they had not brought their 'weekly pence'.

There are two schoolmasters daily log books starting from when the school reopened on 9 October 1882.[21] There were then 28 scholars attending who Mr Bridgland remarks were very backward. The log books give a picture of a very rural community, with strong-minded parents and children, struggling to conform with Church School secular and religious requirements under difficult conditions.

On 16 November there was deep snow and only 16 children attended. In January 1883, a severe outbreak of measles closed the school but in February there were 41 students on the register. At this time, school holidays were very short; for example, the school closed for the Easter holiday at 12 noon on Maundy Thursday for the weekend, but the scholars had to return on Easter Monday morning, but were given the afternoon off. On 9 May, school was closed at midday so that the students could attend the traditional May Fair in Hereford. In June, there were 62 scholars but the master had to attend the County Court because one family were in arrears with their fees and an Order was made by the Court for the arrears to be paid by monthly instalments. The summer holiday began on 22 August to allow the children to help with harvesting. School reopened on 8 October and on the 19th all were taken to the church for the Institution of the new Rector, Rev H.P.M. Dodington, by the Bishop of Hereford, Rev Thackwell having died in April. The Christmas holiday began at 4pm. on Christmas Eve, Christmas Day was a whole day off but the children had to return to school on Boxing Day! In the early years, there were just two classes, the Infants and the senior pupils. After the turn of the century, the classes comprised

Standard I	3 to 6 years of age
Standard 2	7 to 9 years of age

Standard 3   9 to 11 years of age
Standards 4&5   12 to 14 years of age

The general standard of reading and writing at this time was acceptable, but the standard in arithmetic was poor. Indeed, a school inspectors report in December 1885 was quite scathing of the academic standard of the pupils, which led to the resignation of W. Bridgland in February 1886. Another problem concerned the bad time-keeping of the pupils, especially during periods of bad weather. It was therefore decided to start in the mornings at 9.30am. and to finish 30 minutes later in the afternoon at 4.30pm. There were only unmade paths and lanes leading to the school, which in winter were very muddy and caused no end of problems in keeping the school clean as no doormats were provided. When heavy rain or snow prevailed, attendance was very much reduced as many parents could not afford to buy adequate shoes or boots. In winter, the heating was inadequate as there was only one open fire grate. In the summer months the lanes were extremely dusty which again added to the problem of keeping the school clean. All the written work of the infants was done on 'a slate' using chalk but the older pupils were allowed to use pen and ink on paper. The outside toilets were very basic and there was no running water. There was no space for playing games within the school boundary but a limited amount of play took place in the lane outside. Some children went home at lunch time but most of them lived a long way from the school and brought whatever meagre amounts of food that the family could provide.

The minute book of the school managers' meetings is very difficult to read, especially in the period from January 1883 to November 1890 when Rev H.P.M. Dodington was chairman and correspondent. His handwriting was very poor and he often used 'Old English' spelling by using the letter 'f' in words with a double 's', e.g. 'Mifs' for 'Miss' and his own abbreviations for many other words. In these early years there were many meetings of the ratepayers of the two parishes to try to resolve how much each parish should pay for the running of the school. As in all situations like this, there were very heated discussions.

In February 1886, Miss Edith Whitemarsh was appointed as Mistress with Miss Wightman as her assistant. In March, the managers offered the mistress 'a salary of £24 per annum in addition to all the school pence of the Standard children and one half of the gross Government grant.' It was also decided to pay the assistant, in lieu of a fixed salary, all the pence of the Infant children and one-fourth of the Government grant with the Rev Dodington giving her in addition £15 and guaranteeing that the original amount of £30 should not be decreased. As one would guess, this level of salary did not attract the highest grades of teachers and many of them resigned after only a few months or years in the post.

On 1 February 1891, Mr and Mrs A. Davies were appointed master and mistress with a combined salary of £80 per annum. Almost a year later, on 15 January, Mrs Davies died in Burghill Asylum aged 41 years, her death being 'precipitated' by influenza. However, Mr Davies had to keep the school open having given notice that he would relinquish his position on 31 January.

In the midst of this traumatic period, a school inspection took place and the subsequent report stated:

> The discipline of the School seems to be somewhat better than it was at the last inspection and some improvement is manifest in the style of the Reading but with these two exceptions, no advance has been made since last year. The Infant class seems to have been entirely neglected and the elementary work of the Standards is a complete failure. Some allowance must of course be made due to the exceptional circumstances of the past year. Needlework is unsatisfactory throughout. Unless the school is brought into more efficient condition before next examination, it will be my duty to report it inefficient under Article 86. More Reading books are required. Modern maps of the World and Europe are also needed.

Mr and Mrs Sharp commenced their duties as master and mistress on 22 February 1892 and worked hard to improve the academic standard of the pupils for eight years under fairly difficult conditions. An 1894 H.M.I. report highlighted the need for a good blackboard and that damp patches were prominent on the classroom walls and that the lighting and entrances to the 'offices' are very unsatisfactory.

Little work was carried out to the school structure until a grant was sought in 1897 towards the £135 estimate for carrying out essential repairs. The National Society granted £15 for this work, but no other aid was ever sought from the Society.

A presentation from the parishes of Aconbury, Little Birch and parts of Much Birch was made to Mr. and Mrs. Sharp for their work in the school and the community generally at their farewell in 1900.

Several other masters and mistresses were appointed over the next few years but one character should be mentioned. On 16 October 1905, Mr Edmund Sillence and his daughter, Hester, were appointed teachers. A Miss Elizabeth Jones born 1894 and interviewed by John Clench in 1986, aged 92 years, well remembered her time at Little Birch school. She lived at Newtown Cottages at the bottom of Pendant Pitch, which were pulled down and later rebuilt. Her neighbours were the Watkins family with daughters Edie and Beattie. Her best friend was Gladys Humphries who later married another pupil at the school, Noah Cutter, while she, with a glint in her eye, said she had a soft spot for Guy Sillence, son of the master. She produced a copy of the first photograph taken of the 49 pupils with the master, Mr Sillence in 1907/8. This photograph is reproduced below and she is stood on the extreme left at the back with Gladys Humphries next to her. After leaving school, she went into 'Service' at Aberaeron, near Aberystwyth. The H.M. Inspection in 1907 gave a very poor report of the school and of the very frequent absence of the master through 'illness' (he spent a lot of time at the Castle Inn). He resigned in 1911.

Fig. 13.16 School photograph taken in 1907/8. The headmaster on the right was Mr Edmund Sillence. Elizabeth Jones is standing on the extreme left at the back, Gladys Humphries is next to her and Polly Jones is on the extreme right. Others mentioned at this time who may or may not be pictured are Gwen Oliver, Alice Webb, Gladys Verry, Florence Andrews, Annie Hollingworth, Fanny Bruton, Agnes Davies, Mary Jones, Grace Hancock, Oswald Monkley, George Day, William Baldwin, William Prosser, Harold Wanklyn, Harold Monkley, Robert Dyke, David Dyke, George Andrews, William Morgan and Roy Davies

Several of the entries in the Masters Log Book and the Minute Book of the School Managers' meetings are given below to illustrate the day to day incidents over the 100 years of the school.

1882	6 Nov.	Several children kept in 15 mins. after school for neglecting their lessons.
1883	19 Nov.	Attendance very fair, 59 in afternoon. Several girls kept in after school. Annie P's mother came and ordered her home.
1884	13 May	William M. caned for swearing in school hours.
	25 July	Miriam H. kept at home more times this week on the plea of being ill over a subtraction sum last week.
1885	22 May	Arthur J. absent in the afternoon through being kept in 20 mins. and going home late after playing in the road with other children.
1887	7 Jan.	School opened after Christmas with snow on the ground – 34 children, no infants. Snow has been falling all week, consequently attendance very poor; only 1 infant on Wed and Thurs and none on Friday. One girl absent all week with yellow jaundice.
1888	10 Aug.	Eliza M. came to school and brought her sister with her (a baby 1 year and 10 months) as her mother had recently died and the managers consented to try the child at school as there was no one at home to look after it.
	17 Aug.	William Verry and Charles Whitcombe away this week 'binding'.
	15 Oct.	Hop picking being over for this year, more children attended school, 67 being present this morning.
1890	3 March	Scolded the boys for making gaps in the garden hedge.
	24 March	Opened school after very low attendance over last two weeks due to mumps and flu.
	1 Aug.	First day off school for the children to attend Much Birch Flower Show.
1891	6 Feb	Friday – school broke up for a week after H.M. Inspection.
	6 May	Poor attendance today (38/61) due to the May Fair in Hereford.
1892	6 June	Only 40 children present, it being Club Feast at Wormelow Tump(?)
	25 June	Attendance is again bad, partly due to measles and partly to some children detained to help in the hayfields and gardens.
	27 July	School was reopened today by permission of the Sanitary Authorities following redecoration.
1893	2 & 12 May	Half day holidays given for Club Feasts at Little and Much Dewchurch.
1893	30 June	Attendance has been poor this week due to fruit picking and sore throats.
	20 July	Holiday given for tea party at Rectory.
	16 Oct.	Highest attendance so far this year – 71.
	27 Dec.	School opened after short Christmas holiday.
	29 Dec.	The end of school year. Statistics: Total number of times open: a.m. - 206, p.m. – 200, total - 406 Average attendance per day: boys – 25.8. girls – 27.4, total – 53.2

1894	31 Aug.	School dismissed for 4 weeks holiday.
	1 Oct.	On account of the lateness of hop picking, holidays extended 1 week.
	16 Nov.	The School Concert took place today so no school was held.
1895	15 June	Diocesan examination by Rev. Thomas Bevan, Rector of Woolhope.
	30 Dec.	Managers agreed a contract with George Court of Lyston in the sum of £122 to carry out alteration to the school buildings as specified by the Education Department. A 3d rate in the £ to be collected in Aconbury and L. Birch to defray the cost.
1896	5 May	14 children were vaccinated at the school this afternoon due to the prevalence of Small Pox in the neighbourhood.
	15 June	Whooping Cough and Chicken Pox are causing many children to be absent.
	July	National Provincial Bank made another loan of £40 in addition to the £60 already advanced.
	22 August	Afternoon playtime will begin at 3.15 and last till 3.25 until further notice.
1897	23 March	Government Report: 'This school has been at a great disadvantage this year. It was closed on Acct. of sickness for six weeks in the Spring and attendance was greatly reduced in the Autumn from the same cause. Allowance therefore must be made for shortcomings and on this Acct., the Grants are recommended at the same rate as last year, but Grammar and Geography should improve if the higher grants are to be claimed again. There should be more intelligence in Reading and less weakness in writing and Spelling. Discipline should also be stricter, especially in the Infant Class. A beginning has been made with Swedish drill. Two good cloakrooms have been built and the 'Offices' have been enlarged but by the present arrangement, there is only one approach to them for both girls and boys. The Directress reports the Needlework to be fair, but a continuation of the higher grant is recommended on consideration of the special difficulties of the year. Improvement will be looked for in this subject another year.' The Registers must be tested by the Managers at least once a quarter at irregular intervals, as required by paragraph 6 of Appendix 2 of Instructions to Inspectors. Attention is directed to Article 85(d) of the Code. No grant is payable under Article 105 as the Staff during the past year was not sufficient for the requirements of that Article. My Lords are unable to recognise A.F. Sharp under Art. 68 as H.M. Inspector reports that she does not give her whole time to School work, being absent about half an hour every morning after 10 o'clock
		Signed W. Fitzwarine Smith – Rector. March 23rd 1897
1897	3 May	Letter from Bishop calling for the formation of a Diocesan Association of schools according to the Voluntary Schools Act 1897. Agreed to send 2 reps. To a Diocesan Meeting to discuss propositions. The National Society awarded the school a grant of £15 towards a total cost of £135 for repairs and improvements to the building. Public Meeting to be called to discuss a Memorial to commemorate Queen Victoria's Golden Jubilee.

	14 June	A half holiday given today on account of Jubilee Festivities at Bryngwyn Park.
	6 Dec.	School closed for a few days on account of Master breaking his leg.
1898	26 Jan.	Managers decided to call for a rate of 2d in the £ to be collected in May and again in November.
1899	8 Jan.	Drawing Examination held this day. 14th result Award – Good.
1903	Oct.	Board of Education letter objecting to the two teachers being paid a combined salary.
1907	11 Jan	Letter from Education Dept. asking Managers to consider the poor HMI report and also asking the nature of the Teacher's illness. The correspondent feared that he 'imbibed too much' and gave him a written warning.
	7 May	Half day holiday for a Tea at the Gospel Hall.
	23 July	School closed for 5 weeks due to an epidemic of measles then holiday to 24th September to help with the harvest.
	Oct.	Report on the building states that 'There is not a sound window frame in the School.'
1911	28 March	The teacher, Mr. Sillence, resigned and the school closed until July 1st.
1912	11 May	Commenced Gardening Class. Received 5 spades, 2 forks, 3 drag hoes, 3 Dutch hoes, 1 rake and 5 trowels and seeds from Kings Acre Nurseries.
1914	8 Sept.	Demand from Education authority to convert present 'Privies' to Earth Closets and to lay on a water supply. Education Authority would not give any financial help.
1915	April	School Managers agreed that the Whitsuntide holiday this year should begin at haymaking and 5 weeks summer holidays should be taken in the Blackberry Season.
	Oct.	Rev. W. Fitzwarine Smith resigned as Chairman of the managers due to ill health.
1916	31 May	Rev. W.L. Groves elected to the position of Chairman and Correspondent.
	Nov.	School harmonium found to be defective.
1918		HM Inspector's report was very critical of the scholastic standard but conceded that there had been much illness amongst the children.
1924		Managers agreed that anyone using the school for concerts other than for School funds should pay a fee of 5 shillings. Care should be taken as the staging for concerts was rotten.
1925	March	Letter from LEA reprimanding the Managers as the new grate in the school had been installed without their permission.
1928	Feb.	Assistant teacher resigned as she said she could no longer work in the same room as the head teacher.
1929	Oct.	Reconditioned piano bought for £12 from Duck, Son and Pinker and the old one sold for £3-10 shillings. A hanging Aladdin Lamp was purchased for £2-5 shillings for the schoolroom.
1932	March	Piano had become inoperative – the teacher was asked not to place flowers on it.

May	Mr. Leonard Cox of The View offered a portion of ground at the bottom of his field for a playground. The Managers proceeded to the site to inspect it and on their return agreed that, subject to LEA approval, T.A. Matthews, Solicitors should proceed with the conveyancing of the property. Messrs. Paine and Watkins should obtain estimates for a gate and necessary fencing. A letter of thanks was sent to Mr. Cox and it was agreed that the parish should make a dry and sound path from the school to the playground.
Aug.	Mr. Leonard Cox offered a quarter of an acre of his field for the playground. This was gratefully accepted and Messrs. T.A. Matthews were authorised to draw up the Trust Deed.

Fig. 13.17 School photograph of the infant class in 1931/2. This was taken in the lane, notice the Public Library sign beside the door. Those pictured are: Girls L to R: Alice Lemon, Joan Broad, Elizabeth Morgan, Eddie Scrivens, Gladys Scrivens. Boys, middle row L to R: Aubrey Hodges, Peter Thomas, Monty Hodges, Geoff Jones, Bill Andrews.
Boys, back row L to R: Donald Morgan, Ronald Morgan

Fig. 13.18 School photograph taken in 1935. Those pictured are:
Back row L to R: Monty Hodges, Donald Evans, Aubrey Hodges, Fred Wooles,
Geoff Monkley, Dennis Walker, Geoff Jones, Percy Verry
Middle row: Hilda Andrews, Jean Cox, Margery Powell, Dorothy Monkley,
Joyce Haines, Nadine Merrick, Alwyn James
Front row: Gilbert Wooles, Ronald and Donald Morgan, Tommy James,
Bob Morgan, Florence Wooles, Muriel Cox, Peggy Morgan

1933	16 May	Rev. W.S. Groves had recently died and the Managers observed a 'One Minute of Silence' in his memory. The new rector, Rev. J.R. George was welcomed.
1934	1 Nov.	It was agreed by the Managers that the supply of milk for the children should be given to Mr. Trist of Well Orchard Farm.
1935	6 Sept	Agreed that the supply of milk should be passed to Mr. Keating of Well Orchard.
1937	5 Oct.	Miss Pritchard, the teacher, proposed to commence poultry keeping classes. Managers agreed to make a grant of £4 from school funds to enable her to make a start in her new undertaking.
1938	14 June	The chairman was asked to communicate with the County Council and the Ministry of Health with regard to a water supply for the school, asking them to expedite a water scheme for the benefit of the parish and the school. Letter to be sent to Mr. W. Jones asking him to keep his poultry off the school playground.
	11 Aug.	Managers discussed a proposed scheme of the LEA to provide pensions for Supplementary Teachers and a resolution was passed supporting the scheme. It was also agreed to support and cooperate with the scheme for building a Senior School at St. Weonards.
1939	15 June	It was agreed that the wall and gate to the schoolhouse should be repaired also the bell chain.

There is no record of any meetings in 1940 but Rev. George had died and in 1941 Rev. Dyer Wright was welcomed. The other managers were Messrs. Paine, S. Watkins and D.H. Dyke. Mr J. Bibby was elected to fill the vacancy in the management caused by Mr T. Bowen leaving the district. No managers meeting recorded in 1942.

1943	Jan.	Agreed that Miss M.E. Powell be appointed Supplementary Teacher to succeed Miss Lena Bowen who had resigned after 10 years service.
		Education Committee be asked to provide school dinners to those wanting them.
	Aug.	Letter from Education Comm. Re providing school meals if they were paid for. Managers agreed they could not meet the cost.
1944	Dec.	Discussed supply of Calor Gas lighting for the school.
1946	March	Agreed to pay Mr. Bibby £38 for putting water pipes into school and £10 for tapping his private pipeline.
		Severe winter weather with snow and ice – impossible for vehicle to deliver meals from Hereford to the school, so senior boys had to walk to King's Thorn and bring them back.
1947	Oct.	Miss Pritchard retired and managers opened a presentation fund with £5. No subsequent note of the presentation or how much money was raised.
		It was decided to sell the poultry house to Miss Pritchard for £1-10s-0d.
1948	Feb.	It was agreed to sell the surplus furniture in the schoolhouse for £15.
1949	Nov.	Miss Hughes, headmistress, complained of lack of doors on the lavatories and stated that the chimney stack on the schoolhouse needed attention.
	Dec.	Letter from Education Authority stating they could make no grants for structural alterations or repairs.
		Repairs to playground fence; agreed to put wire netting on the inside and barbed wire on the outside.
1950	June	Rev. Siney from Diocesan Education Dept. attended to explain the implications of the new Education Authority with regard to Church Schools.
		Managers decided unanimously that the school should elect to become a State School rather than Voluntarily Controlled.
		Also agreed that Mrs. F.K. Davies should become a permanent assistant teacher.
1953	July	Mr. Bibby resigned as a manager and tributes were paid for his service to the board. A new managers appointment was now in the hands of the Parish Council.
	Aug.	Mr. E. Paine resigned and it was resolved to ask his son, Stafford Paine to fill the vacancy.
1958	Dec.	Mr. Hugh Bowen welcomed as a new manager.
		Letter received from the Local Education Authority with reference to the intended closure of the school by September 1959.

		Over the previous 90 years, the average attendance was about 50 (apart from exceptional circumstances of severe weather or illness) but over recent years numbers had declined.
1959	July	Ministry of Education could not make the final decision date for closure until after July 24th which was the expiry date of the public notice regarding objections to the closure. In practice, the school would, in fact, close on July 24th and the children would be notified that in September the over 11s would go to Redhill Secondary Modern School and the juniors would go to Much Birch school.
		A letter from the Diocesan Board of Finance[22] had been received requesting the Managers that, on the actual closing of the school, to notify them on order that the property might be legally reverted to them and a sale negotiated, if thought desirable.

No reported further meetings were held and the recollections of Iris Lloyd and Anne Rooke are that no celebrations were held and there were no records of presentations to staff. There were only some 18 pupils attending at the time of closure. Mrs Evans, the head teacher, bought the property for £600 and lived there whilst teaching at Redhill School but she then moved into Hereford while Mr Evans remained there until his death in 1976. The property was sold in 1979, completely refurbished and made into one dwelling.

Fig. 13.19 The former school and schoolhouse in 1979 before renovation

14 Recollections of some of the older Little Birch area inhabitants

Early Memories and the First World War

No-one alive today can have first-hand memories of life in Little Birch before the First World War. However, a generation ago there were such people, and one of these was Sidney Powell, the uncle of Bill and Tom Powell of Green Farm. Mr Powell died in 1977 at the age of 84. He had been a gardener and, after his retirement and the death of his wife, he came to live first at Well Orchard and latterly at Green Farm. Before their marriage, his wife had lived at Cherry Tree Cottage (now Cherry Cottage), which belonged to her brother, Joseph Rooke; he had bought it in the 1920s from the Vaughan family, to whom it had been allotted at the enclosure of the common in 1824, though the Rookes seem to have been renting it for a considerable time before they purchased it.

Mr Powell's vivid memories of the productiveness of the garden at Cherry Tree Cottage and of how villagers used their gardens a hundred years ago were recorded in the early 1970s. Throughout much of the twentieth century there were three large damson trees about a metre inside the hedge which separates the garden of Cherry Tree Cottage from Copse Lane. They were of the variety Bradley's King of the Damsons and seem to have been planted about 1920; they finally succumbed to gales in the 1980s. Before they had been planted, according to Mr Powell, there had been a line of cider apple trees there, from the fruit of which in some years as much as 300 gallons of cider had been made. Also in the same hedge there had been a Muirfowl's Egg pear tree (described in Hogg's *Fruit Manual* of 1884 as 'a vigorous small-fruited Scottish dessert pear'). The decaying stump of this tree was still visible when the hedge was laid in the 1980s. There was a fine walnut tree, cut down in the 1950s, and near the front door a fruiting cherry tree that gave the cottage its name and was subsequently replaced by a flowering cherry.

Like most gardens in the village there had been no room for a lawn. Mr Powell recalled that it had been one of the best gardens in the neighbourhood, its produce carrying off many prizes at local shows. At the southern corner there was an area for soft fruit, which produced blackcurrants 'as big as grapes'. As well as a vegetable plot, there was also a flower garden for cut flowers. At the beginning of the twentieth century, before the introduction of old age pensions, their gardens had been the main source of income for the cottagers of the village once they had retired. Mr Powell recollected that an aunt of his had made £80 a year from the produce of her garden. Fruit, vegetables and flowers were taken to Hereford to be sold in the Butter Market. Here various ingenious ways of 'adding value' were employed, of which Mr Powell provided two examples. New potatoes would be carefully cleaned and displayed in small quantities arranged in the outer leaves of a cabbage. Vegetables would often be bought by the wives of local doctors and solicitors; when they bought peas, the stallholder would offer to shell the peas for a small additional sum while they completed their other purchases in the market. What Mr Powell described, looking back in the early 1970s, is exactly what Dr H.G. Bull spoke of when the members of the Woolhope Club visited Aconbury Hill in June 1885 (see p.92).

Some long term residents of the area were interviewed in the period 2003–2006 and their recollections recorded. By 2003, one of the oldest residents was Dulcie Morgan who was born at Old Hall Cottage Pencoyd on 14 August 1908. She always lived and worked in the area, moved into Mount Pleasant on the southern slope of Aconbury Hill in 1956 and died there in 2005. Other long time residents included Geoff Jones (b.1926) of Orchard Green; Margaret Mullins of Castle Fields, Little Birch; Victor Townsend (b.1923) of Willow Cottage; John Evans (b.1930) of Castle Pool Cottage; Ivor Crum (b.1926); and Bert Verry (b.1923) of Ivy Bine Barrack Hill. Geoff Jones was the oldest resident who was born and lived continuously within Little Birch parish until he moved to Hereford in 2006.

Other contributors included Frank Cooke, born at Holme Lacy in 1917, Muriel Saunders (née Cox) born at The View, Little Birch, in 1925, John Walker born at Dinedor in 1934 and Percy Bristow who was the local police constable based at Little Birch in the 1950s and '60s. Frank Cooke came to Parish Lane in 1922, moved to a cottage at the foot of Pendant Pitch in 1947 and then to Daneswood on Little Birch Road in 1984. Perhaps not surprisingly there were some discrepancies between their accounts and the dates when events occurred.

In common with most areas many local men must have signed up for service in the 1914–18 war. Sadly eight men from Little Birch did not return and their names are recorded on the memorial in the churchyard. Several people had recollections and stories to tell relating to the war. Dulcie Morgan clearly remembered German prisoners of war, based at Ross-on-Wye, walking past her school at Holme Lacy to work on the harvest at Ballingham Hall. William Brookes, a relative by marriage of Dulcie and who worked at Aconbury Court farm carried a bullet scar sustained whilst stealing rum from German troops in France. Frank Cooke's father was killed somewhere in France in 1917 and Geoff Jones had an uncle who was gassed there. Margaret Mullins had an uncle who lived at Castle Mead and was an army despatch rider. Percy Verry recalls his father recounting his experiences in the army in France and particularly explaining that masks had to be put on the horses first in case of a poison gas attack. John Walker had two uncles from Dinedor who served in the war. One was in the navy and worked as a stoker on *HMS Hood* and *HMS Orion*.

Leonard Cox, the father of Muriel Saunders, returned from the war and moved to The View, Little Birch, for health reasons. He was a member of the Bretheren Fathers and despite ill health he toured the county giving sermons at interdenominational services. He was also a keen gardener and laid out the garden at The View where many of the specimen trees he planted can still be seen. Despite the slope he managed to level out an area for a tennis court where local people were encouraged to play. Leonard was obviously a well-respected man of many talents including a special interest in spiders and spiders' webs.

The 1930s

A major event in the village was the celebration of the coronation of King George VI and Queen Elizabeth in 1937. It started with a sports day in the field adjoining The View, continued with a tea attended by all the villagers at Little Birch schoolroom and ended with a bonfire and fireworks in the Twenty Acre field owned by Ernest Paine. Local ladies provided tea in the schoolroom. Scouts from Hereford camped around the bonfire to prevent pranksters from lighting it prematurely and joined in the celebrations.

During the 1930s people were poor and times hard. Food was not a particular problem because most grew their own vegetables and kept pigs in the gardens that were slaughtered for meat. By modern standards the local killing of pigs was gruesome. Typically, four strong men held them whilst their throats were cut. Hair was removed using burning straw after which the carcass was scrubbed in water and hung on a tripod to dry. After drying, the carcasses were cut into hams shoulders etc and cured, using salt, because there were no freezers in those days to keep meat fresh. It was common to share cuts of meat with neighbours who returned the favour when their pigs were killed later. Pigs also provided offal and lard used for baking pastry. Chickens were also kept in gardens to provide eggs and meat.

Other sources of food included pheasants and wild rabbits, usually poached in the surrounding area. Rabbits were plentiful and were also sold in Hereford to provide income. They were collected regularly by Capel Beaven who had a shop in West Street or delivered to Harry Quinsey and sold at his shop at Belmont, both in Hereford.

Many people made cider from apples grown in their own gardens. The apples were collected and the juice for fermentation extracted in mills and presses at local farms. Farms with such equipment included Merrivale and Well Orchard. One report talked of making several 40, 60 and 100 gallon, barrels each year. The product was kept in locked cider houses and usually drunk from cow horns, especially at weekends, when a plentiful supply would encourage visits from friends and neighbours.

Around this time few houses had indoor toilets or running water. Toilets were usually situated away from the house and utilised a pit or bucket. Rainwater was collected and heated in a solid fuelled boiler for laundering clothes.

Many residents recall having to fetch their water from local wells, details of which are given on pp.118-120.

Employment

In the 1920s and '30s the gentry living in the big houses and local farms were a source of much employment. Men worked on the farms, whilst the occupants of Kingsthorne House, the Rectory at Little Birch, Strickstenning Hall, Birch House, Much Birch Rectory, Mount Skippett and Lyston Court Wormelow all employed maids. In the early 1930s Major Davy at Lyston Court employed eight gardeners.

In the autumn, bus transport and part time work was provided for hop picking in the Withington area.

At this time many people lived in tied cottages owned by local farms and fared reasonably well. Those not in tied cottages often had a hard life, and many young people slept rough. Towards the end of the decade some joined the territorial army for military training and were the first to be mobilised when the Second World War started. Others left the area for work, including in the South Wales coal mines, and never returned.

In the 1940s about 14 men and boys were based at the Guy's Hospital Estate depot and wood yard at the bottom of the Thorn. They were responsible for the maintenance of all the estate houses. By then the depot was long established and there is an old photograph showing timber being cut in the adjacent Macklins Lane using a steam engine (Fig. 10.2). The depot was the first place in the area to be supplied with electricity and at that time had three sawmills with blades up to 6 feet in diameter. Normally trees were felled in the autumn, the bark removed and left on the ground for 18 months to dry. Softwood was used for fencing and building work on the estate. Hardwood was cut to planks for sale after drying at Holme Lacy. Willow was sold and used for cricket bats.

For several years the estate was managed by a man named Hood who lived at Uplands. Farm and house rents were paid to him in the estate office, a wooden hut located at the estate yard. The hut was moved in the early 1960s and can still be seen on the site just below Crossways Cottage.

There was another sawmill on the Thorn owned by Sid Watkins who employed six or seven people. It was used to point stakes for fencing and provide firewood. Sid was also a regular preacher in the chapel.

A bus service was provided for the many local people who worked at the munitions factory at Rotherwas during the Second World War.

A few residents had skilled and professional jobs in Hereford and further afield. David Dyke of Castle Nibole was an electrician who worked for the South Wales and Shropshire Electricity company that generated electricity in Widemarsh Street, Hereford, now the site of the Do-it-all store. At one time he declined an opportunity of promotion and a move to Stourbridge because he was a keen marksman and the pheasant shooting season was about to start. Others moved from local farms to jobs in Hereford. For example, Geoff Jones, who had worked for many years at Long Orchard farm, moved to the large Post Office stores on Holmer road now the site of a retail park. All the spares needed to maintain the telephone system in the area were kept there until the formation of British Telecom.

Little Birch School from the 1930s
Most of the people interviewed attended the old school at Little Birch and there are many photographs showing pupils standing in groups outside the building that is now a private house. There were two classes, one for juniors, the other for seniors. All recalled the names of two teachers, the head, Miss Pritchard, who lived at the school, and Miss Bowen, who lived at Church Farm. Total attendance was about 40 pupils.

A bell on top of the school-house was used to call pupils to school. (The bell is inscribed with the words 'Come away make no delay'. Intriguingly, the date cast into the bell is 1780, well before the school was built). None of the people interviewed talked about school lessons, but most clearly remembered outdoor activities including nature walks in the woods on Aconbury Hill, playing fox and hounds around the nearby lanes and keeping chickens at the school. It was common for older boys to disappear on nature walks and be caned the next day.

Leonard Cox was concerned that the children had nowhere to play during school breaks and so fenced off part of his field at The View for their use. Many people remember the school sports there, along with the swing that remained until the school closed in 1959.

The Second World War

Unlike some urban areas of the country the Little Birch area was not seriously affected by the Second World War. Food shortages and rationing of food were not much of a problem to people who had already learned to be self-sufficient. Rationing of basic food items was controlled using coupons in books issued to every individual. Managing these coupons must have been very difficult at Castle Nibole which was operated as a long term guest house for as many as 30 people evacuated from London and other cities.

Some men served in the armed forces but most stayed at home because they were exempted as a result of their work on farms and in forestry. Men who stayed at home were required to serve part time in the Home Guard or the AFS (Auxiliary Fire Service) in Hereford. The Home Guard was a military organisation that trained in uniform in preparation for a German invasion. The field opposite the King's Thorn bus shelter, now the site of Corner House, was used for training. In the early days pitchforks were used in drills due to the lack of rifles. Duties included night guard duty in dugouts overlooking the Rotherwas munitions factory, and patrolling the Ross and Monmouth roads. Another group was based at the Harewood End public

Fig. 14.1 The Home Guard (not the complete battalion) taken in front of the Memorial Hall in 1942. Those pictured are:
Back row, L to R: Harold Page, Eric Marshall, Arthur Hart, unknown, unknown, Vic Symonds, Fred Gaines
Middle row: Sidney Simcoe, James Edwards, Stafford Payne, unknown, Bill Townsend, Harold Wilson, Tom Helme, George Hill, Albert Boneham
Front row: Rev Redmon, Dick Dimery, ? Cooke, Lt Durrant, G.W. Godwin, George Parry, Ernie Thomas

house. As the Home Guard became more organised each member was provided with a rifle, 40 rounds of ammunition and iron rations and they had to be ready for immediate action. Training was normally on Sunday mornings with shooting practice at Harewood End. At the end of the war the Home Guard took part in VE (Victory in Europe) and VJ (Victory in Japan) parades, received individual letters from the king and were stood down. All equipment except uniforms had to be handed in.

A searchlight for spotting enemy aircraft was installed in the field opposite Castle Nibole. Around 20 soldiers were stationed there to operate it. Remains of buildings used as toilets and cookhouse are still there. The soldiers slept in tents but moved into a barn at Castle Nibole in bad weather. The searchlight was operated at night when aircraft could be heard or were expected. At least some local residents were concerned that this would invite the attention of attacking aircraft and felt safer when it was switched off.

Dulcie Morgan recalled bombs being dropped on Clover Bank near Aconbury, leaving two large craters. She and others reported a bomb being dropped on a house at Watery Lane in Hereford killing the occupants. The son of the house survived because he was in the garden shed at the time. The blast from this bomb was so powerful that it dislodged crockery from a sideboard at Aconbury Court. Towards the end of the war Dulcie witnessed the crash of an aircraft near Aconbury. It was based at Madley and all the occupants including a local girl being taken for a joy ride were killed.

Generally people felt optimistic about the outcome of the war. Social events continued as normal, although there was some ill feeling from wives and girl friends of conscripted serving men towards those who had been in 'exempted' work. The events were partly used for fund raising for returning troops. There was pride in Little Birch that all those returning were given £20 each as a result of these activities, a lot of money in those days. By comparison men returning to Much Birch received only £5.

Transport

Before the Second World War bicycles were the main form of transport for most people. One report said that in 1937 there were only three private cars in Little Birch. After the war, motorcycles became more popular, particularly amongst young men. Motorcycle service and maintenance was available at The Hall on Barrack Hill.

Public transport to Hereford on Wednesdays and Saturdays probably started with a removable canopy on a lorry chassis by Sid Watkins at King's Thorn timber yard. Dents at the Castle Inn and Phillips at Bannutree also ran buses at various

Fig. 14.2 The blacksmiths shop in King's Thorn in 1915.
(The notice relates to a Parliamentary election)

times. A regular service in the late 1930s was started by Wye Valley Motors, owned by Bill Morgan and based in St Martins Street, Hereford, using Bedford vehicles affectionately known as 'Little Birch Stage Coaches'. At first the service was only available on Wednesdays and Saturdays but increased to daily later on. It was well used by people working or shopping in Hereford. The route started at Hereford bus station and went through Callow village before doing a circuit of Little Birch.

In the 1930s many still relied on horses for transport and people remember the blacksmith at King's Thorn. Many of the shops and delivery services are also remembered well (for details of these see pp.113-115).

Entertainment and Little Birch Hall

Several people recollected sports days being held on Little Birch Road and the field behind The View, but details were somewhat scanty. A flavour of what went on is provided by an advertisement in the *Hereford Times* dated 11 July 1931 for Little Birch Sports to be held on 25 July. Events included horse jumping, motor and push cycling, clay pigeon shooting, air rifle shooting and bowling for a live pig. Also advertised were Gardeners Galloping Horses and Swingboats and King's Radio Band. The organising secretary was Mr J. Morris of Cuckoo Cottage, King's Thorn.

Fig. 14.3 The Memorial Hall in 2000

The King's Thorn Memorial hall was built jointly by Much Birch and Little Birch in memory of those killed in the First World War and opened in 1927. It is now used by scouts, and the rifle club meets in the building behind. Before and during the Second World War it was used for meetings, dances, whist drives and other entertainment. It was a very popular venue for dancing on Saturday nights. Live music was provided by the Diamond Players and the Frederick James Trio. (Frederick James lived locally opposite Much Birch garage). Another popular dancing venue for Little Birch people was the village hall at Sellack.

After the Second World War it was common for young men to cycle to Fownhope at weekends. Their ages were not known in that village and so they would be more likely to be served in the four public houses there. Around the same time groups of youths from various villages congregated in Hereford on Saturday nights. There was much rivalry and frequent fights. One interviewee admitted to being locked in a police cell after being arrested for fighting in Bridge Street and being fined ten shillings in the magistrates court.

The events at the Memorial Hall and whist drives at Little Birch school were used to raise funds for a new hall at Little Birch. It was built on land purchased from David Dyke of Castle Nibole for £65 under an agreement dated 1951. Reclaimed materials were used in its construction including roof trusses from the Rotherwas ordnance factory and oak flooring from the demolished Goodrich Court. Building did not progress smoothly. The original builder went bankrupt and it was finished by Harry Vaughan from Hereford. According to one report the ceremonial opening was performed by Mr Johnson, owner of Callow garage in 1951, but this is not confirmed by the illuminated scroll in old-fashioned script hung in the Hall which reads:

Fig. 14.4 Little Birch Village Hall in 2000

Little Birch Village Hall

This Hall was opened on Sept. 4th 1951
By Captn and Mrs Burdon.
Erected through voluntary subscription and
funds raised by the Parish under the leadership of
Mr. J. Bibby on land the gift of Mr. and Mrs. D. Dyke
For the Enjoyment of All
In Friendship and Good Fellowship

A photograph in the hall shows a large group of people present at the opening although date on the caption is 1954, agreed by all as incorrect. In subsequent years people came from all round the area to events and the New Years Eve dance in 1952 was especially successful. The hall was very prosperous until 1956 when Park Hall Ballroom, Wormelow, was opened by Amos Peel. It was then closed for some time until reopened in 1977 by a committee of local people with a new formal constitution, and registered as a charity in 1978. The timing was probably connected with the Silver Jubilee celebrations for Queen Elizabeth II in that year.

Amongst other things the new and energetic village hall committee started was the monthly *Newsletter* that was delivered to all homes in Little Birch and King's Thorn. It was very successful and in 2005 was renamed the *King's Thorn and Birches Newsletter* when the circulation expanded to include Much Birch.

The use of the hall and popularity of events have varied considerably in the intervening years. Gardening, youth, Evergreen, keep fit, line dancing and other clubs were based there at various times. Pantomimes were very popular and a total

Fig. 14.5 Those attending a New Year Party in the Village Hall in 1952

1	Hilda Andrews, Eden Cottage	24	Betty Jones
2	Jack Bibby, Folly Cottage	25	Geoff Jones, Orchard Green
3	Mrs Bibby, Folly Cottage	26	Miss Lawrence, School House, Much Birch
4	Mr Chapel, Hill House	27	Nurse Miles, Reculvers
5	Ivy Crum	28	Monica Morgan, Waterloo Cottage
6	Mrs Cutter, Folly Cottage	29	Tom Oliver, Yew Tree Cottage
7	Nora Davies, Quarry Cottage	30	Oliver, Yew Tree Cottage
8	Rosalind Davies, Dinedor	31	Mrs Oliver, Wye Cottage
9	Mr Dawson, Glendene	32	Barbara Parry, Rossway Cottage
10	Dawson	33	Amos Peel, Home Farm, Much Dewchurch
11	Jean Evans, Little Dewchurch	34	Mrs Peel, Home Farm, Much Dewchurch
12	Bill Garland, Folly Cottage	35	Beryl Peel, Home Farm, Much Dewchurch
13	Margery Garland, Folly Cottage	36	Merle Peel, Home Farm, Much Dewchurch
14	Lillian Gwynne, Folly Cottage	37	Ivor Perkins, The Glen
15	Ray Gwynne, Crossways	38	Gertrude Perkins (Polly), The Glen
16	Miss Gwynne, Crossways	39	Cathy Perks
17	Eunice Hitching, Sunny Cot.	40	Winnie Price, Dinedor
18	Nonnie Hitching, Castle Pool Cott.	41	Jack Pugh, Dinedor
19	Arthur Iles Fairview, Dinedor	42	Mrs Pugh, Dinedor
20	Dolly Iles Fairview, Dinedor	43	Leonard Smith, Fernleigh
21	Lottie Iles Fairview, Dinedor	44	Doris Verry, Mill Cottage
22	Mr Johnson, Callow Garage	45	Nurse Zappeloni, Reculvers
23	Mrs Johnson Callow Garage		

Fig. 14.6 Members of the Evergreen Club in 1981. Pictured are:
Back row L to R: Frank Short, Edgar Cutter, Wilf Roberts, John Bryant,
Percy Oliver. Front row, Iris Roberts, Daisy Short, Polly Perkins,
Linda MacCartney, Nora Oliver, in front Percy Williams

Fig. 14.7 The pantomime Dick Whittington *in 1978.*
Pictured are: Chris Wilden, John Bryant
and Paul Hitching

of 12 productions were well attended in the hall in the period 1978–1989. The first was *Dick Whittington and his Cat* produced by Phyllis Williams who lived at Hellenswood, and the last was *Arthur and the Court of Camelot* produced by Margaret Stevens (Applewick, Eden lane) and Ann Thomas (Pendant). In the 1980s the Evergreen club put on several shows including *Old Tyme Variety Shows.*

Gardening has always been popular. There was a show and sports on the Glebe field from 1977 to 1986 and annual flower and vegetable shows have taken place in most years since then in the hall.

During 2003–4 the hall committee considered options for the long-term future of the building including refurbishment and even demolition and construction of a completely new hall on a different site. The issues involved were divisive and there followed

Fig. 14.8 The pantomime Dick Whittington *in 1978. Pictured are: Roxanna Walker, Vanessa Lloyd, Kate Walker, Diane Lloyd, Wendy Guerri, Mandy Lloyd, seated John Walker*

several investigations, well-attended meetings and two referenda, required by the constitution and organised by the Parish Council, to reach a resolution. The outcome was to accept the option for refurbishment of the existing building to modern standards based on designs prepared by Robin Derham, a London architect who uses Upper House as a holiday home. Currently funding is being sought for the village hall refurbishment.

Police Constable Percy Bristow

In 1956 a new police house was built next to the village hall. (Earlier policemen and their families lived at Sunny Cot opposite Castle Nibole). The first occupant was Percy Bristow who was, by all accounts, a well-respected pragmatic man who carried out his duties with fairness and humour. He retired in 1964 and at the time of writing is almost 90 years old and still living in Hereford.

Percy was born in Kidderminster in 1917 and joined the Hereford police force in 1939. An earlier application to join the Worcester Force was rejected because he was not tall enough (5 feet 10½ inches). His first job was in the village of Wellington, north of Hereford, where the accommodation provided depended on oil lamps. Because of this he considered resignation and so was delighted with the opportunity to become the policeman at Little Birch. He had three children who went to school at Little Dewchurch. One son worked for Percy Williams on building work and fitted the windows in the bus shelter.

The police area covered from Little Birch extended to Holme Lacy in the east, to Tram Inn in the west, and from Hereford to Llandinabo to the north and south. This large 'beat' was patrolled entirely by bicycle until a small Velocette motor-cycle was provided in the early 1960s.

At that time an important part of the duties of a village policeman was to check on the movement of farm animals. This required Percy to visit farms once a month to check records. During his eight years in the area he never had a serious crime to deal with but did recall two tragedies one of which was also recalled by

Fig. 14.9 This photograph was taken near King's Thorn shop when the road was made impassable by snow in January 1982. The road was eventually cleared by a snow-blower, the first seen in the county

several other people. This latter was a motorcycle accident which occurred in the mid 1950s. Percy Bristow was the first duty policeman to arrive at the scene so his version of events is probably the most accurate. A group of five local youths on two machines returning from Hereford to Little Birch was hit by a Humber police car near the Grafton Inn. The occupants were policemen returning from a cricket match at Ross-on-Wye. Don Evans and Reg Devereux were killed and two others seriously injured, including Roy Gwynne who lived for many years at Corner house. Joan Ingram, then a newly qualified nurse on her first shift in the Hereford hospital casualty department, treated the injured. (She later became postmistress at King's Thorn post office).

According to Percy the accident caused there to be a 'cloud over the village' for some time. It was particularly difficult for him because he was upset at having to recover a severed arm from the grounds of the Grafton Inn. In addition there was bad feeling because a police car was involved. The driver was found not guilty of dangerous driving but according to one source, compensation of £500 was paid to each of the victim's families.

The second tragedy was the accidental drowning of a young girl in a water butt at Cherry Orchard Cottage, King's Thorn.

Like several others Percy recalled bad winters and deep snow during his eight years in the village. During such weather he used to look out of the police house windows in the mornings to check for smoke coming from the chimneys of cottages in the valley. He would then investigate that all was well in cottages where no smoke appeared, especially the ones lived in by old people. He remembered that during one particularly bad winter his children were unable to attend school for three weeks because of the depth of snow.

One incident Percy remembered with delight and in great detail. Cycling towards Caldicot cross-roads he noticed a Rolls Royce car parked beside the wood. He stopped to investigate and discovered that not only was it unlocked but there was a shotgun on the back seat. The gun was removed and taken to the police house for safekeeping. Some time later the local gamekeeper, Leo Naylor who lived at Crossways Cottage, arrived to report the theft of a gun. He was relieved to find that it was safe but disconcerted that Percy would not allow him to return it to its owner. The owner was non other than Sir Charles Clore, a London financier and then owner of what is now the Duchy of Cornwall estate, who was required to visit the police house to identify the gun, sign for it and show his gun licence.

Medical Care

Memories of medical care in the earlier years of the 1900s are very few. Arguably people were more stoical, more medically self-sufficient and less demanding then. One or two people mentioned problems with TB in the area in the 1930s when people built chalets in their gardens to isolate their sick family members. From before this time the area has been served by a doctor based in Much Birch. The names Steele and McMichael were mentioned. Then Dr Maurice McGinn ran a single-handed practice from Wonder View and was joined by his son Michael in the late 1960s. On Dr Maurice's retirement Dr Peter Clark joined Dr Michael McGinn and a new purpose-built surgery was erected next to the church. When Dr Clark left, Dr Peter Garlick replaced him. The local people were shocked by Dr McGinn's death in a car accident on the Callow Hill in June 1976. Dr Clark then returned. One memory of him mentioned by several people was of visits on horseback in the snows of January 1982. On his departure, Dr Michael Davies joined and since then the practice has expanded, including, among others, partners Drs Andrea Johnson and Vanessa England. Surgery premises and facilities have also increased providing excellent local medical care. Many people will have memories, obviously not shared with us, of the care received during illness and dying of loved ones. This care has been shared for much of this time with District Nurses in the area and two well-remembered names from the 1960s were Nurses Zappalloni and Miles who lived in Parish

Lane. Later memories were of Joan Ingram, in particular, who as a midwife was responsible for delivering a number of the residents in the area before she retired when she and her family ran King's Thorn Shop.

Currently, in 2006, we are fortunate in that the majority of the staff at the surgery live locally.

15   Influential People in the Village*

The Reverend Stephen Thackwell

Stephen Thackwell was born in Dymock, Gloucestershire in 1809. The entry in the Parish Records reads: 'Stephen, son of John Thackwell Esq. & Winifred his wife was born 2nd. May and baptised June 11th. 1809 by me E. Evans, vicar.'[1]

It is known that he had five brothers and at least one sister because the same register records twins, John Cam and Ann Cam Thackwell, born in 1807 and a brother James Seabright, (his mother's maiden name), born in 1810. Another brother Joseph Edwin became a general in the army.[2]

It is not known what school he went to, but he matriculated at Pembroke College, Oxford on 21 June, 1827, aged 18. His father is described as a gentleman. Stephen went on to graduate in 1831 and received his M.A. in 1834.[3] While at Oxford he became a good friend of T.W. Webb whose father was Rector of Tretire. Apart from attending lectures and reading, they amused themselves by having tea parties and drinking wine, telling stories and going for long walks.[4]

Stephen next appears in the records when he became rector of Little Birch and vicar of Aconbury in 1855, where he remained until his death on 27 April 1883.[5] There does not seem to be any record of him marrying and the census returns for 1861, 1871 and 1881[6] show him living in the rectory at Little Birch with four servants, a coachman, footman, cook and a housemaid. Although there is anecdotal evidence of him having descendants, this is probably erroneous because when he died his estate was left to his two brothers, John Cam and Joseph Edwin. Probate was granted on 28 July 1883.[7]

As has already been mentioned (see p.169), Stephen paid for building and running a school, having inherited money from his father John who had in turn benefited from the will of Dame Ann Cam, an heiress who lived in Dymock,

---

*Those featured are only a few of the many families who either have in the past or currently still are influencing life in the village. The people featured have been chosen as their descendants no longer live in the parish.

Gloucestershire. She inherited the fortune of her father, William, and grandfather, Joseph, both described as 'Citizens of London', even though their origins were in Gloucestershire.[8]

Evidence of his wealth shows in a mortgage deed of 1861.[9] With his brother, John Cam Thackwell, and Lt. Col. Edmund Roche of Ballymorris, co. Cork (Stephen's aunt was Maria Roche, daughter of the 1st Lord Fermoy), he lent James Gregg of Ledbury, gent. £6,400.

Apart from building and maintaining the local school, he also supported the restoration of Aconbury church which, in 1863, was carried out by none other than Sir George Gilbert Scott at an expense of £756. Most of the cost was borne by the Governors of Guy's Hospital, indeed their then treasurer, Mr Thomas Turner, paid for the shingle belt turret himself, but the Rev Stephen Thackwell donated £125.[10] In 1863, it also became obvious that repairs were needed on the church at Little Birch and Littlebury's *Directory and Gazetteer of Herefordshire*, 1876–7 notes that it was restored at a cost of £700, chiefly defrayed by subscription.[11] This can only have been a patch and mend operation because in 1868 a completely new church had been built, the Reverend Thackwell providing the whole amount necessary, £3,500, a considerable sum of money in those days.[12]

As well as building a church and schoolhouse, Rev Thackwell also built the cottages known as Model Cottages. As mentioned elsewhere in the book, Stephen

Fig. 15.1 Model Cottage (no.2) in 2000. The two Model Cottages were built by Stephen Thackwell on land which he owned behind the school

used his money to help people rather than to accumulate wealth. We have already seen how he lent money to James Gregg and similarly he bought properties from people in financial difficulties such as that belonging to Christopher Seir. These were then rented out.[13] It is a pity that we don't have a picture of this man who was a great benefactor of Little Birch, who devoted 28 years of his life to the parish and its people and whose memory lives on in the buildings which he left behind.

The Waites and the Southeys of Castle Nibole

Both the Waites and the Southeys have, in various ways, contributed to and been involved in the life of the village from the 1850s through to the late 1920s. They were something of a dynasty, holding positions of influence, and providing employment for local people. Although there are few personal memories of them, they have left their legacy in different ways and descendents of the Waites, the Lees, still own Swiss cottage in King's Thorn and come there quite frequently.

The first to move into the area was William Waite. He was the son of John Waite, a wheelwright from Bugbrook, Northampton. They were descended from generations of wheelwrights who had done quite well for themselves, owning a large business and many properties. Even so John was considered to have married above himself (according his wife's family). Their sons, taking advantage of the opportunities of the time, proceeded to adapt their wheelwright skills to those needed in railway construction. The eldest emigrated to USA but the other three travelled throughout Britain. William's travels, in the course of railway construction, took him to such places as Rugby, Stamford and Peterborough then in 1856 he moved to Pontypool where he was an engineer's inspector working under Sir Charles Liddell involved in the construction of the Taff Vale

Fig. 15.2 William Waite

railway extension from Pontypool to Quaker's Yard in Crumlin, which included the Crumlin viaduct and tunnels. His brothers Robert and Thomas joined him here and each became responsible for different constructions on the line, including the Crumlin viaduct. An extension of the line went over a viaduct at Cefn Glas at which Bessie, William's daughter, laid the keystone of the central arch.

William moved the family to Pontypool at this time. Whilst here he came to know and formed an affection for Herefordshire. In 1857, before leaving South Wales, and with a view to early retirement, he bought a small cottage with a few acres in Orcop for the family. Then, when the Castle Nibole site came on the market in 1858, he bought that. There was no house on this site at the time although there were the ruins of a former dwelling. Using his engineering and construction skills, together with the money he must have accumulated, he built a well designed and commodious house in Strawberry Gothic style on the site which he named Castle Cottage. While this was in the course of construction his family moved up to Little Birch, living first at a cottage in Burnt House field near the new house, then at Waterloo Cottage in King's Thorn, a property owned by Charles Macklin — foreman at Guy's estate yard — with whom he had become friendly. In the meantime William was away for two years inspecting parts of the Midland line in Bedfordshire. The family must have moved into 'Castle House' before 1861 as his wife, his son John and daughter Mary were in residence at the time of the 1861 census, (his wife was styled 'landed proprietor'). William was presumably still in Bedfordshire. Meanwhile his son John farmed the land here.

When William returned from Bedfordshire in late 1861 he retired from the railways aged 56. Records in the Parish Minute Book[1] show that an increased rate of £20 became chargeable for 'Castle Niboll' in 1861. William was a Methodist who attended the Primitive Methodist chapel at the top of Barrack Hill.

After William had settled into Castle Nibole, his brothers Robert and Thomas also decided to relocate into the area from Bugbrook, together with their father. The business and properties there had now been sold. They bought The Chimneys in Orcop where they appeared in the 1871 census. Their father had by now died although he had lived to 89, apparently helping with reaping on the farm until then.

At some point between 1861 and 1881 the Waites bought a cottage on the site of Hergest. At that time there was a cluster of cottages there called, variously, Upper Black Pits and Black Pits, one of which was obviously renamed Swiss Cottage. They must have decided to move there and rent out Castle Nibole because the 1881 census records them living at Swiss Cottage. It is not clear which of the houses they were living in at the 1871 census since house names are not recorded. Castle Cottage remained in the ownership of the Waites although it was rented out.

The 1881 census records an Elizabeth Jones (retired timber dealer's widow) and her daughters and grandson living in what was then called Castle Neabo.

William Waite obviously continued to work locally and was involved in the community. In January 1863 he was recorded (in the Parish Minute Book) as being on a committee for 'making the assessments and re-valuation of the Parish for the Poor Law Board.' Then in December of the same year, after the resignation of Mr. Green as Assistant Overseer 'Wm. Waite was chosen to fulfil the office and collect all Rates and Taxes in the Parish at the salary of twelve pounds, twelve shillings per annum.' He continued in the role until 1887 when he gave notice of his intention to resign this post and a replacement was elected. To be in post of tax collector for over 20 years suggests that he must have been very well known in the area and, presumably, well respected or he might otherwise have been removed. He continued to attend, and took an active part in, Parish meetings until 1890 by which time he was 85. Presumably he felt he had given enough by then!

By 1881 he was recorded as living in Swiss Cottage, occupation 'retired builder'. In 1891 he was still there, but a retired carpenter! Interestingly, Kelly's *Directory* for 1891[2] records the name of the house as Castle Hill. He was by now living there only with his daughter, his wife having died. By the time of the 1901 census his son, John, was living there, his father having died in 1895, leaving Castle Nibole to his daughter, Bessie.

William Waite had many children, a number of whom died shortly after birth but two of the surviving children became involved with the Southeys. His son John married Esther Mansell of the Hill Farm, Much Dewchurch in 1864. His farming activities ceased at Castle Nibole as some time after 1871 he became a farmer at The Moors in Orcop parish from which he also operated as the village carrier. He was recorded as living at Garway Hill, where The Moors is located, in the 1881 census. The Castle Nibole land was then tenanted by John's brother-in-law, Thomas Mansell, who lived some of the time at Laburnam House on Parish Lane. The carrier business became well established, running a market conveyance regularly to Hereford, Ross and Monmouth. When John retired from this in 1892 he and his wife left the farm and moved into Swiss Cottage. He looked after his father, who was in failing health, but William died in 1895. John continued to live there (at what was, strangely, called 'Castle' in the electoral register of 1906) while he generally made himself useful at Castle Nibole during the Southeys' residence there. In 1907 his wife died and, since John is not recorded on the electoral register of 1910, it must be assumed that he no longer owned Swiss Cottage and was probably living at Castle Nibole. He knew Bessie Matthews (widowed daughter of Charles Macklin) who was his sister's best friend and who lived at Waterloo Cottage (now Waterloo House). She had inherited this from her father who owned several properties in the area. Some time after the death of his sister John and Bessie Matthews must have come to know each other rather better as they married in 1912. Although John does not appear on the 1914 electoral register for either Little or Much Birch, he and has wife both appear at Waterloo Cottage in 1920.[3] He outlived his second wife also; she died in 1922 whilst John himself died in 1927 aged 88.

John (known to the extended family as 'Uncle John' or 'Grandpa Waite') had a son William who became an apprentice to H.W. Southey (H.W. as he was generally known in the family), eventually rising to the position of Works Director of the *Merthyr Express*. He commuted weekly from here to King's Thorn, having moved his family into a cottage known then as Fern Cottage which his father and H.W. helped to refurbish in some of the Art Deco style as used at Castle Nibole. Fern Cottage was owned by Macklin and, later, William's stepmother who eventually left it to him. It was renamed Swiss Cottage after John's family home in Little Birch which was sold around 1905. (This was subsequently remodelled into the Edwardian style Hergest.) William's weekly commute involved catching the milk train up from Merthyr on a Friday then walking from Tram Inn via Dewsall to King's Thorn — exhausting after a week's work. William, in the family tradition, was also a pillar of the Methodist chapel. William and his wife had a number of

children including Nancy, Bessie, Peggy (born 1913 and still alive) and Basil. Basil also became involved with the *Merthyr Express*, becoming Works Manager until the 1980s. He inherited Swiss Cottage from his father, but, having no use for it, passed it to his sister Nancy, who married a Lee and their three sons, David, Peter and Michael use this Swiss Cottage in King's Thorn as a holiday home.

'Uncle John' Waite was a much loved member of the extended Waite and Southey family, particularly when he moved up to Swiss Cottage in Little Birch. He was well known in south-west Herefordshire through his carrier activities and

Fig. 15.3 John Waite outside Castle Nibole was much respected in the village where he was a staunch member of the congregation at the Methodist chapel at which he led the singing with only the aid of a tuning fork. He was locally known, in certain circles, as a very successful poacher. In fact, it was said that he was lucky not to have been transported to Australia. The fruits of his labours were stored in old barrels at Swiss Cottage in amongst the cider, and this seemed effective at escaping detection. On certain days John Waite would go shopping in Hereford with his pony and trap loaded with 'empty' vinegar barrels. He would complete many errands for local people then, on passing 'Fishy' Gardeners in King Street he would drop off the barrels with a cheery 'here's your vinegar then' and make his way homeward. Presumably payment was forthcoming at some point. Another facet to this likeable character was his poetry writing. He compiled a little book including a series of poems reflecting on the past year and other things written on each birthday from his 75th to 86th years and published in the *Hereford Times*. They are well written and thought provoking as well as humorous. As a lifelong smoker of thick twist (Stanford's shag), he was hardly ever seen without a pipe in his mouth. His couplet relating to this gives one the feeling that one knew him and had conversed with him:

> The pipe, with solemn interposing puff,
> makes half a sentence at a time, enough

William Waite's daughter, Bessie, who was born in 1837, married Harry Wood Southey in 1864 in Hereford Registry Office. H.W. Southey came from Wellington, Somerset and was a relation of the Poet Laureate Robert Southey. H.W. moved to Merthyr Tydfil as a clerk, following an advertisement sent by a cousin in the *Merthyr Telegraph*, a leaflet in circulation there. He found his way into writing articles for this publication and discovered he had an aptitude for it. His work impressed the owners. After the removal of stamp duty in 1854, the production of newspapers became easier and a company was formed to launch the *Merthyr Express*. The directors very soon lost confidence in the management and asked H.W. Southey if he would become manager. He

Fig. 15.4 Bessie Southey (on the left) with her mother, Mary Waite, and her sister, Mary

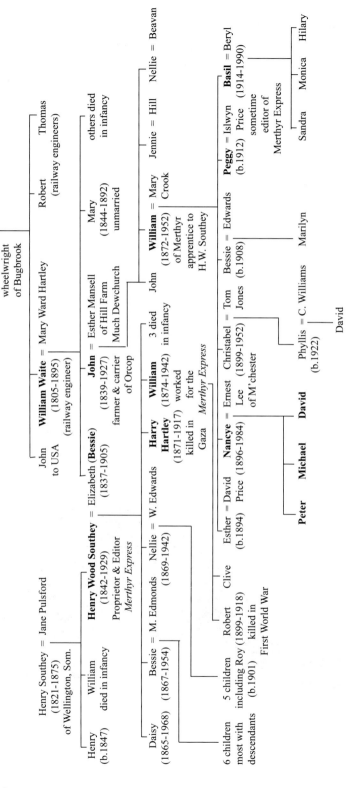

Fig. 15.5 Family Tree of the Waite and Southey families.
Those names in bold are members of the family mentioned in the book

agreed only if could become editor as well. This was arranged and the paper flourished and its owners prospered. Southey was able to buy a half share by 1869 and the rest in 1874, becoming the sole proprietor. New premises were built and the paper enlarged. Southey's fair and even-handed dealings with staff and others, his informative but independent editorials and his championing of causes, particularly in education, earned him respect throughout Merthyr. The only official position he held in the community was that of magistrate. He did, on an anonymous basis, act as *The Times* correspondent from Methyr during the time of the closure of the steel mills.

The industrial smoke and fumes in the area around Merthyr Tydfil began to take their toll on Bessie Southey's health and, during the 1880s, it was arranged that the Southeys would take over Castle Nibole, still owned by Bessie's father William. Castle Nibole was the name chosen from the selection of previous versions by H.W. Bessie and some of their children then lived there most of the time while H.W. commuted weekly to Merthyr Tydfil. He would 'put the paper to bed' on a Thursday evening then catch the night train and alight at Tram Inn where his 'man' Innes of Lower Black Pitts would meet him in his spring cart and transport him

Fig. 15.6 Castle Nibole before the 1880s' extension was added. Pictured are H.W. Southey in the centre, his son, Harry, on the grass, Bessie in the window and Daisy on the right

Fig. 15.7 The invitation sent out by the Southeys to their Silver Wedding party in 1889

to Castle Nibole. He would then return on Monday having worked on writing over the weekend.

During H.W.'s residence at Castle Nibole many alterations and enlargements were planned and undertaken. A large wing was added to the west end of the house at the end of the 1880s and many interesting stained glass panels installed, probably painted by a local man. Interesting tooled leather panels were also inserted into the woodwork, particularly on the staircase. In addition, handsome marble fireplaces were installed. The Southeys entertained regularly at Castle Nibole, often having house guests. These always found it an hospitable, relaxed and yet well organised home, a compliment to the character of Bessie. The Waites and Southeys of the younger generations were always welcome there and frequently returned at holiday times. A large party was held to celebrate their Silver Wedding and 25 years of the *Merthyr Express* in 1889.

H.W. became part of the community, living in some style and employing local people in the house and grounds. He even paid his brother-in-law — Uncle John — who was remembered for always being at Castle Nibole doing odd jobs. (The land at this time was being farmed by Thomas Mansell.) Having retained his independence of council and political matters in Merthyr, H.W. obviously felt free to indulge in these in Herefordshire. He became 'a stalwart rallying leader for Liberalism over a very wide district',[4] became a J.P. and also organised local government under the Act of 1894, becoming Chairman of Little Birch Parish Council, a post he held for 20 years. His firm, flowing hand graces the Parish Council Minute Book[5] throughout this time. In this role, he obviously helped to organise the refurbishment of Higgins Well to commemorate the Diamond Jubilee of Queen Victoria in 1897, and a plaque to this effect with his name at the bottom remains at the well to this day (see Fig. 10.6). The community must have been very grateful to have a motivator in their midst giving them this improvement. The letters on the plaque were originally engraved and filled with lead. The Parish Council minutes record

Fig. 15.8 The invitation sent out to villagers to a Coronation Celebration in 1902

the theft of some of this, presumably for profit, and offered a five shilling reward for information. All lead has long since disappeared so this must have been an unsolved crime! Bessie, meanwhile, became 'a household word in the parish for her kindness and thoughtful consideration for the poor old people and children'.[6]

A national celebration gave cause for another party when H.W. and his wife invited the villagers (men separately to women!) to Castle Nibole to celebrate the coronation of King Edward VII in 1902.

Bessie continued to live at Castle Nibole with their daughter Daisy but, after a lengthy infection, she died in 1905 aged 68 and was buried in Little Birch churchyard. This must have been a very sad time for H.W. He continued to come to Castle Nibole regularly but his daughter travelled to and fro with him now. Their other children had left home and married long since. Further tragedy was to follow when his much-loved son Harry, a partner in the firm, a much-respected local man and a Major in the Territorial Army running a unit in Merthyr, died in 1917 of wounds received at Gaza in Palestine. H.W. must have found this hard to cope with as did so many others in similar situations. As many others at that time, H.W. developed an interest in spiritualism to help him make contact with those whom he had lost. He must have attended and held séances regularly down in Merthyr where he met, and became friendly with, Conan Doyle. Indeed, Conan Doyle is known to have visited Castle Nibole and taken part in a séance here. An aunt of the Lees, a child at the time, remembers peeping down the stairs and seeing the great man at the table. At another séance the mother of the Lees remembered dangling a button on a string out of an upstairs window so that it tapped against the window of the room where the séance was being held (the scepticism of youth!). Various stories of hauntings were around at that time but not too many people took them seriously.

Castle Nibole, now owned by H.W., continued to be a 'home-from-home' for the extended Waite and Southey family but as H.W. became older, his visits to

Castle Nibole became less frequent and towards the end he rarely came. He died in Merthyr in 1929 aged 86 but was buried in Little Birch churchyard alongside his wife. The *Merthyr Express* carried a fulsome obituary together with a lengthy life story — a fitting tribute to a much respected person. He had been Proprietor and Editor for over 60 years.

His son William inherited Castle Nibole but had no intention of living there so it was sold in 1933 (presumably at a 'knock-down' price — see Fig. 9.5) leaving the only connection with the village being that of the Lees.

The *Merthyr Express* continued to flourish although ownership eventually passed to a national company. William Waite's great-granddaughter married a journalist, Islwyn Price, who became editor for a while. The paper has provided a good training ground over the years for many well-known broadcasters, including John Humphrys, all of whom owe their success in some small way to the enterprise of H.W. Southey.

As an interesting addendum, a cousin of John Waite went into partnership in a grocery business with his brother-in-law a Mr Rose. This went from strength to strength building up a large chain — Waitrose — which was eventually bought out by John Lewis.

Appendix 1

The will of William Higgs, rector of Little Birch, Herefordshire

(Transcribed by Dr D.L. Potter)
Orig.: Hereford Record Office: Probate 4/2/6 (8 July 1664)

IN the name of God, amen. The fourteenth day of June in the fourteenth yeare of the raigne of our most gracious soveraigne lord king Charles the second, 1662, I William / Higgs of the parish of Little Byrch in the county of Hereford, beinge somewhat infirme in body but of good and perfect memory, thanks bee given to almighty god, considering the fra[g]ilety and incertainty / of this transitory life and beinge therefore resolved to settle my Temporall estate in order and to prepare my selfe to bee ready when it shall please almighty God to call mee out of this / transitory world. I doe therefore make and declare my last will and testament in manner and forme following, that is to say first and above all things I commend my soule into the hands of almighty / God my creator, …astly beleaving and assuring my self, through the merits and bitter passion of his only sonne Jesus Christ my saviour and redeemer, to obtaine remission of all my sins and to bee / in …. of everlasting life and glory in his heavenly kingdome and my body to the earth wherewith it was made, to be buried in fitting manner. ITEM, as concerning my temporall estate / wherewith it hath pleased Almighty god to give mee, I give and devise in manner following, that is to say, First I give and devise unto my son William Higgs and his heirs and assigns for ever, ALL / that messuage or tenement, garden, orchards, …. pastures and hereditaments with all and singular the hereditaments …. ….. being in the parish of Little Byrch and in the county of / Hereford heretofore purchased of one William Gynny; and also I doe likewise give and devise unto my said son William Higgs his heirs and assigns all my lands, tenements and hereditaments / with thappartenants, which I purchased of one Richard Gwatkyn, Thomas Gwatkyn, John Gwatkyn, Hugh Gwatkyn and also James Gwatkyn deceased together with all and singular / my lands tenements et hereditaments situate, lyeing and being in the said parish of Little Byrch or elsewhere within the County of Hereford and all deedes, evidentes and writings touching or / concerning the same, which I have in my possession or custody and all deedes, leases, writings which any other persone or persons have or hath in this or theire possession, possession or custody / in his or their name or names in trust for mee, my heirs, executors, administrators or assigns touching or concerning the premises or any parte thereof. ITEM, I doe give and / bequeath unto my son John Higgs the somme of one hundred pounds and one feather bed to bee paid and delivered unto him within one yeare next after hee shall accomplishe the / age of one and twenty yeares if the said John Higgs shal bee then living. Also my will is that in case my son John shall not bee … and apprenticed in my life time, my son William shall lay / out ten pounds of [his?] money for the setteing him to a trade over and above the said hundred pounds. ITEM, I doe give and bequeath unto my daughter Flizabeth Berrow twenty shillings to be payed within a yeare after my deceae. Also I doe give and bequeath unto William Willym and … ry Willym my grand children ten shilligs a yeere. I give unto Thomas Byncks of / Merrifould the younger, ten shillings and to John Gwatkyn my neighbour, ten shillings. I give to Elizabeth Pegg my servant ten shillings if she bee living with me at the time of my decease. / Also I give to Anne Powell my servant five shillings and to my servant Thomas Prosser five shillings if they are living with me at the time of my decease; and my will is that hee or she that shalbee / departed our of my service as my servants shall have noe bequests. Also I give and bequeath unto the poore of my parish of Little Byrch [seventy?] shillings, all which severall sommes shalbee / payed within a yeare after my decease by any executor heareafter named, PROVIDED always and my will and meaning is and I doe hereby will and devise, that if my said son William / his heirs and assigns shall make default of payment of the said one hundred pounds and not well and truly pay the same unto my son John, within a yeare after hee shall accomplish the / age of one and twenty yeares if hee bee then living, according to the true meaning of this my last will and Testament, then my said son John and his assigns shall and may enter into all and / singular the above devised tenements, hereditaments and premises with thappurtenances and shall and may enjoy the moitye or one halfe thereof and have and receive the rents, issues and profits / thereof to his owne use until my said son William Higgs, his heirs and assigns shall well and truly satisfy and and pay unto him my said son John the said one hundred pounds of lawful / English money at one whole and entire payment. ITEM, I give and bequeath unto my said son William Higgs all and singuler my goods and catles, personall estate whatsoever unbequeathed xxxxxxxx / AND of this last will and testament I doe nominate, constitute and ordaine my said son Willliam Higgs my sole executor. And finally I doe renounce and revoke all former and other wills which I have heretofore made in whose hands or custody soever they are and this only to bee executed by my said executor.

Signed, sealed and published in the presence of:

JOHN GWILLYM
JAMES WILLIAMS   JOHN ROGERS
The marke of
THOMAS WEAVER

Appendix 2

Incumbents of Little Birch 1306 to the present

Incumbents	Assistant Clergy	Patron
1306 John Hobart		
1308 Walter, son of High de Westone (39 yrs)		
1349 Stephen de Castello		
1357 John de Northeme		
1367 Richard Dewall (35 yrs)		
1402 Edward Child – resigned 1413		
1413 John ap Adam		
1420 John Snell – resigned 1437		
1437 William Tompkins		
1441 Robert Huggyns		
1460 Richard of Gloucester – resigned 1516 (56 yrs)		
1516 John Gregge (54 yrs)		

Post-Reformation

Incumbents	Assistant Clergy	Patron
1570 John Yonger – died 1611 (41 yrs)		Parry
1611 William Higgs – died 1664 (53 yrs)		Powell
1664 William Hallowes	1674 Thomas Barbour	
1692 John Finch	1679 Titus Neave	Chandos
1706 Richard Traherne		Chandos
1731 Thomas Willim, also vicar of Much Birch?		Chandos
1750 Richard Reece		Guy's
1767 Richard Gomond		Guy's
1777 William Whitmore		Guy's
1792 William Henry Barry		
1810 Richard Lucas	1813 James Scudmore	
1833 William Pepperell Hutton	1824 Cudworth Bruch	
1835 Thomas Phillips	1827 A. Jones	
1838 Henry Hampton	1843 C.M. Hesilsige	Guys
1850 W.H. Joyce	1844 W.W. Trumper	Guys
1851 Vernon Guise	1846 James Archibald	Guys
1852 Richard Georges Foot		Swire of Liverpool
1855 Stephen Thackwell		himself
1883 Henry P.M. Dodington		John Cam Thackwell
1890 Walter Fitzwarine Smith		HMPD

Little Birch joined to Much Birch

Incumbents	Assistant Clergy	Patron
1916 William L. Groves	1915 Edmund Jones	
1933 John R. George	1920-1933 C.E. Ind	
1941 G.H. Dyer Wright		
1956 A.W. Butterworth		
1968 John Pitchford	1972–1970 Leslie H. Rhodes	
1980 Peter G. Newby	1981–1986 Frank Morley	
1989 C. Hollowood	1986–1994 Paul Wilson	
1993 Alan Jeavons	1992–1994 David Enoch	
2003 Kay Garlick		

Appendix 3

Little Birch Churchwardens

Year		
1725	John Evans	
1840–2	James Bennett – New Mills	Thomas Preece - Bromley
1846–7	William Bennett – New Mills	William Crompton – Church Farm
1850	John Lawrence – Church Farm	
1851	William Paine – New Mills	John Lawrence – Church Farm
1852	T. Roberts – Bromley	John McMullen
1853	William Green – Green Farm	Benjamin Carey
1854&5	William Green – Green Farm	Daniel Biggs
1856–1861	William Green – Green Farm	John Lawrence – Church Farm
1862&3	William Green – Green Farm	George Bonnor – Church Farm
1864	William Hillier – New Mills	George Bonnor – Church Farm
1866–73	William Hillier – New Mills	William Davies – Well Orchard
1874	William Whittingham – Bromley	William Davies – Well Orchard
1875–6	William Whittingham – Bromley	James Maskell – New Mills
1877	William Whittingham – Bromley	Daniel Paine – Church Farm
1878–9	William Whittingham – Bromley	George Pickering
1880&1	Arannal Williams	George Pickering
1882–4	Thomas Watkins – Church Farm	George Pickering
1885	Thomas Watkins – Church Farm	A.J. Payne – New Mills
1886	Thomas Stallard	A.J. Payne – New Mills
1887–9	W. Bridgland – School House	Thomas Stallard
1890	G. Trupp	Thomas Powell – Green Farm
1891&2	Richard Trupp	George Pickering
1893–6	Charles Woodruffe Sharp – School Ho.	Arthur James Jones – Lower House
1897–1900	Charles Woodruffe Sharp – School Ho.	Thomas Hudson – Walls Pool
1901–3	John Fox	Thomas Hudson – Walls Pool
1904–21	John Blashill – Church Farm	Thomas Hudson – Walls Pool
1922	J.W. Woodthorpe	Thomas Hudson – Walls Pool
1923	J.W. Woodthorpe	T. Thomas
1924–26	J.W. Woodthorpe	T.P. Bowen – Church Farm
1927&8	F.W. Woodthorpe	T.P. Bowen – Church Farm
1929–39	Woodthorpe	T.P. Bowen – Church Farm
1940&41	J.S.Wilson	
1942–46	J.S.Wilson	Hugh Bowen – Church Farm
1947&8	David Dyke – Castle Nibole	Mrs D. Dyke
1949–64	David Dyke – Castle Nibole	Ernest Rooke
1965	David Dyke – Castle Nibole	Mrs Hewitt
1966–68	W.J. Badham	Mrs Hewitt
1969–73	David Dyke – Castle Nibole	Roland Creed
1974–9	David Dyke – Castle Nibole	Christopher Marshall – Withycombe

1980-6	John Bryant – Kings Thorn	David Enoch – Fayre Oaks
1987–97	John Bryant – Kings Thorn	Stephen Turner – Crossways
1998	John Bryant – Kings Thorn	
1999–2000	John Bryant – Kings Thorn	Miss J. Coles
2001	John Bryant – Kings Thorn	John Bulbeck – Crow's Nest
2002	John Bryant – Kings Thorn	
2003	John Bryant – Kings Thorn	James Gould
2004&5	Susan Mason – Merrivale Farm	James Gould
2006	James Gould	

Appendix 4

Little Birch School Teachers

1858   John Preece

1861   William Baker

1871   James Liddington, Elizabeth Liddington (sister) – taught sewing

1882   W. Bridgland, Mrs Bridgland – Assistant

1886   Miss Edith Whitemarsh, Miss Wightman – Assistant

1887   Miss Wightman resigned
       Miss Christine Brace – monitress to 7 April

1890   Miss Green Ada Williams – monitress from 8 April

1891   A. Davies, Mrs Davies – Assitant, died 18 January 1892

1892   Charles W. Sharp Mrs Amy Sharp – Assistant

1897   December – Mr Sharp broke leg; Mrs Sharp deputised till Feb 1898

1900   Thomas Rowe, Mrs Rowe – Assistant

1902   Thomas Kingdon, Mrs Blanche Kingdon – Assistant

1905   Edward Sillence, Hester Sillence (daughter) – Assistant

1911   W.T. Varley, Mrs Varley – Assistant

1916   Mrs L.H. Woodbine, Miss J.M. Preece – Assistant

1917   Miss Preece resigned, Dorothy Dyke – Assistant

1919   Mrs Helen Tyson

1920   Miss Minnie Snasdell

1924   Miss Nellie Pritchard

1925   Miss Alice Cutter appointed assistant teacher

1926   Miss Mabel Gough appointed assistant teacher

1929   Miss Terry appointed assistant teacher

1930   Miss Olive Pocknell appointed assistant teacher

1933   Miss Catherine Bowen (Church Farm) appointed monitress and later
       appointed Assistant Teacher

1944   Miss Marjorie Garland – Assistant

1948   Miss Constance Hughes

1956   Mrs Mary Evans, Miss Freda Davies (Sunnybank) appointed Assistant

Appendix 5

Members of Little Birch Church Sunday School 1941

Margaret Dyke
Margaret Yapp
Peggy Davies
Gillian Field
Doris Rooke
Evelyn Rooke
Jean Rooke
Lillian Gwynne
Nell Gwynne
Margo Wooles
Joyce Devereux
Marigold Kirby

Colin Davies
Norman Hocknell
Leslie Hitching
John Walker
Bill Walker
John Wilson
Michael Kerton
John Evans
Jean Wooles
Patricia Bishop
Connie Hirons
Marion Kirby

Bibliography

Arnold-Foster	Arnold-Foster F, *Studies in Church Dedications*, London 1899
Atherton (1992)	Atherton I, (ed.), *Sir Barnabas Scudamore's Defence*, Akron 1992
Atherton (1999)	Atherton I, *Ambition and Failure in Stuart England*, Manchester 1999
Bannister	Bannister A.T. (ed.), *Diocese of Hereford Institutions*, Hereford 1923
Bartrum	Bartrum P.C. in *Transactions of the Honourable Society of the Cymmrodorion* 1948
Burnham and Wacher	Burnham B. and Wacher J, *The Small Towns of Roman Britain*, London 1990
Collingwood and Wright	Collingwood R.G. and Wright R.P., *The Roman Inscriptions of Britain* Oxford 1965
Chandler	Chandler J. (ed.), *Travels through Stuart Britain*, Stroud 1999
Coates and Breeze	Coates R. and Breeze A., *Celtic Voices, English Places*, Stamford 2000
Coates and Tucker	Coates S.D. and Tucker D.G., *Water Mills of the Middle Wye Valley*, Monmouth 1983
Coplestone-Crow	Coplestone-Crow B., *Herefordshire Place Names*, Oxford 1989
Davies (1978)	Davies W., *An Early Welsh Microcosm*, London 1978
Davies (1979)	Davies W., *The Llandaff Charters*, Aberystwyth 1979
Doble	Doble G.H. (ed. Evans D.S.) *Lives of the Welsh Saints*, Cardiff 1971
Elton	Elton G.R., *England under the Tudors*, London 1955
Faraday (1972)	Faraday M. (ed.), *Herefordshire Militia Assessment of 1663*, London 1972
Faraday (2005)	Faraday M. (ed.), *Herefordshire Taxes in the Reign of Henry VIII*, Hereford 2005
von Feilitzen	von Feilitzen O., *Pre-Conquest Personal Names of the Domesday Book*, Uppsala 1937
Fenwick	Fenwick C., *The Poll Taxes of 1377, 1379 and 1381, Part 1*, Oxford 1998
Foster	Foster J. *Alumni Oxonienses 1500-1714*, reprinted Liechtenstein 1968
Gray	Gray H.L., *English Field Systems*, London 1969
Hill D.	Hill D. in *Antiquarian Journal 2000* 196-206
Hill M.	Hill M., *A True and Impartiall Account of the Plunderings, Losses and Sufferings of the County of Hereford by the Scottish Army*, London 1650
Hodges	Hodges G.J., *Owain Glyn Dwr*, Logaston 1995
Home	Home J.H.(ed.), *Diary of Lady Mary Coke*, Edinburgh 1889
Hoskins and Stamp	Hoskins W.G. and Stamp L.D., *The Common Lands of England and Wales*, London 1963
Jones G.	Jones G.R.J. in Finberg H.P.R. (ed.), *The Agrarian History of England and Wales 1.ii AD43-1042*, Cambridge 1972
Jones T.	Jones T. (ed.), *Brut y Tywysogyon*, Cardiff 1952
Laslett	Laslett P., *The World We Have Lost Further Explored, (third edition*, London 1983
Lloyd	Lloyd J.E., *A History of Wales (third edition)*, London 1948
Long	Long C.E. (ed.), *Diary of the Marches of the Royalist Army during the Great Civil War kept by Richard Symonds*, London 1859
Margary	Margary I.D., *Roman Roads in Britain (third edition)*, London 1973
Matthews	Matthews J.H., *Collections towards the History of the County of Hereford in Continuation of Duncumb's History: Hundred of Wormelow (Upper Division Part 1)*, Hereford 1912
Morris	Morris A., *Numismatic Arrivals in Herefordshire* in *A Herefordshire Miscellany*, Hereford 2000
Noble	Noble F., *Offa's Dyke Reviewed*, Oxford 1983
Orwin and Orwin	Orwin C.S. and Orwin C.S., *The Open Fields*, Oxford 1938
Parry	Parry J.H. (ed.), *Registrum Johannis de Trillek*, Hereford 1912
Poole	Poole A.L., *From Domesday to Magna Carta*, Oxford 1951
Rees	Rees W., *A History of the Order of St. John of Jerusalem in Wales and on the Welsh Border*, Cardiff 1947
Rivet and Smith	Rivet A.L. and Smith C., *The Place Names of Roman Britain*, London 1979
Robinson	Robinson C.J., *A History of Mansions and Manor Houses of Herefordshire*, London 1872
Salway	Salway P., *Roman Britain*, Oxford 1981
Shrewsbury	Shrewsbury J.F.D., *A History of Bubonic Plague in the British Isles*, Cambridge 1970
Siddons	Siddons M.P. (ed.), *The Visitation of Herefordshire 1634*, London 2002
Skelton	Skelton R.E. in *Woolhope Club Archaeological Section Report 1987*
Smith A.H.	Smith A.H., *The Place Name Elements*, Cambridge 1970

Smith B.	Smith B., *Herefordshire Maps 1577-1800,* Logaston 2004
Smith L.T.	Smith L.T. (ed.), *The Itinerary of John Leland,* Carbondale 1964
Stanford	Stanford S.C., *The Archaeology of the Welsh Marches,* London 1980
Tate	Tate W.E., *The Parish Chest,* Cambridge 1953
Taylor C.	Taylor C., *Fields in the English Landscape,* Gloucester 1987
Taylor E.	Taylor E., *Kings Caple in Archenfield,* Logaston 1997
Thomas	Thomas C., *Christianity in Roman Britain,* London 1993
Wacher	Wacher J., *The Towns of Roman Britain,* London 1974
Webb	Webb J. (ed. Webb T.W.), *Memorials of the Civil War...as it affected Herefordshire...,* London 1879
Whitehead	Whitehead D., *A Survey of Historical Parks and Gardens in Herefordshire*, Worcester 2001
Whitehead and Shoesmith	Whitehead D. and Shoesmith R., *James Wathen's Herefordshire, 1770-1820*, Logaston 1994
Whiteman	Whiteman A., *The Compton Census of 1676,* Oxford 1986
Wightman	Wightman W.E., *The Lacy Family in England and Normandy 1066-1104,* Oxford 1966
Woodward	Woodward C.W.O., *Dissolution of the Monasteries,* London 1966
Wrigley and Schofield	Wrigley E.A. and Schofield R.S., *The Population History of England and Wales 1541-1971,* Cambridge 1989

References

Abbreviations

AJ	*Archaeological Journal*
ASC	Whitelock D., Douglas D., Tucker S. (eds), *The Anglo-Saxon Chronicle,* London 1961
CSPD	*Calendar of State Papers Domestic*
DB	Thorn F. and C.(eds), *Domesday Book Herefordshire*, Chichester 1983
DBH	Galbraith V.H. and Tait J. (eds), *Herefordshire Domesday* (Balliol College MS 350) London 1950
DNB	*Dictionary of National Biography 2004-6,* (on-line version)
Enc Act	*An Act for Inclosing Lands in the Parishes of Much Birch and Little Birch in the County of Hereford,* 1812
HCL	Hereford City Library
HMC	Historical Manuscripts Commission
HRO	Herefordshire Record Office
LLEvans	*The Text of the Book of Llan Dav,* ed. Evans J.G., Oxford 1893
LLRees	*Liber Landavensis* ed. Rees W.J., Llandovery 1840
NLW Mynde	Catalogue of the Mynde Collection in the National Library of Wales
NA	National Archives Catalogue (formerly PRO Catalogue)
OS	Ordnance Survey
Population	*Comparative Account of the Population of Great Britain in the Years 1801, 1811, 1821 and 1831,* London 1831
RCHM	*Royal Commission on Historical Monuments England, Herefordshire Vol. 1 South West,* London 1931
SMR	Herefordshire Council Sites and Monuments Record (on-line resource)
TWNFC	*Transactions of the Woolhope Naturalists' Field Club*
VCH	*Victoria County History*

Section 2 The Pre-history of AconburyHill

1. Webb ii, pp.342 and 217; HRO (microfilm) BN 13
2. TWNFC 1883-5, p.296; HRO, AW28/47/5; Smith B., p.122
3. HRO, AW28/47/9, C99/III/318
4. AJ cx 1954, pp.1-87; cxxvii 1970, pp. 82-129
5. AJ cx op cit; SMR 910
6. Stanford, p.104; AJ cx op cit; SMR 6479
7. AJ cx and cxxvii op cit; Stanford p.107
8. Salway pp.542-52
9. Stanford p.96; SMR 476, 8405
10. AJ cx op cit
11. Collingwood and Wright p.703; Morris pp.179-81
12. Stanford pp.119-21; Rivet and Smith p.381; Mr Peter Reavill, local Finds Liaison Officer of the Portable Antiquities Scheme, has kindly given advice on pre-Iron Age boundaries
13. AJ cx op cit; Taylor E p.6

Section 3 The Roman Period

1. Burnham and Wacher pp.70-6
2. TWNFC 1999 pp.143-5
3. A full account of these roads can be found in Margary. According to his system of number classification they are: 63a, 6c, 612a, 613. For Antonine Itinerary see Rivet and Smith pp.150-80
4. TWNFC 1970 pp.49-54
5. Taylor E. p.7
6. Salway op cit pp.542-52
7. SMR 4071, 4092, 6408, 6422, 6434, 6440, 6459, 6461, 6472, 10477, 10660, 30554
8. AJ cx and cxxvii op cit

Section 4 Archenfield

1. ASC p.14; LL Evans pp.141-3; LL Rees pp.383-5
2. Wacher pp.418-22
3. Doble pp.56-87; LL Evans pp.78-86; LL Rees pp.323-31; Thomas pp.267, 278; Arnold-Foster ii pp.198-200, iii p.358
4. Rees, Coplestone-Crow and Taylor identify 'Henlann super ripan Gui' with Llanfrother, Evans and Davies with Dixton near Monmouth
5. Davies 1978 pp.65-107; Rivet and Smith pp.257-8; ASC p.63
6. Discussed in detail in Davies 1979
7. Rivet and Smith op cit; Doble p.84; LL Evans, LL Rees op cit
8. ASC p.30; Jones T. p.2
9. LL Evans pp.43, 363; LL Rees p.376; Bartrum pp.296-8; Shelton pp.26-9
10. Shelton op cit; DB 1.55, 29.20
11. LL Evans p.170; LL Rees p.417; Coplestone-Crow p.64; LL Rees p.316. (NB Evans does not agree with the identification of Llandinabo.) LL Evans pp.164-5; LL Rees p.410
12. ASC p.63
13. Noble; Hill D.; SMR 850, 851; Taylor E p.18
14. DB A 1-10
15. Lloyd i pp.359-71
16. Lloyd op cit; ASC pp.130-1

17. DB 1.49, 24.3, 24.5, 25.6
18. Davies (1978) pp.24-42; Jones G. pp.281-382
19. Coplestone-Crow p.34; HRO L97/B; NA E326/2982, E326/2983
20. Arnold-Foster; Coates and Breeze pp.303-14; Thanks are due to Mr John Freeman for the explication of 'Wenleys'; NA E326/3103, E326/4097; HRO G87/23/8
21. Jones G. op cit; Davies (1978) pp.54-6; NLW Mynde pp.223-224
22. ASC p.136; Lloyd op cit
23. DB 1.49
24. DBH p.20; DB 1.58
25. Jones G. pp.303, 307; DBH p.19
26. DB Endnote 2; Wightman pp.116-70
27. von Feilitzen p.219
28. DB
29. Coplestone-Crow p.22; Coates and Breeze p.379

Section 5 Aconbury Priory

1. Matthews pp.13-14
2. DBH p.20; Arnold Foster i pp.349-61; Matthews pp.30-3, 73
3. Matthews p.34
4. Poole pp.315, 481
5. Matthews pp.13, 34-5; Coplestone-Crow pp.22, 34
6. Matthews p.34
7. HRO Monastic Records i pp.10, 21-2; Matthews p.35
8. Rees pp.60-1
9. HRO Monastic Records i pp.5, 24; Matthews p.55; NA E326/2982-3
10. Mr John Freeman has kindly provided advice on the earliest forms of this name; DB note 2
11. NA E326/3103; HRO Monastic Records i Aconbury Cartulary
12. Coplestone-Crow p.64; NA E326/4097
13. Coates and Tucker pp.30-3; Matthews pp.40, 47; NA E326/2982-3
14. SMR 3760, 11031, 16090, 16539, 16540, 16543, 16545, 43050
15. Matthews pp.40-57
16. Hodges p.113; Taylor E. pp.83-4; HRO Monastic Records i pp.59-60
17. Elton pp.176-179
18. Elton pp.188-190
19. Woodward pp.64-67; Matthews pp.37-38
20. TWNFC 1962 p.139
21. Matthews p.58; Woodward p.124; VCH Gloucestershire iv p.57; Faraday (2005) p.280
22. Woodward pp.79-80, 135
23. Robinson pp.282, 19; HRO AL2/26; Siddons p.34

Section 6 Peace and War

1. HRO AG 64/1
2. Atherton (1999) pp.220-245; Webb i pp.17-33
3. Atherton (1999) op cit
4. Atherton (1992); Webb ii p.81; NA C115/C5/1068
5. Webb ii pp.67-9; Atherton (1992) p.7; CSPD 1644 pp.397-9
6. Webb i pp.194-6

7. There is no satisfactory study of the Scottish siege, and the primary sources are limited; Webb ii pp. 196-230, 378-99 probably contains most information but is confused. For Dinedor, see Whitehead and Shoesmith.
8. Webb ii pp.391-7
9. Hill M.
10 Hill M. *op cit*; Faraday (1972) pp.179-80
11. Faraday (1972) pp.175, 173-174
12. e.g. *Scottish Dove* 15-23 August 1645
13. TWNFC 1972 p.386
14. Atherton (1992) pp.10-6
15. HRO O68/I/38; Webb MSS in HCL; HMC 13th report App. 1 p.263
16. Atherton (1992) p.26; HRO AG 64/1
17. Long p.240; HRO L97/B
18. There are several contemporary accounts of the events of 17/18 December 1645. Scudamore's own account is reproduced in Atherton (1992). This also contains an account of his later years and references to all the other primary sources
19. HRO AG64/1
20. Foster i p.708; HRO Probate T4/2/51; 4/2/6
21. Faraday (1972) p.179; HRO Probate 4/2/6; HD 5/14/54
22. HRO AG64/1; Probate 4/2/6
23. HRO AG64/1; Foster i p.708; Atherton (1992) pp.28-9

Section 7 Population and the Pattern of Settlement before the Nineteenth Century

1. Information on census procedures, counts of communicants etc. and national annual tables of population are taken from Wrigley and Schofield. See also Laslett pp.106-21; Tate pp.80-2
2. HRO AG64/1; HG5/14/54
3. Faraday (2005) p.393; Population p.109; Whiteman p.253; HRO AG64/1; HG5/14/54
4. It is worth noting that one of the curious features of the Little Birch parish register for 1709-1718 is that the number of burials recorded is much lower than the number of baptisms. In fact the difference is greater than in any other parish in the deanery of Archenfield. This suggests that the birth rate could have been higher than the national average and thus the parish's population lower than this estimate. On the other hand, a proportionately high birth rate would be consistent with inward migration by people in economically active age groups, and this would be likely to cause an increase in population, though the growth might occur over a slightly longer period. Only calculations based on baptisms reflect the growth between 1676 and 1811 – years for which we have more secure data. Using Tate's cruder method for calculating from baptisms would give a figure for 1713-4 of 129. All estimates from register entries are liable to a 10% error either way. (HRO HD/5/14/1-217)
5. See Hoskins and Stamp p.52; Smith L.T. iii p.47
6. HRO AF96/2; HD5/14/62; Whiteman p.253; HRO HD5/14/40
7. HRO QR1/34

8. Parry ii pp.373-82; Shrewsbury p.71; Fenwick p.360; Matthews pp.55, 74
9. Stanford p.107; HRO HD5/14/1-217

Section 8 The Ownership & Use of Land from 1540 to 1840

1. OS (1831 edition); HRO (microfilm) BN13; L97/B; QR1/34
2. HRO C99/III/23,24; Atherton (1999) p.63; Enc Act p.12
3. HRO L97/B
4. HRO From an account of deeds in the possession of the owners of Bromley prepared by the County Archivist
5. Robinson p.4; Siddons pp.122, 37; Faraday (1972) p.179; DNB; TWNFC 1980 pp.91-116
6. Robinson p.22
7. DNB; Home iii p.104
8. DNB; HRO AH24/71; Robinson pp.138-43; HRO L97/B; N11/3
9. See NA catalogue Series details C115 – separated material
10. Orwin and Orwin; Gray pp.139-56
11. HRO C99/III/227; TWNFC 1949 pp.55-67; Matthews p.58
12. HRO Monastic Records i p.84
13. TWNFC 1949 *op cit*
14. See section 5 above; HRO Monastic Records i p.31; HRO L97/B; Taylor C. p.123; see section 6 above
15. HRO C99/III/227; L97B; S385; OS 1904 (1:2500)
16. Matthews p.58; Lovelace D. History of Aconbury Woods (for Duchy of Cornwall) 2001; HRO AW28/47/5; C99/III/318
17. TWNFC 1986 pp.450-68; NA C115/63/5561
18. TWNFC 1986 *op cit*; Chandler pp.196-8
19. HRO L97/B
20. Faraday (2005) p.393; HRO AG64/1
21. HRO L97/B; Faraday (1972) p.179; Matthews p.25; Robinson p.22
22. HRO Probate T4/2/51; Faraday (1972) p.179; HRO K2/III/198-202
23. NA Probate 11/198
24. Faraday (1972) p.179; NA Probate 11/207
25. NA Probate 11/273
26. Faraday (1972) p.179; HRO J38/18/5; Probate 4/2/6; L97/B; QRelii/18/1-30 HD5/14/54
27. Faraday (1972) p.179; HRO Probate 4/2/6; L97/B; RCHM i p.22; NA Probate 11/273
28. HRO Probate 4/2/6
29. Deeds in the possession of Mr. W. Powell; Bannister p.117
30. Faraday (1972) p.179; HRO Probate 4/2/6
31. HRO Probate 4/2/6; G87/29/27; A28/2-11; L97/B
32. HRO G87/29/16A; Smith A.H. i p.79-80
33. HRO L97/B; OS (1904 1:2500)
34. HRO G87/23/7; G87/23/11; L97/B
35. HRO G87/23/8; G87/23/10
36. HRO K2(Introduction), III/198-202; L97/B
37. HRO L97/B
38. HRO A28/2-11; OS (1831); Enc Act
39. HRO AW28/47/5

40. Matthews p.17; HRO C99/III/26
41. Whitehead pp.viii, 3, 165
42. HRO QR1/34; Enc Act; HRO (microfilm) BN13; Deeds in the possession of Mr and Mrs J. Elphick
43. HRO AH24/1-71; AG64/2-6

Section 9 The Development of Farms after 1840

1. TWNFC 1883/4/5 p.297
2. Sale Particulars of Part 2 of Home Lacy Estate 1909 (HRO LOWU 4493-6)
3. Sale Particulars of Athelstan's Wood and Crabb's Castle Cottages 1923 (HRO M5/22/21)
4. Sale Particulars of Upper House 1920 (HRO M5/21/32)
5. Lascelle's *Directory* 1851 (HRO)
6. Kelly's *Directories* 1891, 1905, 1917 (HRO)
7. Much Birch Women's Institute – 25 years of the village, Much Birch, Little Birch, Kings Thorn 1952-1977, Mrs D. Rowan – '25 years of Crossways Nursery'
8. Sale Particulars of Part 2 of Home Lacy Estate 1909 (HRO LOWU 4493-6)
9. Sale Particulars of Athelstan's Wood and Crabb's Castle Cottages 1923 (HRO M5/22/21)

A large amount of information was also taken from the Tithe Map for Little Birch 1841 (HRO L 97 (B))
The following people contributed information about their own or other's properties:
Mr Mark Roberts – Bromley Court
Mr Victor Townsend – Kings Thorn
Mr Gerald Skyrme – Sycamores
Mr William Powell – Green Farm
Mrs Margaret Mullins – Castlefields
Mr and Mrs John Dillon – Castle Nibole
Mr and Mrs John Bulbeck – Crows Nest
Mr Michael Morley – Uplands
Mr Geoffrey Jones – formerly of Orchard Green
Mrs Susan Jones (Fernleigh) and Mrs Diane Smith (Fern View)

Section 10 Social and Economic Development of the Parish

1. Population, p.109
2. Heather Hurley, *The Pubs of Ross and South Herefordshire*, Logaston Press 2001 p.201
3. Norman Barber, *A Century of British Brewers 1890-2004*, Brewery History Society
4. Cutting from the *Hereford Times* 1900 (HRO BN 57)
5. Little Birch Parish Council Minute Book 1894-1941 (HRO BL 57/1)
6. Faraday (1972) (includes Hearth Tax Returns for 1664)
7. RCHM p.22

Use was made throughout of:
The Tithe Map for Little Birch 1841 (HRO L 97(B))
Censuses from 1841-1901 HRO
Mr Jim and Mrs Muriel Tonkin made a most valuable contribution with their comments and observations on some of the older properties in the parish
Much information was gathered from many local residents whose names are included in the Acknowledgements

Section 11 Poverty in the Parish

1. Hereford Militia Assessments of 1663: Hearth Tax return, Lady Day, 1664 (HCL)
2. Robinson
3. Census Returns for Little Birch, 1851 (HRO)
4. Arthur Armitage, Report on the state of cottages on the commons belonging to Guys Hospital, 1857 (HRO AW/28/45/129)
5. http://www.thepotteries.org/dates/poor.html
6. Little Birch Overseers account book, 1784-1792 (HRO N 11/3)
7. Cam Parish Overseers Papers Goucestershire Record Office (P69 OV 3/1/23)
8. see note 6 above
9. *ibid.*
10. http://users.ox.ac.uk/~peter/workhouse/Hereford/Hereford.html
11. *ibid.*
12. see note 5 above
13. Little Birch Parish Minute Book (HRO)
14. see note 6 above
15. Information from the Reports of the Commissioners appointed in pursuance to various Acts of Parliament to enquire concerning charities in England and Wales. Herefordshire, 1819-1837. Unfortunately the copy of the Commissioner's Reports in HRO is missing a preface, if there ever was one, so it is not clear what the significance of the Parliamentary return of 1786 is. Presumably it was a previous attempt by government to record and possibly regulate charities in England and Wales
16. Enclosure Award for Little Birch (HRO Q/R1/84)
17. Little Birch Parish Register (HRO AG 64)
18. Will of William Higgs (HRO)
19. *Public Health*, IX, 10 January, 1897 p.286
20. *Merthyr Express* 9 November, 1929 from Merthyr Tydfil Lbrary and Record Office
21. Merthyr Tydfil Record Office

Section 12 Roads, Tracks and Transport

1. Alfred Watkins, *The Old Straight Track*, Methuen 1925 p.81
2. Heather Hurley, *The Old Roads of South Herefordshire*, Newent 1992 p.6
3. Enclosure Award and map for Much and Little Birch 1824 (HRO Q/R1/34)
4. Surveyors drawing for 1st OS map 1816, South Herefordshire, in British Library, microfiche in HRO BN 13
5. Aconbury Gate Accounts (in James Hereford's documents) (HRO P82 LC 9013)
6. Enclosure Award and map for Much and Little Birch 1824 (HRO Q/R1/34)
7. Parish Council Minute Book 1894-1941 (HRO BL 57/1)
8. Little Birch Parish Minute Book (kept locally)
9. Much Birch Parish Minute Book (kept locally)
10. Census 1871 (HRO)
11. Heather Hurley, *The Pubs of Ross and South Herefordshire*, Logaston 2001 pp.122-123

Section 13 Church, Chapels and Schools
1. LL Rees
2. Court Rolls of the manors of Aconbury and Caldicot
3. Rev Preb Seaton, *History of the Deanery of Archenfield*, p.77
4. Presentments for the Bishop's Visitation 1716 (HRO 1/DE/14/54)
5. Little Birch Church early Parish Registers 1557-1741,1742-1812 (HRO AG 64)
6. Little Birch Parish Minute Book (held locally)
7. Tate
8. The notes were recorded in the trade magazine, *The Builder*, 24 July 1869
9. Jakeman and Carver's *Directory* 1890 (HCL)
10. Thomas Coombe, Illustration of Baptismal Fonts (reference in notes of Cmdr H. Bromby in HRO BN 57)
11. Scudamore, Stanhope and Moffatt, *The Church Plate of the County of Hereford* (reference in notes of Cmdr H. Bromby in HRO BN 57)
12. Letter of consent for sale from Wesleyan Church Committee, Manchester (HRO BH 28/4/5)
13. Primitive Methodist Records (held at St John's Methodist Church, St. Owen Street, Hereford)
14. Sunday School registers (held by Little Birch Methodist Chapel)
15. The National Society for Schools, Westminster, London
16. Little Birch Parish Minute Book (held locally)
17. Deed of 12 February 1857 for School at Little Birch, Diocese of Hereford
18. Guy's Hospital Estate Records, Report of Arthur Armitage 1857 (HRO)
19. *The History and Directory of Herefordshire*, 1858
20. Minute Book of meetings of School Managers 1882-1939 and 1941-1959 (held locally by Little Birch Parochial Church Council)
21. School Masters' Log Books 1882-1907 and 1907-1929 (held by Little Birch Parochial Church Council)
22. Letter dated 28 April 1960 from Ministry of Education re sale of Little Birch School, Hereford Diocesan Board of Finance

In addition to the above, information was taken from:
Censuses for Little Birch 1841-1901 (HRO)
Littlebury's *Directory* of Herefordshire 1876-7 (HCL)
Kelly's *Directory* 1891-2 (HRO)
History of our Village, Much Birch, Little Birch and Kings Thorn, Much Birch, Women's Institute, 1978
Notes on 1857 School at Little Birch by Mr J. Clench (held locally)
Notes of Cmdr H. Bromby (copies held locally and in HRO BN 57)
Notes on Little Birch Church by Rev David Enoch (held locally)
Little Birch Church Baptism Register 1813-1884 (HRO AG 64/3)
Little Birch Church Burials Index 1813-1834 (HRO BO 36/3)
Little Birch Churchwardens register and briefs (HRO N11 1-3)
Overseers Account Book (HRO N11/3)
Trustee Meeting for Methodist Chapel (HRO L31/89)

Chapel papers for Wesleyan Chapel (HRO BH 28/4/6)

Chapter 14 Recollections of some of the Little Birch area older inhabitants
Those who have contributed to this section include:
Percy Bristow, b.Kidderminster, 1917
Ivor Crum, b.Much Dewchurch, 1926
John Evans, b.Wormelow, 1930
Geoff Jones, b.Green Cottage, 1936
Iris Lloyd, b.Poplar Cottage, 1945
Dulcie Morgan, b.Pencoyd, 1908
Margaret Mullins
Muriel Saunders (née Cox), b.The View, 1925
Mariuon Turner
Victor Townsend, b.Bromley Cottages, 1923
Percy Verry, b.Upper House, 1923
John Walker, b.Dinedor, 1934

Section 15 Influential People in the Village
Stephen Thackwell
1. Dymock Parish Records (Gloucestershire Record Office)
2. J.E. Gethyn-Jones, *Dymock down the ages*
3. Joseph Foster, *Alumni Oxoniensis 1715-1886*
4. Reverend T.W. Webb, Diary (Hereford City Library)
5. A.T. Bannister, *Diocese of Hereford Institutions etc. (A.D. 1539-1900)*
6. Census Records for Little Birch, 1861, 1871, 1881 (HRO)
7. Sale deed of Wesleyan Chapel in Little Birch, 1861-2 (HRO BH 28/4/5)
8. Report of Arthur Armitage on school building in Herefordshire to Thos. Turner Esq. Treasurer of Guys Hospital (HRO)
9. Mortgage Deed 15 Feb. 1861 (HRO AR 69/51-5)
10. Robinson
11. Littlebury's *Directory*, 1876-7 (HCL)
12. Little Birch Parish Minute Book (kept locally)
13. Deeds of Crow's Nest (summary from Mr and Mrs J. Bulbeck)

The Waites and Southeys of Castle Nibole
1. Little Birch Parish Minute Book (kept locally)
2. Kelly's *Directory* 1891 (HRO)
3. Electoral Registers for 1906, 1910, 1914, 1921 (HRO)
4. Life story in *Merthyr Express* (see below)
5. Little Birch Parish Council Minute Book 1894-1941 (HRO BL 57/1)
6.

Some of the information was taken from the Censuses for Little Birch 1841-1901 (HRO)
Much information about the life of W.H. Southey was obtained from his Obituary and Life Story published in the *Merthyr Express*, 9 November 1929, a copy of which was kindly provided by the Merthyr Tydfil Library and Record Office.
A large amount of invaluable information and help has been provided by Mr Peter Lee, Swiss Cottage, Kings Thorn and members of his family.

Index

There is an index of people, secondly of properties and thirdly a general index,
which we hope makes navigating the index easier
Figures in italics refer to illustrations

Index of People

Index of Properties

General Index